Shalom

One Man's Search for Peace

•

A Filmmaker's Autobiography

Warren M. Marcus

Thomas Nelson Publishers
Nashville, Tennessee

Copyright © 1993 by Warren Marcus

All rights reserved. Written permission must be secured from the publisher
to use or reproduce any part of this book, except for brief quotations in
critical reviews or articles.

Published in Nashville, Tennessee, by Thomas Nelson, Inc., and distributed in Canada by Word Communications, Ltd., Richmond, British Colum-
bia, and in the United Kingdom by Word (UK), Ltd., Milton Keynes,
England.

Unless otherwise noted, Scripture quotations are from The Holy Bible,
KING JAMES VERSION.

Library of Congress information

Marcus, Warren M., 1949–
Shalom / Warren M. Marcus.
    p.   cm.
ISBN 0-8407-6790-0 (pbk).
    1. Marcus, Warren M., 1949–   . 2. Converts from Judaism—
United States—Biography.   I. Title
BV2623.M37A3   1993
248.2'46'092—dc20
[B]   93–2551
                                                        CIP

ISBN 0-8407-6790-0

Printed in the United States of America
1 2 3 4 5 6 7 — 98 97 96 95 94 93

*This book is dedicated
to the memory of my dad:*

Charles Marcus

●

Special Acknowledgement to the following people:

*Richard Gallagher, James Tate, Pat Robertson,
Gwen and Wally Odum, Sid Roth,
Jerry Falwell, John Deegan,
Rick Amato*

●

A special thanks to:

Donna, Tara Lynn, and Joseph Charles

●

*According as He hath chosen us in Him before the foundation of the world,
that we should be holy and without blame before Him in love . . . (Eph. 1:4).*

Introduction

THE MAIN EVENT

The sign on the door read: "INTENSIVE CARE—KNOCK BE-FORE ENTERING." I hesitated slightly, praying once more that God might give me the right words to utter to my dying uncle. As I approached the bed, I noticed how thin and frail he had become. Once so full of life, the cancer had taken its toll. It seemed to have happened so suddenly. I thought to myself, *Life is too short*.

His eyes were wide open as they met mine.

"Uncle Ben, it's Warren. Do you recognize me?" I heard myself ask.

He nodded his head slightly as if to say yes. He couldn't talk. There were tubes in his throat and nose. One look into his eyes and I could see that he was frightened. The other patients around him were dying. I continued talking as I hovered over his frail figure.

"Uncle Ben, I drove all the way from Virginia to see you. It took me seven and a half hours to get here."

He nodded. He turned away to look at the oxygen machine on the opposite side of his bed, as if to catch a moment of time alone. As he turned back to face me, I could see from his pained expression that Ben knew he was dying. However, God was giving me an unusual sense of peace as the proper words flowed from within.

"I love you, Uncle Ben," I said gently as I bent over to kiss his forehead. Tears welled up in his eyes.

"And I know you love me. But, Uncle Ben, even greater than our love for one another is God's love for you. He loves you so much that He sent his Son to die for you that you might live forever."

Ben would have had an abundance of retorts if the doctor hadn't placed an unappetizing plastic tube down his throat. The most innocent mention of a belief in God would have propelled him into his routine of blasphemy and destructive loquacity. Not only was my uncle a Jew, but a confessed atheist. To me, this seemed to be a great contradiction; the ability to be both a Jew and an atheist.

In spite of his past attitude, I told him that God is real and that there is eternal life—if only he would believe. I asked Ben if I could pray for him and I extended my hand toward his. To my surprise, he lifted his weakened hand and I grabbed it. Leaning close to his ear, I began to pray, reaching deep into my spirit for God's anointing.

"Oh God of Israel, I come in the blessed name of *Yeshua Ha Maschiach* (Jesus Christ) and ask You to give my Uncle Ben a peace in his heart. I pray You will take away any fear he might have. Dear God, I know how much he hates hospitals, but God, I pray that You would comfort him and make Yourself known in a special way. May You reveal your Son Jesus, in a vision if need be, that Ben might believe. Let him know that if he asks Yeshua into his heart right now that he will have eternal life in the kingdom of heaven. Now in the mighty name of Jesus I pray that You would comfort Ben with a peace that defies reason."

I opened my eyes and saw tears streaming down Uncle Ben's cheeks. He was touched deeply by the prayer. I continued to minister with the realization that I was probably the only person who had ever prayed with him in his entire life. What a privilege and awesome responsibility to know the living God of Israel. It remains a mystery how God could use such an unworthy vessel as me to make manifest His love toward Uncle Ben. Still holding his hand in mine, I leaned forward and kissed his forehead and told him I loved him.

Remaining close to him, I began to speak softly into Uncle Ben's ear, "It's time to stop fighting God, Uncle Ben. Are you ready to accept Jesus as your Messiah? If you are, squeeze my hand as tight as you can."

I felt his hand tighten around mine. Tears filled my eyes as I began to audibly thank God for this miracle, the miracle of salvation.

After the prayer, God gave me more words for Ben, as I boldly told him that he didn't have to fight any longer. It was time to rest. He had been battling all his life, and now he could rest in the arms of God. How marvelous are the ways of God! His mercies are never-ending! Although Ben mocked the name of God his whole life through, it took one moment of turning to God and confessing belief in Yeshua the Messiah for him to receive forgiveness.

As I said my good-byes, I thought about the thief who was crucified alongside the Messiah. What a life of rebellion against God he had led, stealing and cheating others, committing crimes against all things decent and godly. Yet in his final moments of life, a simple confession of belief erased a lifetime of sin, enabling him to enter paradise with the Messiah of Israel. God's amazing grace!

My Uncle Ben died less than a week after I had prayed with him.

Before I believed in Yeshua, I knew nothing of God's amazing grace. The God of Israel was an impersonal force that existed somewhere in the cosmos. I doubted if He were able to hear my prayers, even though I prayed out of desperation. Sometimes I questioned His existence in the face of the world situation—war, sickness, starvation, misery. It seemed that mankind was on a hopeless path of ultimate destruction. I noted that every solution mankind discovers for the problems that plague us results in the creation of new, more complex problems. I concluded that if there was a God, then why all this confusion and suffering? I was no different from Uncle Ben—except that he was more vocal with his unbelief.

It appears as if each of us is born with this fighting spirit of rebellion. The truth is that we discern the world around us from our own selfish viewpoints. That which does not fit into our own opinion of right and wrong is labeled dogmatism.

Views are conflicting between us, and, if we are honest, they are self-serving. As we grow up there are many voices calling out to us defining truth—that which is right and wrong. As children, we learn that an object is too hot, often by getting our fingers burned. This method of trial by fire often becomes our only device to formulate an ever-changing code of ethics. Too often, our code of ethics vacilates with each day to suit our ego. We are gratified, discovering others who parrot identical philosophies. It is comforting to hear our opinions shared by others. We read newspaper editorials, listen to the radio, and watch television programs to reinforce our mind-set. We desire to be reassured of our sanity by siding with majority opinion, yet all the while pretending to be individualists. The media often become an opiate to suppress the void within us that cries out for answers. Unconsciously, we choose to accept the rationale of human beings who are as miserable as we, applauding as they declare, "This is the way; walk ye in it."

The fact is that we don't want to judge that which we've never experienced for fear of being called a dogmatist. Honestly, what modest person considers himself supreme in forging rules for others? The answer to our dilemma is never realized. Often, we find ourselves confused by the myriad of voices which clamor out their half-baked ideas. In this state, we search for an escape—through drugs, sex, arts and crafts, or intellectualism.

The Bible puts it this way: ". . . wide is the gate, and broad is the way, that leadeth to destruction, and many there be which go in thereat: Because strait is the gate, and narrow is the way, which leadeth unto life, and few there be that find it" (Matt. 7:13–14).

There is a way that is true and right, though no man has formulated it. God Himself is the only one capable of discerning absolutes. There is only one God, the God of Israel, and He is a jealous God. A jealous God, because His love for us is like that of a husband for his bride. Though many voices cry out trying to seduce us, God is ever-present from the day of our birth crying, ". . . *This is the way, walk ye in it . . .*" (Isa. 30:21).

Throughout my life God has sent people to point the way, circumstances to cause me to turn to Him for help and His Spirit to compel me to be a part of His kingdom. This is a story of my own struggle—a conflict between the voices of this world pulling me into a pit of destruction versus God's perfect love drawing me into life everlasting.

Every time God reached out to me, bringing a messenger to me, a trying circumstance or a beautiful miracle, God's enemy, Satan, also sent his evil messengers to try and steal the blessing. The Bible says that Satan comes only to steal, kill, and destroy. Throughout our lives, we are given a choice. A choice to believe in God or to reject Him. And by rejecting Him, we embrace the very enemy of God.

This is the story of His mercy toward me, a rebellious young man. It is a reminder of how God can use the most unlikely situations, miracles, and other people to carry out His perfect will. This is a story of God's sovereignty, for in spite of my weaknesses and frailties, He has used me to be His instrument in reaching millions of others through television and films.

It is my prayer that you might see His hand in your own life through reading this autobiography. No matter who you are or what you've done, God will not only forgive you, but He will reveal to you His special plan for your life.

• ONE •

A TREE GROWS IN BROOKLYN

Brooklyn, New York: November 20, 1949
"It's a boy!" cried the doctor, or so my mother tells me.

Still under the influence of ether, she lifted her head to take a peek. Mom remembers that the hospital was being remodeled, the hammering creating a distracting din. Sawdust was drifting into the hallways. The nurses quickly removed the little bundle from my proud mother and carried it to sterile quarters. That little bundle, of course, was me, and Mom became quite upset because they didn't let her see me again until the following day. She had no idea that the hospital was in such chaos.

Within a week, I was circumcised in obedience to Jewish law. According to my parents, my *brith* took place at their apartment on Green Avenue in Brooklyn. A large group had gathered in the tiny rooms. Every room was filled with the smell of cigar smoke and scotch whiskey, and Mom says pandemonium reigned as everyone tried to outshout the others.

Dad's family was large. He had a total of ten brothers and sisters, and their spouses. Then there was my mother's side of the family, and my brother, Stan, and sister, Fran, and all the friends of the Marcus clan. The whole *mishbuka* (clan) had gathered to witness the special religious event. The *brith* was not only a part of Jewish tradition, but it was commanded by God himself in the Torah (the five books of Moses). I was naked as they lifted me into the air. Thank God I was too little to remember it because all eyes were upon me as I was dedicated to the God of Abraham, Isaac, and Jacob. The *mohel* (ritual circumciser) spoke the blessings in Hebrew. Then, as an outward sign of the newly-formed covenant, a portion of foreskin was cut off. All those assembled applauded as the *mohel* announced that Wolf Mayer (Yiddish for Warren Marcus) was now a son of Abraham, and his name had been entered into the Book of Life.

The *mohel* made his way through the crowd to my mother, holding a vial of white powder in his hand. He tried to find a quiet place to talk without having to shout. They finally moved into the hallway.

"Don't hold the child near you until tomorrow. If your son should bleed, then put on some of this powder. And Mrs. Marcus, *mazel tov* (good luck); may the God of Israel bless you for your good disposition."

The *mohel* was referring to my mother's patience with such a rowdy crowd. She thanked him, though she couldn't quite hear all his words as the clamor permeated the hall with echoes of laughter, arguing relatives, and the ear-splitting singing of my father. The scotch often caused him to react like this.

Mom says I rested quite comfortably in my cradle after the rather traumatic experience until one of my aunts couldn't resist picking me up to cuddle. She touched the sore spot, and I began belting out harmony to my father's favorite song with a loud wailing cry. In ran my mother to the rescue. Seeing the blood, she reacted with a Jewish mother's typical composure.

"He's bleeding! What do I do? Oh God! See if you could catch the *mohel!* No, call the doctor! *Oy vey!* The ambulance! Quick!"

Suddenly, she remembered the vial of white powder. It was just what the rabbi had ordered. The commotion was over, but they tell me it became the main topic of conversation.

"Oh, the poor baby," said one aunt.

"I don't understand why we should continue such a barbaric tradition," said a well-meaning friend.

"It's not barbaric, it's a command of God," interjected my orthodox Jewish grandfather.

"Oh, the *kindala* (child) won't remember any of this. They're so innocent at that age," said my grandmother. Am I ever glad Grandma was right!

These days, many Jewish people do not understand why their children are circumcised. They continue the tradition because they feel it's the right thing to do. Those who believe that mere men wrote the Torah argue that circumcision was established for health reasons. Hospitals today recognize this fact, and even Gentile babies are now circumcised. However, for those who truly understand, the rite is ordered by God in the Torah as an outward sign that the child is in covenant with Him. It is the seal of the contract that binds the child to obey the teachings of the Law. It is supposed to be a serious commitment before God that parents make for their child. They are responsible to teach the child the Jewish way of life. However, I am certain that my parents, along with most Jewish people, did not realize the seriousness of this event. Nevertheless, this was my first introduction to the religion of my forefathers. I was born a Jew, and the rite of circumcision was the external symbol binding me to Judaism.

Two

IT'S A MAD MAD MAD MAD WORLD

It was as if my mother and father were direct opposites. Their family upbringing was poles apart. My father's family came from Eastern Europe—both his father and his mother from Romania. They immigrated to the United States before World War II. Had they waited, there might not have been a Marcus family because most Jews were exterminated by Hitler's Third Reich.

In Europe, their family name was Lurch, but like so many immigrants of the time, they changed their name when they arrived at Ellis Island in New York, the entry point for millions. It is a mystery why they chose the name Marcus. After World War II as the 1950s began, much of the family moved from Brooklyn to New Jersey, where large developments of affordable housing were being constructed almost overnight, seeming to fill almost every vacant lot and farm. It was the beginning of the great American move to suburbia, and our family was no exception to the mass migration. The Marcus side of the family was not a religious group. My father's dad, Joseph Marcus, always claimed to be an atheist but called for a rabbi to make confession on his deathbed. Just as some families pass down biblical values and doctrines, Joseph passed down the values and doctrines of secular humanism. Grandpa Marcus's denial of God resulted in my father's never receiving religious instruction nor being *bar mitzvahed* (a ceremony performed when a Jewish boy attains religious adulthood). I am told, however, that my grandfather was very well-read. By trade he was an upholsterer, and examples of his work still survive. His shop in Roselle, New Jersey, was on the street level; the home was above.

As mentioned earlier, my father's family was large. He had six sisters: Claire, Anne, Edith, Ethel, Ruth (nicknamed Cookie), and Ernestine. He also had four brothers: Morris, Gilbert, and the twins, Sol and Benjamin. When you added Dad, that meant there were eleven children in all.

The family called Dad Charlie. He was the oldest of the brothers. It was his responsibility to help with the family business. He once told me, "I worked very hard for my father, and what little I earned immediately went to take care of feeding and clothing the rest of the family." Dad was not very happy with the arrangement, often letting his father know about his displeasure. They argued frequently.

My father once told me, "I had a dream to make my mark on the world. I wanted to be known by others—to become famous." This desire had led him to pursue a boxing career. He started in the amateur circuit and won a number of bouts, including a state of New Jersey championship fight. In this last bout, his face was bruised, and his mother begged him to give up boxing. Reluctantly, he promised he would, because he loved her.

Things worsened at home with arguments between Dad and Grandpa Marcus getting worse. My dad decided to leave. He moved from New Jersey to New York City. He took a room in Tin Pan Alley—the world-famous music-writing and publishing district. His cousin, Mickey, lived there with him.

When Dad hung out on Times Square, it was the place to be in New York, not the crime scene it is today. The square was the Hollywood of the East with grand premiere galas promoting new movies. The area was nicknamed "The Lights of Broadway."

An uncle once told me about the time he visited my dad during those early days of his independence.

"Your dad was always dressed in the latest fashion. And was he a real joker!"

"It was a trait that never left him, as all the family can testify to," I interjected.

My uncle laughed and continued his story:

"Charlie took me on a walking tour of Times Square at night. The lights were bright; the movie marquees flashed their exciting advertisements of the latest motion pictures direct from Hollywood. And Charlie pretended to know everybody!"

My uncle explained that my father played the part so perfectly that he really thought Dad had become famous.

"Your dad pointed to a cab that stopped nearby and began to

yell excitedly, 'Hey—there in that taxicab—it's Jimmy Stewart!' The man inside the cab resembled the famous Hollywood actor," my uncle explained.

"Then your dad waved and shouted at the man in the cab, 'Hey Jimmy, how you doing?'"

I asked, "Did the man in the cab hear him?"

"Of course," replied my uncle, "and the poor person in the cab, thinking that it was someone he must have met somewhere, waved back. Warren, everybody would laugh at your dad's practical jokes."

There seemed to be no limit to how far my dad would go to impress his friends and make them laugh. One night, there was an opening of an important new film on Times Square. Thousands of people lined up on both sides of the entrance, applauding as celebrities arrived and went inside the movie palace. My dad was dressed in the latest fashion—white spats and a big fedora hat. It was the same attire that the infamous mayor of New York, Jimmy Walker, loved to wear. Dad told his friends, "Mayor Walker is supposed to be here. I told him we were coming, and he's got tickets to give me."

While his friends were busy watching the excitement, my father slipped away and hailed a cab a block away. The cab pulled up outside the theater. He stepped out of the cab with his head down and dressed like the mayor. The throng of people started yelling, "There's the mayor; it's the mayor!" as they waved to him. With great fanfare, Dad accepted the accolades and waved back. Then, even bolder, he grabbed the arm of a famous actress and escorted her inside the theater, the crowd still screaming their approval.

Of course, once inside, he was found out and he was ousted. But the crowd was forgiving and appreciative of the practical joke. They applauded and laughed loudly for him. My father's friends just couldn't believe he had the *chutzpah* (guts) to pull it off.

My mother, Pearl Rubinson, came from a totally different kind of family. Her mother, Becky, and her father, Sam, were born in Russia. They arrived in America in 1905, when Russia was in turmoil. Sam and Becky settled on a small farm in New Jersey, but found farming to be difficult in America. My grandparents moved to Brooklyn, where they sold from push carts on the streets to survive. It was a hard life in this promised land. Yet, no one ever heard a complaint from the mouths of Becky or Sam. Hard work was part of what was expected.

Unlike my father and the Marcus side of the family, my mother's parents were devout Orthodox Jews. My mother's grandfather was a Kohan (a descendent of Aaron, the first Jewish High Priest). They lived according to the rabbinic and talmudic laws of Jewry. In their synagogue in Brooklyn, only Hebrew was spoken. Women and men could not sit together. The men sat on the main floor, and the women were seated in the balcony. Though my grandfather's income was meager, he never turned away a family member or even a stranger who needed a meal or a place to stay. My dad could not understand such actions. He told me this story:

"One time your grandparents let these people into their apartment in Brooklyn. They claimed to be their long-lost relatives. I was dating your mother at the time.

"While your grandparents were out of the house, I watched this guy looking through the drawers of the kitchen. Finding where some money was hidden, he took it and stuffed it into his pocket!"

My father said he became very angry because he knew that Sam and Becky worked hard for every cent they made. My father's face was intense as he continued the story.

"I told your mother about the incident, but she didn't want to believe me. Your mom thought they just didn't look like thieves. When I told your grandparents, they remained calm.

"I couldn't believe what your grandmother told me: 'If they need the money so bad, then they need it more than we do!'"

I often listened as the Marcus side of the family ridiculed my grandparents' seemingly naive ways, but the Jewish Law commands such charity, and Sam and Becky were determined to practice the Law.

This meant that the keeping of a kosher (ritually clean) home was a must. All meat had to be slaughtered by the *shochet* (Jewish butcher) according to strict rabbinic methods and given an okay by the rabbi. Certain methods to prepare the meat at home were necessary also—such as salting the meat so all blood would drain from it before cooking and eating, as commanded by the Torah.

There were separate sets of dishes and silverware—one for use with meat and one for use with dairy products. The two could not be mixed because of a certain talmudic interpretation of a passage in the Law of Moses. The Jewish high holy days, Yom Kippur and Rosh Hashanah, were celebrated. *Yahrzeit* candles were lit for dearly departed family members on the anniversary of their death. Many more customs were followed by my grandparents.

My mother, Pearl, her older brother, Joseph, and her younger brother, Jack, all pitched in to help my grandparents with their business. As a teenager, my mother helped by selling hot dogs from the pushcart. An entourage of boys would hang around just to get to know her and ask her out, but she would shoo them away. They nicknamed her: "Pearl, Pearl, the hot-dog-girl!"

"If you're not here to buy a frank, then beat it!" she'd snap at them. It seemed the meaner she treated them, the more hot dogs they bought. My grandfather thought she was just good at sales.

One of the boys, Max, gained twenty pounds as well as Pearl's heart. His persistence paid dividends for my grandpa, whose bank account grew richer, and for Pearl, when Max asked for her hand in marriage. Max bought her a beautiful engagement ring. They were headed toward marriage, until Charlie stepped into the picture. From the moment Charlie set eyes on her, he vowed to make Pearl his wife. He began to visit her, dressed in the latest fashions. He even borrowed money from his mother to pay the cab fare to take Mom on dates.

"Warren, for some time I secretly dated Charlie without letting Max know," Mom told me. "I just didn't want to hurt his feelings."

Pearl was beginning to fall in love with Charlie. They were two very opposite kinds of people, but as the saying goes, "Opposites attract!" Here was Charlie—a clown and a jokester, a man who had left his parents, an agnostic with no clear goal in life. On the other hand, Mom was a deeply religious woman with close family ties. She was sensitive and empathetic, and she spoke Yiddish fluently. All of her life she heard Hebrew as read from the holy Scriptures, and watched and loved all the rich Jewish traditions such as her mother's lighting the Sabbath candles every Friday night.

Charlie exposed her to an exciting world that she never knew existed. They spent late nights at New York City's posh night clubs.

My mother loved to dance the Charleston and the jitterbug, something my orthodox grandparents would never have approved of.

There was a time when Max was crushed when she broke off the engagement. Soon after, Pearl and Charlie were married.

THREE

LOST WEEKEND

My parents began their married life in a cramped apartment on Green Avenue in Brooklyn. The neighborhood was mostly composed of blue-collar Italians and Jews. In those days, the streets were safe enough for the children to go outside and play without supervision.

Years earlier, Dad had learned the tool-and-die-making trade from his cousin, the father of actor Edward G. Robinson. His excellent training allowed Dad to land a job with a large New York jewelry manufacturing company, designing dies for processing equipment. There was, however, one hitch Dad did not like but had to accept. Because the Jewish people were so heavily discriminated against in the jewelry industry, he had to change his last name at work to Marco.

The family began to grow, first with the birth of my brother, Stanley, in 1934. Then came my sister, Fran, five years later. Now contented with being a homemaker, Mom was no longer interested in painting the town red with my dad. However, a quiet domestic existence was far from what Dad wanted and he soon grew extremely bored with staying home. With the alias "Marco," he became friendly with the surrounding Italian community. It wasn't long before he began frequenting the bars, drinking with his newly found buddies, who thought my dad was one of the *paisano* (Italian for family). Though a number of them were involved with the Mafia, my father stayed clear of their "business arrangements," but managed to build a rapport with them. He felt important just knowing them, seeming to bask in what he perceived as the glory of their lifestyle and power.

Once my Aunt Annie told me, "Charlie would openly boast to the rest of the Marcus family that he knew these famous gangsters.

He felt important being called their friend. He'd say, 'I was just out with so-and-so. We had a few drinks together. You know, he's a big gun in the Mafia!'"

Aunt Annie told me that she was extremely worried for Dad's safety and lectured him for bragging about his friendship with these thugs.

A tragic event occurred that would change my father's life drastically. When word reached him that his mother had died, his world fell apart. She was only forty-seven years old when complications from an operation claimed her.

During this period, my dad developed a life-long habit. After laboring hard all day at the factory, he would drop in at the neighborhood bar and grill. He would often stay out late getting drunk with his Mafia buddies. Yet, somehow, throughout his life he never failed to provide, always holding a steady job. And fortunately for the whole family, he never became mean or abusive like many alcoholics do.

Dad was working at a lucrative job, unusual for a Jew in those days, so we always managed to have some of the latest things from cars to clothes, and even the very first television set on the block. All the neighbors would come to our apartment and gather around to watch that early black-and-white magic box. The "Golden Age" of TV had come, and ours was one of the first families to get in on it!

Then, my father began bringing home some of his drinking buddies. A number of them were gangsters. Knowing this, Mom became upset. However, because of her servant's heart and obedient personality, she warmly welcomed whoever accompanied my father. There was always delicious, home-cooked food on the stove and a pot of coffee brewing for anyone who was there. The door was always open. My father's friends all liked my mom, and, because of her, they thought Dad was the luckiest man in the world.

One day, he brought a nice gentleman home who made a very favorable impression on my mother.

"Charlie," she said, "why don't you hang around with more people like him? Why don't you . . . I mean, he's a gentleman, a nice man!"

Words cannot describe mom's shocked expression when she

looked in the newspaper three weeks later. There was this nice gentleman's photo plastered on the front page. He was charged with murder! No, you never knew what to expect from my father's friends!

He was beginning to experience some serious repercussions from all of his drinking. Dad found any excuse to get drunk, whether it was to celebrate, or to console his damaged spirit when enduring the vicissitudes of life. One night he was so soused that he fell in the street, breaking his arm.

On November 20, 1949, when I was born, my father promised my mother that he would try to mend his ways. He wanted to be a good father to his newborn son. My mom was forty years old when she bore me. Ten years separated me from Fran and fifteen years from Stan. Yet, good intentions could not help my dad give up his addiction to alcohol. His drinking binges continued unabated until he faced the greatest challenge of his life, the nightmarish hallucinations of the d.t.'s. To this day, my sister cannot forget the night he came home in a drunken stupor:

"I was awakened from sleep as he came into the house screaming for Mom. He yelled, 'Pearl! Pearl! Pearl!' Mom couldn't figure out what was wrong with him. He was as white as a ghost, and his eyes were open so wide it seemed he saw the devil himself."

Yet, what scared my mom and sister the most was when he began to describe who drove him home.

"Pearl, I swear to you, I didn't drive the car! I just sat there. It was black hands that drove me home. Pearl, they took control of the wheel."

Needless to say, that was not original equipment on the car! On another occasion, he came home so drunk that he saw bats flying around the room, and in terror he cried out for help.

"The bats—they're after me, they're after me!" Dad screamed. As a result, he wound up going to the hospital to dry out.

My brother and sister tried to get out of the apartment as much as they could. Their form of escape was the local movie theaters. In those days they showed cartoons, a news reel, two feature films, and sometimes even included live entertainment.

I was only three years old as I sat with my teenage brother and sister in the movie house. I observed them as they lighted their cigarettes, then inhaled deeply, and finally let out bellows of smoke. I loved the two of them and wanted to be just like them. "I want one!" I said loudly. They tried to quiet me. "You're too young," reasoned my sister.

"I want one!" I yelled so loudly all in the theater could hear.

They tried to appease me by buying a candy bar, but I had a one-track mind. They were denying me my rights. My brother handed me an unlit cigarette, which I sucked on, blew into, yet no smoke appeared.

"I want smoke!" I screamed. People turned around, annoyed at my outbursts.

Finally, my brother lit the cigarette, just so I'd shut my mouth. I didn't inhale but was able to draw the smoke into my mouth and blow it back out. Standing on the seat, I was proud and wouldn't switch places with anyone in the world!

On the way home, one could imagine a three-year-old shrimp, walking down the Brooklyn sidewalks, smoking a cigarette. My brother and sister were embarrassed as heads kept turning. Defiantly, I blew smoke at the spectators, enjoying the attention.

My newly formed habit was quickly broken when my father came home from work. As I ran to greet him, he picked me up and smelled the telltale smoke.

"What's that I smell? Tobacco?"

Afraid of his stern, booming voice, I coughed up the truth, shaded in my favor, of course.

"Stanley gave me a cigarette," I admitted, pointing toward my brother.

"I had to give him it. He was acting like an idiot in the movie theater! Wasn't he, Fran?" my brother said, turning to my sister for support.

Unbeknown to my brother, Fran had slipped out of the room to avoid a confrontation. This left my poor brother defenseless and stuttering.

Dad didn't give him any further chance to explain. He barked and screamed out his displeasure all evening long. It would be a long, long time before I would even touch a cancer stick, let alone smoke it.

It is by the living example of others that children are most influenced. What we are taught orally is important, but what we observe is what teaches us most. My brother and sister smoked cigarettes, so I desired them too.

The God of Israel wanted His people to clearly understand his commandments and to teach them to their children. It is written in the Torah, in the book of Deuteronomy, chapter 6, verse 7:

> And thou shalt teach them diligently unto thy children, and shalt talk of them when thou sittest in thine house, and when thou walkest by the way, and when thou liest down, and when thou risest up.

According to this, there seems to be no time left to do anything else but talk to our children about God's commandments. What God is really asking us to do seems fanatical: "Teach your children my Word from the moment they wake up, throughout the day, until they go asleep." In reality, He is admonishing us to be living examples to our children. In the New Covenant in the book of James, chapter 1, verse 22, the same concept is stated this way:

> "But be ye doers of the Word, and not hearers only, deceiving your own selves."

Most of us have no concept of what God is telling us here. Even the most "religious" concern themselves more with keeping observances, rather than living godly lives on a daily basis. Traditions are beautiful when they are observed with understanding, but *blind* tradition often keeps us from truly knowing God's perfect will for our lives.

In Judaism, the child was to learn about his faith from his parents and through the traditional observances of the Jewish high holy days—Rosh Hashanah, Yom Kippur, and *Pesach* (Passover). My parents did not have an in-depth understanding of their religion. Like so many modern Jewish families, holiday celebrations were just part of the heritage passed down by tradition.

My mother's orthodox Jewish parents' understanding of the Torah was limited to the practice of observances and blind tradition. The reality of God was never to be questioned, yet seldom did they truly sense His presence. This was their scope of understanding: Rosh Hashanah is the Jewish New Year; Yom Kippur is the

Day of Atonement when we fast and receive forgiveness for a year full of sin; Passover is the Seder, when we eat a symbolic dinner celebrating Israel's deliverance from Egypt under the leadership of Moses. To my grandparents' credit, they were deeply devout and quite humble. They lived in obedience to the letter of the Law and practiced charity toward the poor. My mother learned more by witnessing her parents' actions than by any of the religious observances she was forced to observe.

My dad claimed to believe in God, but seemed to have a disdain for organized religion. Judaism held little meaning for him. Grandpa Joseph was an avowed atheist. Dad was never bar mitzvahed and seldom attended the synagogue. Only upon my mom's insistence did he pay for my brother's Hebrew school education and his bar mitzvah.

"I think this whole bar mitzvah business is ridiculous. In this day and age, what do we need it for?" I'd hear him argue with my mother.

"But Charlie, it's for my mother's and father's sake. It's tradition!" my mother would argue back.

My mother's servant-like attitude helped her to cope with my father's eccentricities. Her limited understanding of God—but great faith—made her strong enough to be the backbone of the family. Her tenderness and ability to look only at the best side of a person's character gave her children the means to continue respecting and loving their father, even under the most difficult of circumstances.

• Four •

The Godfather

By 1952, Brooklyn was changing. The neighbors with money were leaving in droves for the suburbs of New Jersey. My father began questioning the price of his friendship with his mobster friends. Dad often related a frightening incident that convinced him it was time to leave Brooklyn.

The event happened in a crowded neighborhood dive. My father was sitting at the bar with a young man named Sparky, a Mafia gofer. A stranger in the establishment tapped my father hard on his shoulder. This was something you just never did to an ex-boxer.

"You're sitting in my seat!" the man said. My dad stared into his cold eyes without flinching. He turned back to his friend, ignoring the stranger's rudeness. Frantically, Sparky motioned to my father, trying to stop him from messing with this stranger.

This time, the man tapped harder, "Did you hear what I said?" My father continued to talk to Sparky, ignoring his demands. The man pulled at my father's jacket trying to yank him off the seat.

Suddenly, Dad spun around, hitting the man with a hard left jab to his solar plexus. He doubled over on the floor, the wind knocked out of him.

"Charlie, come on! Let's get out of here!" Sparky yelled, hoping to avoid any further confrontation. Dad stood his ground, his adrenaline flowing. Slowly, the stranger rose to his feet, pulling a stiletto (dagger) from his pocket. Now with the crowd's attention, my father took a boxing stance, avoiding the knife with fancy footwork. He pounded the man with a combination of right and left hooks as the crowd in the bar went nuts, egging Dad on. Finally, he left the stranger bleeding and unconscious on the floor. Sparky was shaking as he ushered my father from the bar.

"Charlie, I tried to tell you not to mess with that guy. He's a made man! You know, a hired gun in the family!"

My father turned white as he realized the danger he was in by tangling with a Mafia killer. Then Sparky told Dad that he knew some people in high places in the mob and the best thing would be for him to try and get a Mafia trial. Otherwise, my father would be the target of a vendetta.

Sparky set it up, and the trial was held in an abandoned warehouse. My father told me how he felt as he entered the darkened room and approached the two empty chairs which were set in the middle of the large room.

"I wondered if this was really a trial, or whether I would be killed on the spot. Nobody gets away with touching a made man in the Mafia," Dad explained to me. "I was shaking on the inside, but I pretended to be calm and cool as I sat down in the wooden chair. My life was now in the hands of the Mafia. I wasn't a religious person, but right then and there, I said a silent prayer to God, begging Him to get me out alive."

The hired gun entered and sat down in the chair opposite my dad. He had a black eye and his face was bandaged from my father's pummeling. A dozen mob leaders—the judges—faced the two as the head mobster asked to hear both sides of the story. The hit man began with his lies.

"This dirty Jew came over to me and called me some names. There's no way I was gonna take that garbage from him."

On and on he lied about the fracas. Before the meeting, Sparky instructed Dad to remain cool and to keep his eyes off his adversary, looking constantly at the leader of the mob.

My father's turn came. He was comforted by the fact that he knew at least five of the twelve judges. He told exactly the way it happened. The stranger was cocked tight as a trigger and interrupted my father a number of times, calling him a liar. Carefully coached by Sparky, my dad ignored these outbursts.

Following Sparky's advice, my father closed with these words, "I really had no idea who he was. If I had known that he was a made man, I would have given him the seat. I'm really sorry for what I did to him."

Without warning the hit man shot out of his seat and went after my father. Dad just sat calmly as the others pulled the man away.

The leader was furious at the hit man's actions. One of the judges, who knew Dad, used the incident to speak up on my father's behalf.

"Hey, I've known Charlie for years. This guy's all right. He's not a hothead."

Several others chimed in with good words concerning my father's character.

The leader warned the two men on trial to sit perfectly still in their chairs. He wanted to meet privately with his men. He stared right into the eyes of the made man.

"If either of you gets out of your chair, or even says anything to the other," he said calmly, "I'll personally kill the two of you!"

Fortunately for my father, he was known as a peaceable person, while the stranger had the reputation of starting fights. The ruling came down: If either of them were ever seen in the future talking to the other, both would be executed immediately. Dad, the agnostic, silently thanked God for his deliverance.

Yet, it took one more incident to convince Dad to move out of Brooklyn. After a hard day's work at the factory, he stopped to talk with Sparky, who was sitting on the front steps of their Brooklyn apartment.

"Nice day, huh Sparky? Feels like spring," my dad said.

"Yeah, buddy! It's good to be alive!"

My dad slowly strolled into the apartment building. As he climbed upstairs to his apartment, he heard the pop-pop-pop of gunfire. He rushed outside, and what he saw would remain with him for the rest of his life. There on the ground was Sparky—dead! Dad began shaking uncontrollably as reality hit him. If he had stayed with Sparky one second more, he would have been lying there too, a victim of a mob shooting! Dad needed no more lessons to get the message.

My mother, however, had mixed feelings about leaving Brooklyn. Her beloved parents lived close by and they would *never* leave Brooklyn. My sister, Fran, and my brother, Stan, were in high school and would miss their friends. But my dad knew he had to get out of the city. One question remained: where would he go? Some of the Marcus family had started a manufacturing company in New Jersey named Margrove Manufacturing. It was established during World War II and they were now making watches, eyeglass frames, and jewelry. However, times were still hard, and the little company was struggling to stay solvent.

Dad gave my uncles at Margrove Manufacturing an idea for an original design that he had created for the giant New York company he was still working for. He told his brothers to wait a while before selling the product so that the New York company could release it first. For whatever reasons, Margrove, the fledgling company, hit the market first with the design and my father lost his job. The family asked him to work for them and my dad gladly accepted. I was just three and a half years old when he moved our whole family to Linden, New Jersey. Dad joined Margrove Manufacturing as the head tool-and-die maker, a position he held until he retired 33 years later.

From an environment of increasing crime, bad friends, and negative influences upon my father, there was now what must have seemed like heaven on earth: Linden—a New Jersey community of nice suburban homes, quiet streets, a growing population of people busy rearing families, new businesses, and jobs. The Jewish community was strong there. The middle class had arrived! As in the rest of America, the move to suburbia and the baby boomer generation had begun in earnest! And the Marcus family was there in force, all eleven Marcus brothers and sisters with their husbands, wives, and kids, playing their part in mid-twentieth-century history!

My father now had a fresh arena in which to make friends. It was a new environment, but Dad retained the same old urge to meet and know important people. However, this time he stayed away from the criminal element, making friends instead with politicians—the mayor, councilmen, district attorneys—and the police.

As far as my parents were concerned, moving to Linden, New Jersey, from Brooklyn, New York, was like the Jewish people escaping Egypt and going to the Promised Land! Our new split-level home was located on Lenape Road. It was a typical suburban development with newly constructed houses, all similar, except for the colors and landscaping. The local legend was that there used to be an Indian reservation on the very street on which we lived. Hence, it was named Lenape Road for the Lenape Indians.

It was an interesting community, a true melting pot of people from various ethnic backgrounds and cultures: Protestants, Catholics and Jews living side by side. And there were many nationalities: Polish, Rumanian, Hungarian, Italian. Prejudice certainly existed; the blacks and Puerto Ricans lived on the other side of the tracks. Linden was indeed segregated. The only place we would come in contact with such minorities was in high school. Besides that tragic fault, for the most part Linden was a great place for a Jewish boy to grow up in.

My father was very happy, especially since his drive to work took only ten minutes. His name again returned to being Charles Marcus—since we were a community that had, at least on the surface, no anti-Semitism. It was here that I mixed with a group of friends of various ethnic backgrounds. We set out to play together on the streets—baseball and all the fun games that suburban America fostered.

FIVE

HEAVEN'S GATE

It was a hot summer afternoon in 1954. At the age of five, I remember playing catch with my neighborhood friend Bob Pirigyi in front of my house. We were enjoying one another's company when suddenly we heard the sound of thunder off in the distance. The sky darkened and a storm was brewing. Bob perked his head up in fear.

"What's wrong, Bobby?" I asked.

"Did you hear that?" he replied, his blue eyes open wide with fear.

"It's only thunder," I laughed.

Another clap sounded. This time it was much louder. Bob screamed so loudly it frightened me. He dropped the ball and began crying.

"Mommy! Mommy!" he called as he ran quickly toward his house.

"Oh, come on, Bobby! Thunder can't hurt you," I shouted after him.

"Oh yes it can!" he shouted back as he ran into the arms of his mother just outside his house. Another louder clap sounded, driving Bob into hysteria.

"Mrs. Pirigyi, he thinks thunder can hurt you!" I yelled over to her.

She shouted back, "Thunder can't hurt you, but lightning can *kill* you. You better go into your house!"

Bob and his mother went inside their home. I was left alone. I looked up at the darkened skies wondering about the truth of what I was told. Suddenly, a flash of lightning lit the sky all around me. The loudest clap of thunder in the world seemed to shake the very ground I stood on.

I began to cry as I ran as fast as I could toward my house. The rain poured down as I slammed the door behind me. My sister, Fran, was fifteen years old. She immediately came over to me to find out what was wrong.

"The lightning can kill me," I cried as she stooped down, embracing me.

"No, no! Don't be afraid! It can't hurt you," she said emphatically.

"Yes it can! Mrs. Pirigyi said it could kill me!" I yelled.

A flash of lightning filled the house, and a clap of thunder plunged me into major panic. Fran held me tighter and tried to comfort me.

"Lightning can't hurt you, because God will protect you," she said softly.

I pulled away from her, puzzled—God? I had never heard that word before. "What is *God?*" I asked her.

"He's your friend. You can't see Him. He lives in a place called heaven. Yet, He is everywhere," she answered smiling warmly, stroking my head tenderly.

I remember looking around the room, newly conscious of a presence I could not see. It was comforting, yet frightening at the same time. I totally forgot about the thunderstorm. All I could think about was this new person called God who was supposed to be near me wherever I went even though He was invisible. Shortly thereafter, I had a dream. I found myself in what I perceived to be heaven. It was beautiful, and I was approaching these unearthly clouds which began to part from the center outward. Suddenly, a bright light moved toward me in the form of colored rays. It frightened me, and I stopped my approach. The source of the light had a pattern I would later recognize. It was shaped exactly like the tablets in Cecil B. DeMille's *The Ten Commandments*, though I did not see the movie until years later!

And then, I heard a soothing voice. It seemed to surround me yet be inside me as it said, "I am your friend. Don't be afraid. I will never hurt you."

I did not want to wake up from the dream. It was so real and comforting!

The next day in kindergarten class I tried to draw a picture of what I had seen in my dream. I used a yellow crayon, and became very frustrated because I couldn't draw it better.

A little boy next to me asked what I was drawing.

"I'm drawing a picture of God," I told him.

"You can't draw a picture of God. No one can see Him," the boy said, laughing.

"Well, I saw God," I told the boy quietly.

Suddenly, my classmate started shouting at me for all the class to hear.

"You can't see God! He's invisible! Teacher! He said he saw God!"

I was embarrassed. I remember feeling all eyes on me. I began to cry.

"I did see God—in my dream!" I told her tearfully.

She quieted the class down as she came over to me. I remember her taking the drawing from my desk and staring at it. She then looked at me with a puzzled expression. To this day I wonder how it affected her.

I am reminded often of this incident. I now realize I had seen the Lord God Almighty in my dream and was trying to draw a picture so I could show others His reality. Little did I know, years later, that I would still be "drawing pictures" of God's reality, not with kindergarten crayons and construction paper, but rather on the canvas of motion picture film. Nothing could make a little five-year-old boy desire to communicate to others the reality of God, unless God himself planted that urge deep in my being. God's plan for my life was made evident through a childhood dream. The Bible says that God chooses us before we are ever born. "According as He hath chosen us in Him before the foundation of the world . . ." (Eph. 1:4). God's plan for my life, now revealed, would take years to begin realizing its full potential.

SIX

FIDDLER ON THE ROOF

After several years of living in Linden, our family was comfortable in the new surroundings. My brother, Stan, had landed a job in Elizabeth, New Jersey, as an assistant manager of a Pep Boy's Auto Store. My sister, Fran, had graduated from Linden High School and was embarking upon a career in nursing, attending the School of Nursing at the Brooklyn Jewish Hospital.

Dad worked hard at his new job. He still frequented the bars, but now it was with his political buddies and the law-enforcement crowd. My mother had the hardest time coming to grips with the move. I remember walking into her bedroom one day. She lay sobbing on her bed.

"Mommy, what's wrong?" I asked.

She tried to hide her tears as she hugged me.

"Nothing, baby. Mommy's all right."

"But why are you crying?"

My concerned little voice helped her compose herself.

"I just miss Grandma and Grandpa," she replied as she kissed me.

My orthodox Jewish grandparents refused to leave Brooklyn, even though my mother begged them to come to Linden. Brooklyn was their home. It was also the home of all their orthodox Jewish friends, and it was in Brooklyn that they had their business selling fruit at the local farmer's market. Several times a year, my mother would take me back to Brooklyn to visit them during the high holy days. I would look forward to these visits, even though it would mean separation from my father who remained in Linden to work.

For a seven-year-old, the bus trip from Linden to New York City seemed interminably long, although it only took an hour. Maybe the excitement of getting to the city kept me conscious of the time. Every minute I'd ask my mom if we had arrived yet. Finally, she'd get so annoyed with my persistence that she would beg me to take a nap.

The next thing I'd know we'd be getting off the bus at the Port Authority Bus Terminal. The New York throngs amazed me. They were a fascinating diversity of people: well-dressed business men, construction workers, winos lying in the gutters. I wanted to stop to help the poor street people, but my mother would tug at my arm assuring me they'd be all right. The buildings overwhelmed me as I craned my neck to see their height. We'd walk the streets from the terminal to a Times Square subway station. On the way, my innocent eyes would survey all the action. It was here where I witnessed the *street prophets*. They stood on soapboxes shouting out the words, "Repent and be saved." Others carried signs: "The end is near." Still others handed out tracts I couldn't read. My mother would grab them from my hands and promptly toss them in the nearest trash receptacle.

One man was there year after year. I'd look for him walking the streets with his sign fastened to his chest. He'd hold a Bible in his hand and stop to stare at people. I'll never forget his piercing eyes when they met mine as my mother and I were stopped at a *Don't Walk* sign. His face broke into a friendly smile and he winked at me. I couldn't help but smile back.

He pointed to his sign and read aloud, "Read the Bible—repent and be saved."

"Mom, what does it mean, 'repent'?" I asked as we crossed the street.

"Where did you hear that word?" she retorted, puzzled because she had been preoccupied with other matters and didn't hear the man.

"That man said it!" I shouted as I pointed him out.

"Oh, he's just a nut that thinks the world is coming to an end," she replied.

"Why does he think the world's gonna end?" I asked with a new concern splitting my brain.

"I don't know. He's just crazy. All of those people holding signs are crazy."

But I kept wondering what those people were doing. They were talking about God, getting saved, and that word *repent*.

Soon the excitement of riding on the subway train removed thoughts of God from my head. Again, it was the people who would fascinate me. One man sitting across from me was talking out loud to himself, but the other people on the train paid no attention to him, just as if he didn't exist. His babbling didn't make any sense, but I'd listen closely with the hope of understanding. The train would break out from the dark underground of Manhattan to the bright daylight on the Williamsburg Bridge. I'd stand by the door, watching the scenery of old, dilapidated buildings pass by as we traveled on the elevated tracks—so many buildings squeezed together in this dirty city of concrete. The people were just a blur of faces, but I'd occasionally wonder what it would be like to know the lady standing on her fire escape or the little boy sitting all alone on the curb.

By the time we'd walk from the elevated station to my grandparents' apartment on Humboldt Street, I would be exhausted. However, walking up the tenement stairs, I'd revive as I smelled my grandmother's chicken soup.

As I gulped down soup, I'd hear my mother pleading with my grandma to leave Brooklyn and come to New Jersey.

"The neighborhood is not good, Mom," she'd say.

"God will protect us" my grandmother would reply.

"I'm not worried about God! It's those gangs that scare me," Mom interrupted.

My stay would be a bit boring, though, because my mother didn't like me going out to play. She feared my being knifed by Bernardo from *West Side Story,* or sexually abused by some wino. Occasionally, I'd sneak out, saying that I was going upstairs where my grandmother's sister, my Aunt Lena, lived.

I hated going up there, because all Aunt Lena and her husband Nathan would do was squeeze my cheeks and call me *kindala* (Yiddish for child).

"Here's some cookies, *kindala!*" Aunt Lena would tell me.

I hated their cookies because they were always stale. No matter how much I refused, Aunt Lena would shove one into my mouth, and watch closely as I struggled to chew it. The only thing I hated more was Uncle Nathan's watery tea served in an unwashed glass that I swore he kept his false teeth in.

"I have a glass of hot tea for my little friend!" Uncle Nathan said as he carefully handed it to me, "Now, drink it up—all of it!"

The two of them would scrutinize my every sip until every drop was gone. Immediately after I emptied the cup, I would jump out of my seat and say, "Goodbye," before they could offer me another award-winning cookie or lousy glass of tea. The moment I left their apartment, I'd run downstairs and outside to freedom. It was in my grandparents' neighborhood that I met a thirteen-year-old black boy named Louie. I was playing in the park outside the apartment complex, when three teenage blacks approached me and threatened to beat me up. One of the boys began pushing me, hoping to spark a fist fight.

"Hey, you punks! Leave my friend alone!" Louie yelled as he came to the rescue.

"What do you mean, *your friend*? He's a white boy," the older one mouthed off.

"You just leave him alone or else," Louie threatened them.

The teenagers backed off and reluctantly left the scene. Louie was good to me and would protect me from the bad elements on the street. We became the best of friends and I'd look forward to seeing him. The experience gave me a real appreciation for the black race. One Sunday, Dad drove to Brooklyn to take Mom and me home, and I told him about my brave protector, Louie. On the way to our car, I pointed him out to Dad.

"Okay. You go into the car with Mom," I heard my dad say.

While inside the car, I watched my father stroll over to Louie and some of his friends. At first the group seemed panicked, their eyes opening wide with fear, as this tall white hulk of a man loomed over them.

"Which one of you is Louie?" Dad asked without emotion.

His friends were quick to point him out, not willing to tangle with the dude who towered over them.

"Louie, my son Warren tells me that you've been a good friend to him. I want you to have this," Dad said as he handed him a ten-dollar bill.

My father always showed his appreciation toward others through his billfold, and this made my mom extremely upset.

She gave him a piece of her mind the moment he stepped into the car.

"Charlie, you gave him ten dollars? Couldn't you give him a dollar or two? But no, you had to take that fat billfold of yours out. Those kids could have knifed you!" she exhorted.

"Pearl, I could have beat up the whole gang of them, even if they pulled a gun on me. I don't want to hear anything more about it!" Dad said, ending the conversation.

They sat in complete silence all the way home to New Jersey.

Year after year, Louie would be waiting for me, outside my grandparents' apartment building, until finally the neighborhood got so bad his family decided to move to Jersey.

The very best part of my visits to Brooklyn were my trips to the indoor marketplace where Grandpa and Grandma sold fruit and vegetables. I'd love to sit with them behind their crudely built fruit stand. Grandpa Sam could not see well, so I'd warn him of the wise guys who'd steal an apple or two. Later, I'd help him close up. Then, at home we would count the change and fold all the shiny coins into bank rolls.

My grandparents continued to be quite devout in their religious practice. I sat on Sam's knee as he listened daily to the Brooklyn Jewish radio station. I couldn't understand a word of the Yiddish broadcast, but I enjoyed hearing Grandpa laugh at something funny the announcer said. And at *their* apartment, I ate only kosher; that's ritually clean food. I watched as my grandmother, Becky, used two sets of dishes—one for meat and the other for dairy. On Friday night, I was mesmerized as I observed the candles being lit by Becky as she sang a Hebrew prayer ushering in the Sabbath.

On Yom Kippur, the most solemn of all the Jewish holidays, no food would be cooked or eaten in their house. As a child, this was difficult for me to understand, and there were no answers given. There was nothing for me to do. No radio or television was allowed. Electricity for lights was forbidden. Only twenty-four-hour candles flickered, creating eerie shadows on the wall. I think the silence would have driven me nuts, if we had not left the house and gone to the synagogue.

That, however, was a mixed blessing for a restless kid like me. Early-morning *minyan* took place from seven-thirty to twelve noon.

Then, we'd go back to the apartment for a nap, only to have the services begin again at two o'clock in the afternoon and last until five o'clock.

The synagogue was in the poorest section of the neighborhood. The buildings around it were falling apart. And most of the congregation seemed to be as old as the building itself. Being a child, I had a choice where to sit. I could go upstairs and sit in the balcony with the women or downstairs with the men. In Orthodox Judaism, women and men could *never* sit together. That was all right with me because running up and down the stairs kept me from falling asleep.

I'd sit for a while with my grandfather and try to follow the service. Every word was in Hebrew, including the songs, and there was no English translation in any of the prayer books. My grandfather followed the service word for word. He'd nod at the same time the other men nodded. I couldn't figure out whether they were all frowning because of boredom or whether it was part of the tradition. For the most part, these old men gave the appearance of being sincere and attentive. Yet every time I'd ask a question, Grandpa would hush me:

"Can't talk now!"

I would listen to all the empty stomachs growling around us, since it was a day of fasting. The variety of noises was hilarious. One time, I actually counted the number of coughs versus sneezes. There were approximately 58 coughs and 13 sneezes in the morning service. Finding the counting game too boring, I'd run back upstairs to see my mom and grandma. It was the opposite scene— mouths were moving a mile-a-minute, but not for prayer. Every subject would be discussed except religion, and all the women seemed to have this *yenta* (women who like to gossip) complex. Yet even in this, I was left out because the juicy parts were said in Yiddish.

By this time, enough was enough! On the holiest of days, I found myself walking out of the sanctuary into the entrance hall— and found a host of other Jewish children. We instantly became friends even though our ages ranged from three to fifteen. We'd talk about everything *but* religion. We had a good time until one of the elders would come out of the sanctuary to rebuke us for being too loud. We moved outside to the steps, and it was here where I met what I took to be my first anti-Semitic confrontation.

A seven-year-old Puerto Rican boy came to the bottom of the synagogue steps.

"Hey, what are you people doing in there?"

"What do you mean?" asked one of the older Jewish children.

"Why are all those people inside?"

"It's a Jewish holiday. They're worshiping God," answered another Jewish friend.

"You people can't worship God. You killed God."

I sobered as I heard this. What was this boy talking about? The other kids angrily told him to get away, but I began to press for clarification.

"What do you mean *we* killed God? *We* didn't kill God," I said.

"The Jews killed Jesus!" he retorted.

The other Jewish children laughed at the boy and then angrily shouted at him.

"Jesus isn't God. Anyway, we Jews didn't kill him. It was the Romans."

The boy stood his ground, "Oh no, the Jews killed Jesus, and he *is* God."

We all went back into the synagogue and went our separate ways, but I was *quite* disturbed about the incident.

Who is Jesus? I asked myself. How can a man be God? Why was this boy saying we Jews killed him?

I didn't tell my parents until Sunday, when my father drove in from New Jersey to pick us up and take us home.

"Dad, who is Jesus?" I asked.

Everybody stopped talking and all eyes were on me. I knew I had struck a chord with that name.

"Why? Where did you hear that name?" Dad asked.

"At the synagogue," I said.

"At the synagogue? What are you talking about? It's impossible!" Mom shouted loudly.

"This little boy told me that we Jews killed God, and that Jesus was God," I cried out as the tears rolled down my cheeks.

"To think at that age to be an anti-Semite. The kid must hear that talk from his father." My dad cursed, yelling in a rage.

He then told me that Jesus was not God—only a man. He assured me that the Jews did not kill him—it was the Romans. He was upset about it the rest of the night, bringing up the subject several times on our drive back to our home in Linden. I wondered whether there was more to this man Jesus than meets the ear, but I was too afraid to ask.

When the holiday of Passover would come, my father drove us into Brooklyn to my grandparents' apartment to celebrate the Passover *seder,* or dinner. Some of my mother's family would join us there, including her brother, Jack, his wife, Lottie, and their two children, Arthur and Lorraine.

My grandfather would read the entire service in Hebrew, and we would follow along with a prayer book called the *Haggadah.* We would partake of the ritual food laid out before us. When the *Haggadah* told us to eat the bitter herbs, we ate. When it was time to drink a cup of wine, we drank.

My father was a jokester who couldn't take much of anything seriously. The only part of the event he didn't interrupt was drinking the cups of wine. Throughout the seder he would become quite verbose, making wise cracks or funny faces at us kids, causing us to laugh and get yelled at by the others. My mother was constantly kicking Dad under the table, or elbowing him in his side, trying to shut him up. "Charlie, please, this is a religious service. Be serious!" my mother would plead.

Dad would put a laced doily on his head and contort his face as he answered in a comical voice.

"Serious? Of course, Pearl, I'm always serious! What makes you feel I'm not?"

All of us kids would laugh, until Aunt Lottie would scream for Dad to stop ruining the seder.

I felt sorry for my aunt and uncle as they struggled through the ritual, only to be disrupted again and again by my father's joking.

One of his favorite antics was scaring us kids with Elijah's cup. This was the cup of wine that was filled at the seder's beginning but was never to be touched. It was reserved for the coming of the spirit of Elijah, who as tradition goes, would enter the door to take a drink. When the appointed time came my mother would open the apartment door to let the spirit of Elijah in.

Dad began to set us up for the kill. He'd use a spooky voice, as if he were a mystic from some horrible Hollywood *Grade-B* movie.

"Now watch the door, kids! Watch as the spirit enters!"

While we stared out the door in anticipation, Dad had sneaked a huge gulp of the wine from Elijah's cup, as he continued to control us.

"Look closely at the cup, he has already taken a drink!"

"He's right! He's right! Look! Some of the wine is gone," cousin Arthur shouted in excitement, his eyes open wide.

We all turned and stared at the cup, chills running up and down our spines.

Then in a very soft whisper, my father would guide us further into his deceit.

"Now keep a close eye on the cup, and you'll actually see him sip more wine."

We all sat perfectly still, giving Dad our every attention as he permitted a moment of very dramatic silence.

Then, without warning, he'd suddenly slam his hand down loudly on the table and scream: "There, did you see it! He sipped the wine!"

We'd all jump out of our seats in fear. At that point, Aunt Lottie and Mom would have taken all they could. They'd begin yelling at Dad, blaming him for ruining the seder.

While this seems humorous to me today, it was sad as well. After the commotion was over, I would always ask what the Passover was really about, and my mom would answer, "It's just tradition."

I am thankful that my uncle and aunt did one year remind me that there was a reason for the tradition.

"It's the celebration of God's deliverance of our ancestors from slavery in Egypt," Uncle Jack explained.

Of course, I already knew that from looking over the English part of the Passover *Haggadah* and I was happy that God delivered our people from slavery. However, deep inside me there was a desire to know what the celebration of Passover meant for us today. Was it just tradition or did the observance have a greater significance?

Little did I realize that the answer was sitting right in front of me, symbolized in the entire observance of the seder meal. This was the feast that the suffering Messiah used to point to Himself as the sacrificial Lamb who would take away the sins of the world. Here He would institute a new meaning to the breaking of the unleavened bread called matzoh and to the third cup of Passover wine which we would drink.

Years later I would learn that, like my Jewish brethren who blindly keep the tradition of the seder, most Christians do not understand the full meaning of communion, which the Messiah instituted during his final seder. Few seem to realize that Yeshua (Jesus' name in Hebrew) did this for very good reasons.

Passover was a festival commanded by God to be celebrated by the children of Israel yearly. This was to commemorate their deliverance from the bondage of slavery in Egypt by Pharaoh, just as my uncle told me. But that was just the beginning.

In the Torah, we read how each household of God's chosen people was to take an unblemished, or perfect, male lamb and sacrifice it. They were to apply the blood of the lamb to the door posts of their houses, so that the angel of death would pass over their homes, sparing their firstborn male children from death. The angel of death, seeing the blood of the lamb on the doorposts, *did* pass over their homes while all firstborn males of Egypt met death. This was the most horrible of ten plagues brought upon Egypt by God all because of the stubbornness of Pharaoh, who would not free the children of Israel

Israel's deliverance from the bondage of slavery was indeed dramatic as God parted the Red Sea, while he kept Pharaoh's attacking army at bay, using a pillar of fire from heaven. Once Moses and his people were on the other side, God allowed Pharaoh's armies to continue their pursuit. The same waters that were parted by the hands of God now came crashing down upon the enemies of Israel, creating a watery grave.

God commanded Israel to keep the Passover festival to remind future generations of God's mercy on His people.

Matzoh, the unleavened bread used in the ceremony, is the type of bread the children of Israel prepared to feed themselves as they escaped Egypt in haste. It is devoid of *leaven*, which the ancient rabbis said signifies sin.

At my grandmother's seder dinner, I would sit staring at the three pieces of matzoh that sat before me on a plate. I was puzzled as to what the meaning of these three matzohs were.

My grandfather would remove the middle matzoh, and, following the tradition, break it in two. Not one person in my family could tell me why this was done, year after year. Messianic Jews point out that the three pieces of matzoh represent the three personalities of the one God of Israel, God the Father, God the Son, and God the *Ruach Hakodesh* (Hebrew for the Holy Spirit).

It was the middle piece, representing the Son of God, which was broken in two. One half was covered with cloth for use later as the *aphikomen* (Hebrew for that which comes last). The other half was the piece of matzoh most likely used by the Messiah when he said, ". . . Take, eat: this is my body, which is broken for you: this do in remembrance of me" (1 Cor. 11:24).

What splendid symbolism—the unleavened bread represents the Messiah, whose sinless body was broken according to messianic prophecy in the Hebrew Scriptures.

The second half, the *aphikomen* which was covered with cloth, is later hidden in the room for the children to hunt and find. When the children find this piece of matzoh, they are rewarded with money. The hiding of the matzoh represents the hiding away of the Messiah's dead body in the grave. The finding of the matzoh, and the reward derived, alludes to the discovery by the believer of the resurrection—the reward of eternal life guaranteed to all who believe.

Another mystery that puzzled me as a child concerning the seder was why did we drink so many cups of wine? Messianic believers know that it was the third cup of wine, called *the cup of redemption*, that the Messiah drank and gave to His disciples as He said: "This cup is the new testament (or covenant) in my blood: this do ye, as oft as ye drink it, in remembrance of me" (1 Cor. 11:25).

No one who gathered at my grandparents' apartment truly understood the meaning of the cup of wine called Elijah's cup. Obediently every Passover, the door was opened to let the Spirit of Elijah in. My Dad's *kibbitzing* (joking) overshadowed the real meaning of this sacred moment. That cup of wine awaits the lips of the prophet Elijah, who, according to Malachi, chapter 4, verse 5, is to announce the coming of the Messiah.

Yet, the most significant portion of the Passover celebration is no longer observed by modern Jews today. The only remnant of this is the bone of the lamb, placed on the seder plate, but rarely understood fully. It was required every Passover that a representative of each Jewish household bring an unblemished lamb to the Holy Temple in Jerusalem for a blood sacrifice. When the sacrifice was completed, the levitical choir chanted *Hallel*, Psalms 113 through 118. It included these verses of Scripture which are a prayer for the coming of Messiah, the greatest hope for any Jew at Passover:

"Save now, I beseech thee, O Lord: O Lord, I beseech thee, send now prosperity. Blessed be *he that cometh in the name of the Lord.* . ." (Ps. 118:25–26).

The sacrificial lamb was the greatest symbol of the Messiah, represented today only by the shank bone sitting on the Passover plate. No longer do the Jewish people have a temple to sacrifice the lamb. John the Baptist, seeing Yeshua (Hebrew name for Jesus) said, ". . . Behold the lamb of God, which taketh away the sin of the world" (John 1:29).

The Messiah was likened to the unblemished lamb that our ancestors sacrificed and whose blood was placed on the door posts of each Jewish home. And God said in the Torah: ". . . the blood shall be to you for a token upon the houses where you are: and when I see the blood, I will pass over you, and the plague shall not be upon you to destroy you . . ." (Ex. 12:13).

The Messiah's sacrificial death, when he was nailed upon the tree on Passover, was not an accidental appointment. As a fulfillment of the messianic prophecy contained in the Jewish Scriptures, according to Isaiah chapter 53, the God of Israel would look upon the blood shed by the suffering Messiah, and our sins would be forgiven.

Just as Israel escaped the bondage of slavery to a wicked ruler, Pharaoh, we would now be freed from the bondage of our sins and our enslavement to the wicked ruler named Satan. Just as Israel looked forward to the Promised Land they were to possess, we who believe on the Messiah and His sacrifice for us can look forward to our dwelling forever in the promised land of heaven for all eternity.

Yet, as a young boy sitting at my grandparent's seder table, I would have to be content with my mother's answer to my questions about the Passover: "It was just tradition!"

SEVEN

I NEVER PROMISED YOU A ROSE GARDEN

How well I remember our neighborhood in Linden, as my friends and I would stay out late on a hot summer night. We'd lie on our backs on my front lawn and gaze up at the stars, talking about such concepts as who is God and what keeps the stars hanging in the sky. We talked about life on other planets and all agreed that there had to be a God who had created such a wonderful universe—a universe we could only catch a small glimpse of.

At eight years old, I was hearing ideas from the older kids about the reality of God. There was quite a mixture of thought, as the group included Protestants, Catholics, and Jews. Larry Wasser, a fellow Jew, would express a view that we Jews hold dear, namely that God is one God, not many. Though we kids had diverse opinions, we never argued with one another. Without defining it, we displayed mutual respect, welcoming inquisitiveness about one another's beliefs.

I became a close friend of Stanley Hecht, another Jewish boy who lived down the block. His mother and father were both survivors of the Holocaust. I'll never forget the first time I saw their concentration camp numbers, still visible where they had been etched on their arms twenty years before. From the Hechts, I first heard about the German atrocities against the Jewish people. Stanley showed me some gruesome pictures of the Holocaust from his large copy of *The Rise and Fall of the Third Reich*. I was reminded of the sobering fact of my being Jewish every time I passed the Hecht home. It wasn't a pleasant feeling to be reminded of the reality of anti-Semitism and the fact that I could have been a victim of a concentration camp had I lived in Germany in the 1930s and early 1940s.

During my elementary school years in Linden no Christian ever witnessed to me. When I think about this, it surprises me. I know there must have been some evangelical Christians in my school, but none of them told me about Jesus at a time when prayer was still allowed in the public school. Every morning a student would be appointed to read Psalm 23 from the Jewish Scriptures or the Lord's Prayer from the New Covenant.

One day stands out in my memory. A student, when asked to read the Lord's Prayer, told the teacher, "I am not allowed to read the last sentence of the prayer in the King James Bible."

The teacher asked him why?

He replied, "I'm a Catholic, and it's against our religion."

The teacher told him that he could read it without the last part. She told the others in the class that they could recite the rest of the prayer if they liked. I recited the prayer with the rest of the class and noticed that the Catholics made the sign of the cross, while the other Christians did not. The Catholics remained silent when it came to the last part of the prayer.

I was curious about the difference. I asked the Catholic boy, "Why can't you read the whole prayer?"

He leaned over and whispered, "The Catholic Church teaches that the verse was not included in the original version of the Bible."

The time passed slowly that day as I sat waiting for the dismissal bell to ring. All day, my eyes were on the King James Bible that sat on a wooden table by the window. I just couldn't wait to read the verse for myself. When the bell finally rang, I ran over to the teacher and asked, "Will you please open the Bible to that Lord's Prayer?"

She obliged, and it was the first time I had ever looked at a Bible. As I read the prayer for myself I was surprised to find that Jesus was the one teaching the prayer to others. I had no idea that there were any of his words recorded. I didn't realize that there even was an Old *and* New Testament. To me the Bible was the Torah (the five books of Moses). The controversial last line read: ". . . For thine is the kingdom, and the power, and the glory, forever. Amen" (Matt. 6:13). This seemed so harmless a prayer. I shrugged my shoulders, perplexed at all the fuss. This was my first exposure to the disunity of the church of Jesus Christ. I thought to myself, *If the Protestants and Catholics can't agree, then surely their God is a false one.*

On Christmas Eve, now nine years old, I was invited to the home of my Catholic friend, Bob Pirigyi. I loved the beautiful decorations, the wreaths and Christmas stockings, and, of course, the lovely Christmas tree. As I sat near the tree, I couldn't take my eyes off the hand-carved creche. I asked Bob what it was; he told me that it was the stable where Jesus was born. I had no idea what Christmas was all about. It was never explained to me. "Who are these people?" I asked.

Bob handled the pieces as he explained, "This is the baby Jesus. These are Mary and Joseph. These are the wise men."

I was perplexed, "Why is this under your tree?"

Bob looked up at me strangely. "Because it's Christmas." Just then, his mom entered the room. She had been listening to our conversation from the kitchen.

I was determined to understand.

"But *why* is it under the tree?" I persisted.

"It's Christmas. That's what Christmas is all about, the birth of Jesus," Mrs. Pirigyi explained.

Still not satisfied I asked, "So *why* is it under the tree?"

Mrs. Pirigyi became upset, raising her voice to end the discussion, "Because that's what we believe! We believe in Jesus. The Jewish people don't!"

I was too embarrassed to ask any more questions. What I was really groping for was an explanation of the true meaning of Christmas. Who was this baby Jesus that was being honored with such festivity? Why was he so important? My questions would have to wait until another day.

One year later, I remember having a serious discussion concerning Jesus. It was one that again included Bob Pirigyi and this time my other Catholic friend, Jerry Canavan. We were sitting on a front lawn when we began talking about God.

"You Catholics believe in three gods while we Jews believe in one," I said, repeating what I had been told by my parents.

"No we don't! We believe that God is one in three persons. God the Father, God the Son, God the Holy Spirit," Jerry replied.

I couldn't understand the distinction between three in one and three *separate* gods. I snapped back, "That's what I mean. You believe in three gods!"

They both got upset with me for not understanding. I apologized, but told them that I really wanted to understand what they meant. Each took his turn trying to explain the Trinity apart from what he had memorized in catechism class. The more they tried to explain it the more they seemed to question it themselves. I felt satisfied with what my parents had told me. The Trinity was something that was a mystery all right—especially since my Protestant and Catholic friends couldn't explain in any satisfactory manner how God the Father, God the Son, and God the Holy Spirit can be one God.

An encounter with anti-Semitism occurred when I followed Bob Pirigyi and one of his Catholic friends to explore the Rahway River, several blocks from my house. We climbed down to the river, and walked along twisted paths running beside it. We were having a wonderful time. We began climbing back up the bank near Saint John's Catholic Church. Suddenly a teenage gang of Catholic school children appeared at the top.

"Hey, you guys, what are you doing by our river?" the leader shouted down to us.

Bob shouted back, "Nothing! We're just walking and looking." The gang made its way down toward us.

"No one is allowed to walk by our river unless they ask permission," the leader shouted as he slid down the bank toward us.

He made his way up to Bob's friend, Red Renaldo, trying to pick a fight with him. One of the other gang members recognized Red Renaldo as the younger brother of one of his friends. "Aren't you a Renaldo?"

He answered that his brother went to Saint John's with them.

"I guess you're all right!" the leader declared, then addressed Bob Pirigyi, "What about you?"

Bob quickly mustered enough courage to speak. "I don't go to Saint John's school, but we go to church there."

The leader gave his approval to Bob.

Then he turned to me, "What about you, you go to church there?"

I blurted out the truth: "No. I'm Jewish!"

The gang started laughing and jeering me, "A Jew boy! We can't allow any Jews around here!"

I looked around. There was nowhere for me to run.

One of the gang began to shout, "Throw him in the river!"

Another told the leader, "Just beat the pulp out of him."

The pictures that Stanley Hecht had shown me of the emaciated Jewish people in the concentration camps suddenly flashed through my mind. At that moment, I understood a little of what it was like to be hated just because I was Jewish.

The members of the gang grabbed me and pushed me into the river. I broke out crying. They continued to make fun of me. I got out of the water and looked closely at each of their faces. I was determined to get revenge someway, somehow. That day would come.

Bob and I walked home in silence. There were no words he could say to comfort me.

When I was in the fifth grade, I developed a bad crush on a Protestant girl named Susan Krietz. I had it bad! I couldn't pay attention to my teacher. All day long I'd continually glance over at her and daydream. I envisioned myself with her, walking on the beach, doing the things that I'd seen couples do in movies—the innocent movies of those days—the montage sequences where one image dissolves into the next—holding hands, bicycle riding. There was another boy in the class, a Catholic named John Haliday.

I told him one day during recess, "John, can I tell you a secret that you promise you'll never tell?"

John nodded his head yes.

I mustered up the courage and let it out, "I have a crush on Susan."

John started to smile.

"Hey, I know where she lives. Do you want to go over to her house with me after school?"

I was reluctant, but he prodded me on. He told me that he had played basketball at her house in the past.

"She has a basket hoop in her backyard."

After school, we rode our bicycles to Susan's house. I couldn't believe it. There I was—playing basketball with her in her yard. There was no way I could concentrate on the game. I felt so good just to get close to her.

After the game, she briefly went inside, and John dropped a bomb on me. "Warren, can you keep a secret? I like Susan too!"

I was devastated because I considered John my friend. John had an idea.

"Hey, Warren, why don't I ask her which one of us she likes better?"

Before I could object, Susan had come back out. In spite of my hoping that John would forget to ask her, he popped the question.

Susan smiled, then dropped her head in embarrassment. Finally, she looked up. "I like you both!" she said enthusiastically.

John couldn't leave well enough alone.

"But out of the two of us, who would you let be your boyfriend?"

I could feel the color of my face turning red with anger. If there was a way of punching John in the nose without Susan seeing it, I'd have done so.

Susan didn't take long to respond.

"I'd have to say John, because Warren's Jewish."

Pains of rejection shot through my stomach as I blurted out, "But my parents don't care who I go out with! Besides, John's a Catholic, and you're Protestant."

"You're a nice person, Warren, but if things got serious we could never get married. It would never work out! I could never marry a Jewish boy. John and I at least believe in Jesus."

I felt my mouth begin to quiver. I tried to hold back the tears. I felt the pain of rejection and learned that being Jewish certainly made me different. I really had no opportunity to reject the Messiah since I really didn't understand who he was. And no Christian seemed to want to tell me.

After this, I began paying more and more attention to the difference between the Christian and the Jew. I wanted to understand what was this thing that was preventing a girl like Susan from entering into a deeper relationship with me.

I remember watching the school Christmas pageant very closely that year. The whole elementary student body was assembled in the auditorium. The houselights dimmed, and the choir members marched in unison with flashlights made to look like candles. I remember the beauty of that whole procession as they moved from the back to the front of the hall, singing a Christmas song as they climbed the stage and gracefully took their positions.

I searched the choir until my eyes fell on Susan. She looked beautiful—like some angel. I couldn't take my eyes off her. I watched her singing, listening intently to every word, trying to understand what Jesus and Christmas were all about.

They sang "The First Noel." I couldn't understand any particularly brilliant message hidden in the words. Suddenly, the words of the chorus sounded, "Born is the king of Israel."

I couldn't understand why they were referring to this baby as a king. And especially puzzling was how this baby could be the king of *Israel*. I figured it was just part of their mythology. I was further puzzled by the song "Emmanuel," in which another reference to Israel was made, "O come, O come Emmanuel, to ransom captive Israel." Again, however, no one took the time to explain to me the meaning of Christmas. Today, I wonder how much they really understood about the One whose birthday they celebrated, and how He can change one's life forever.

If the character of Jesus was alive in His spiritual body called the Church, then it must have been invisible, because I couldn't see it manifested in the lives of my Christian friends. There was absolutely no difference between their lives and mine. We listened and danced to the same rock music. We watched the same television shows and attended the same movies. We even told the same dirty jokes. If God was going to reach me with the truth concerning His reality, He would have to use some extraordinary means.

EIGHT

THE LOST WORLD

By the time I reached eleven years old, my mother begged my father to send me to Hebrew school for several years of religious instruction. My father didn't like the idea. He felt that religion was just *big business* and all the synagogue was after was his hard-earned money. As far as I was concerned, I hoped my father would win the argument, otherwise I'd have to give up two days a week of playtime and sit in Hebrew school. After months of arguing over the issue, my father relented, and I was enrolled at the Suburban Jewish Center for religious instruction.

I really hated going to Hebrew school. Every Monday and Wednesday immediately after public school, I would sit in a classroom at the synagogue to learn about my faith. I found that there were many people in my class who had the same feelings as I did. The leaders didn't teach us anything in terms of the meaning of our faith. The instruction mainly concentrated on how to read Hebrew, but we were not taught how to understand what we were reading.

The Jewish holidays were also discussed in terms of why our ancestors kept these traditional observances, rather than any discourse as to what relevance they might have for our lives today. The main reason for this was that most modern non-Orthodox Jews don't believe that the stories related in the Torah were real events. Rather, they are considered a collection of stories teaching important moral lessons. Our Hebrew teachers conveyed to us that the main reason for continuing these religious observances was merely to keep Judaism alive as a religion, and nothing more.

I listened as the teacher talked about the benefits of keeping a kosher home (the eating of prescribed foods that are sanctioned by the rabbi). We were not to eat pork or shellfish.

I thought to myself, *Tell that to my father who loved to eat a juicy ham sandwich and slurp down raw clams.*

I quickly realized that Hebrew school was not a place for getting to know God better. It was merely preparation for my future bar mitzvah. I don't remember any significant lessons taught at Hebrew school, nor were there any moments of challenge given to seek a closer relationship with God.

The services were no different. The Suburban Jewish Center was a conservative synagogue; this meant it was more liberal than the Orthodox synagogue my grandparents attended in Brooklyn. Women, men, and children were allowed to sit together during the service. The songs and prayers were all in Hebrew, but the rabbi spoke in English so we could understand the lessons. The services lasted several hours. The tragedy was that, for the most part, there was no actual feeling of the presence of God dwelling in the services.

I *did* enjoy singing the congregational hymns, even though they were in Hebrew and I didn't understand a word. The melodies of the songs did something to my spirit when I sang them. Little did I know that many of the songs were directly lifted from Jewish Scriptures and were songs of praise to God. There was one line of Hebrew that every Jew sang with all his heart and with understanding. It was simply known as the *Shema*. In this one moment, you could sense that every voice was focused on singing this Scripture: "*Shema, Yisroel, Adonai, Elohenu, Adonai Echod.*" The words in English meant "Hear, Oh Israel, the Lord our God, the Lord is one."

The rabbi once spent a whole service explaining the importance of these words. He said, "The heathens of the world worshiped many gods. Yet, the God of Israel made himself known as *one*, not many. Even our Christian neighbors believe in three gods, the Father, the Son, and the Holy Spirit. We as Jews reject the belief in three gods or even two. The Shema declares that God is one."

Yet the rabbi was not telling us the true meaning of the Shema. The Scripture does not teach against the Trinity. Nor does it teach that God is not two or three gods, even though it is true that the God of both Jews and Christians is monotheistic. The true meaning of the Shema deals with the fact that there is only *one true God*, the God of Israel. Most Jewish people would defend others' rights to believe in the god of their choice. The argument would be that one could call God Buddha or Krishna and still be reaching the one true God.

However, the Shema points out that the only true God is the God of Israel, that all other gods are false. The rabbi never pointed out to the congregation the many times Israel itself was judged by God for worshiping other gods. If other gods were a path to the one true God, then why wouldn't the God of Israel allow His people to worship these other gods? This is a very hard truth for most people to accept. How could God have chosen only Abraham to reveal his reality to? Is it possible that only the nation of Israel was worshiping the one and only true God of the universe, while the rest of the world was serving false gods? To this day, this concept has become a stumbling block to many.

In the Torah, Genesis chapter 12, verses 2 and 3, we read the promises that God made to Abraham:

And I will make of thee a great nation, and I will bless thee, and make thy name great; and thou shalt be a blessing:
And I will bless them that bless thee, and curse him that curseth thee . . .

So far these promises were made concerning the tiny nation of Israel only, but then God reveals His plan for the rest of the world: ". . . and in thee shall all the families of the earth be blessed."

The ancient rabbis agreed that this spoke of the coming of a Jewish Messiah who would bring the reality of the one true God, the God of Israel, to all the nations.

At the Suburban Jewish Center, whatever the rabbi taught, right or wrong, was accepted by the congregation. There was no personal attempt by us to study the Scriptures for ourselves, nor was it encouraged by our religious authority.

We were supposed to go to the synagogue every Friday night and Saturday morning. For the most part, the Marcus family seldom attended.

The exception was a high holy day like Yom Kippur, the Day of Atonement. Almost every Jew in town would show up for this most holy day. It was tradition that this was the one day that a Jew's sins for the year could be forgiven and we could obtain a fresh start. The service lasts all day. We were to abstain from eating all food from sundown the day prior until sundown of the day ending the holiday. Drinking water was permissible. The service was long and tedious.

Many of the adults would not even be listening to the service. They would talk and socialize with friends and relatives they hadn't seen for a long time. The religious few would always turn around and try to quiet them down. Their cries for silence often went unheeded because most Jewish people do not realize how truly important this service is. Most of the crowd felt that just by attending the synagogue on this most holy day, they were insured forgiveness. The concept of repentance was never communicated.

Often the children would wind up leaving the service to go outside. There, many interesting things would happen—arguments, fistfights, and boys trying to get dates from the well-dressed girls. An elder of the temple would often come out to yell at us!

"It's a holiday! What are you doing out here? The Gentiles will see you!" As if they'd care.

The original meaning of the holy day was never explained to us. Today, I understand it. The Torah clearly lays out the importance of this day in Leviticus, chapter 17, verse 11: "For the life of the flesh is in the blood: and I have given it to you upon the altar to make an atonement for your souls: for it is the blood that maketh an atonement for the soul."

God in the Torah demanded the daily sacrifice of an animal for sins committed by an individual. He made it clear that only the shedding of blood can restore a man's fellowship with his God. There was no other way prescribed by God for the forgiveness of breaking God's commandments. The animal suffered death in the place of the one who sinned.

Actually, Yom Kippur was not meant for the forgiveness of an individual's sins, but rather, for the forgiveness of the entire nation of Israel.

According to the Torah, two male goats were selected. Each had to be unblemished. One was the goat to be sacrificed. The other was the "scapegoat," the one set free.

The twelve elders, one each from the twelve tribes of Israel, would lay hands on the goat to be sacrificed. These elders represented the entire nation of Israel. The sins of the entire nation were transferred in God's eyes to the male goat. The high priest killed the goat and collected its blood in a basin.

The other goat was then set free, symbolizing that the price had been paid for forgiveness and the nation was set free from the penalty of sin.

The Day of Atonement was the one time of the year that the *Kohan Gadol* (high priest) could enter the holiest part of the tabernacle, or temple. This innermost place was called the Holy of Holies. This is the place in which God's actual presence dwelt, called the *shekinah glory*. If any man other than the high priest tried to enter, he would immediately die by the almighty hand of God.

The high priest would carry the basin of blood into the Holy of Holies. He was the intercessor with God for the entire nation. On his breastplate were twelve stones which represented the twelve tribes. A rope was tied to one of his feet, so that if he was overcome by the presence of God, he could be pulled out to safety.

When he entered the Holy of Holies, the shekinah glory of God would illuminate and reflect off the faceted stones on the high priest's breastplate. The sight must have been glorious for the high priest to see. The blood was then applied by the high priest to the ark of the covenant. Then and only then was God's wrath totally satisfied against the nation.

It is my belief the Jewish people are not taught the truth concerning this holiday by the rabbinical authorities because every Jew would quickly realize that without a temple, which contains the Holy of Holies, we cannot obtain God's forgiveness, according to the Torah.

The truth concerning the real meaning of this holy day I was never taught, and millions of Jewish people today blindly follow a non-traditional celebration of this most important holy day.

At the age of eleven, I attended a cousin's bar mitzvah. The service ended, and the family gathered in an adjoining gym for the catered bar mitzvah party. A band played contemporary rock music. Except for the traditional hora, a Jewish folk song both sung and danced, there was no religious music. Hard liquor was flowing. Many of the men in the family were getting soused. I could tell that my father had his fill when he burst out in song for the entire gathering to hear. They laughed and encouraged him to continue singing, on stage at the microphone.

Trays of kosher food were heaped high: Matzoh ball soup, krepla, kishka, prime rib, and an entire table of non-dairy desserts!

I asked myself, *Where is God in all this?* I silently slipped out of the banquet and made sure my yarmulke was still sitting on my head.

I made my way into the now empty synagogue. The lights were off except for the eternal light, an oil lamp which hung before the Ark of the Torah.

I walked slowly toward the middle of the empty room. I believed in God. The boyhood dream I had as a five-year-old had been so real to me, but where was God now? I wanted to see Him again and talk to Him face to face.

I looked upward toward heaven and spoke to God, "God of Israel, where are You? Why aren't You here in this place? Why can't I see You like Moses could see You? I can't feel Your presence. Is this the way the synagogue is supposed to be?"

In the book of Proverbs, chapter 29, verse 18, we read: "Where there is no vision, the people perish: but he that keepeth the law, happy is he."

Another way of translating this verse is, "Where there is no *hope*, the people perish." If any people have had their hope dashed from them, it has been the Jewish people—persecuted in captivity, despised, and rejected as a nation dispersed throughout the world. Our ancestors were killed in eastern European pogroms, as so-called Christians locked Jews in their synagogues, set them on fire, and watched them burn, while marching around singing Christian hymns. Hitler imprisoned and killed more than six million Jews in the Holocaust. After years of persecution, our people have lost their hope and even their faith in a real God.

The Jewish people no longer believe in the reality of miracles. What hope can they have when they or their loved ones face terminal illness? What hope is there against cancer, if there is no faith to be found? What hope is there if the God of Israel is impotent as to performing miracles?

No longer do the Jewish people understand the seriousness of disobeying God. Some rabbis today tell us that *sin* is a Christian concept, never embraced by Jews. If that is so, why does so much of the Torah talk about the sacrificial system and a priesthood that exists no more?

Today, I think about how lonely I was that day as I stood in the empty sanctuary of the synagogue. If only the rabbi had taught me then about the fact that God has promised the Jewish people a new covenant, not like the one given to us by Moses in the wilderness. He could have shared what is written in the book of Jeremiah, chapter 31, verses 31 through 34:

> Behold, the days come, saith the LORD, that I will make a new covenant with the house of Israel, and with the house of Judah:
>
> Not according to the covenant that I made with their fathers in the day that I took them by their hand to bring them out of the land of Egypt; which my covenant they brake, although I was an husband unto them, saith the LORD:
>
> But this shall be the covenant that I will make with the house of Israel; After those days, saith the LORD, I will put my law in their inward parts, and write it in their hearts; and will be their God, and they shall be my people.
>
> And they shall teach no more every man his neighbor, and every man his brother, saying, Know the LORD: for they shall all know me, from the least of them unto the greatest of them, saith the LORD: for I will forgive their iniquity, and I will remember their sin no more.

If only the rabbi would have shared the greatest hope of all, the promise of a Jewish Messiah.

Blind tradition and observances in the synagogue have taken the place of seeking after the reality of a living God—the God who talked to Moses—a God who desires to communicate with us and meet our needs. Is it any wonder why there are so many Jewish people asking, "Has God forsaken His chosen people?"

NINE

THE TEN COMMANDMENTS

I could not find God in the synagogue, nor was there any meaning in the modern way we celebrated our Jewish religious observances. Nor was God manifested in the lives of my Christian friends. Yet, just as God revealed Himself to me in a childhood dream, He would reveal Himself again, but this time on the screen of the Linden Movie Theater.

My mother took me to see the motion picture epic, *The Ten Commandments*. I was riveted to the screen for the entire movie. I did not even leave my seat during the intermission to get more popcorn, because I was afraid we would return late and miss a portion of the movie.

There was God, bigger than life, talking to Moses from the burning bush. When Moses' staff turned into a snake, I realized that the God of Israel was a God of miracles.

God manifested Himself as the judge of the unrighteous as the ten plagues fell upon the Egyptian nation.

I marveled at the pillar of fire as it held back the great armies of Pharaoh and as the Red Sea dramatically parted allowing the children of Israel to walk to the other side on completely dry ground.

I cheered as the sea closed on the pursuing Egyptian army, destroying the enemies of Israel.

My heart pounded within me with an unexplainable fear and wonder as I watched Moses confronting the God of Israel face to face on Mount Sinai. I truly sensed the reality of God as His fingers carved the Ten Commandments on the stone. There I was in a movie theater, yet I felt the presence of God all around me. It was the same feeling I experienced in my childhood dream. The voice of God in the movie was just like the voice I heard in my dream. Even the magnificent countenance of God in the form of light was similar to His appearance in my dream. I could feel my heart beating quickly and hard.

Suddenly, I remembered what God had told me in the dream, "Do not be afraid, I am your friend."

I thought to myself, *This God who can part the Red Sea is my friend?*

An immense supernatural peace seemed to flood my being. Then, I beheld the children of Israel rejecting God below the mountain, thinking Moses was not coming back. They partied and worshiped the golden calf.

No preacher could have ever delivered a sermon as powerful as what I witnessed with my entire being in that movie theater. The reality of God had overtaken me. Not only was my God a God of miracles, but He was a God of judgment. I gaped in awe as He opened the earth to swallow those of Israel who worshiped the golden calf.

The sense of God's reality went home with me from the movie theater. Weeks later, at the synagogue I heard the rabbi talking about the movie. He tried to make apologies for the Torah which describes the parting of the Red Sea in the same miraculous manner as the film.

Dressed in his black religious robe of authority he addressed the congregation, "The Torah is full of wonderful stories with great moral teachings. Some of the events are based on true events, others are oral tales, later embellished by the writer. Of course, we don't take these stories literally."

I felt like a deflated balloon as the rabbi spoke. Could it be what gave me such hope and joy is nothing but a story?

The rabbi continued, "I once heard an Israeli scientist describe a theory of how the Red Sea could have parted. It is reported that once every thousand years a great mystery of science prevails in that area of the Middle East. The Red Sea dries up and parts become low enough to walk over. So, the actual event was something very commonplace, but the timing of this natural scientific phenomenon made it a miracle."

As the rabbi smiled at the wisdom he imparted, I was deeply troubled. He might have explained away the parting of the Red Sea, but how did this prevent Pharaoh's armies from pursuing the children of Israel? The Torah lesson I had heard said that they were all destroyed as the water came down upon them.

Another motion picture which had great impact upon me was *Ben Hur*. Again, it was my mother who took me to the theater to see it.

I instantly became engrossed in the scope of this epic picture. The biblical story line pictured the person of Jesus Christ in a compassionate but mysterious way. We never saw His face, but His presence was revealed in brief glimpses throughout the story.

I was deeply moved as Jesus gave the meek and thirsty main character, played by Charlton Heston, a drink of water. You could only see the hand of Jesus, but the glow on the face of Charlton Heston as he looked into the eyes of Jesus conveyed the majesty of the Messiah's presence.

Yet, nothing could prepare me for the deeply moving scenes of the final hours of Jesus. The passion of the cross overtook me as I witnessed a beaten form of a man carrying his cross. I was moved to tears as Charlton Heston carried the cross for Jesus.

The dramatic climax took my breath away as I silently watched Jesus agonizing on the cross with nails in his hands and feet. Tears began to roll down my cheeks as I asked myself, *Why did they have to kill this innocent, gentle man?*

The glorious conclusion of the movie raptured me into another world; a sense of the reality of God's presence began to fill my being. It all seemed so real as the sky darkened and the lightning flashed and the thunder rolled. Before my eyes, the lepers were healed, and somehow I knew that I had met a great man of God in Jesus.

After the movie was over, I asked my mother if Jesus was real. I wanted Him to be real. I wanted the story to be true, but she turned and said, "No, it was just a story."

Yet, the reality of God had once more overtaken me through the viewing of a motion picture. The movie screen had a way of transcending reality unlike any other medium. Through the use of the camera, lighting, sound, and editing, the story transports us right into the very screen. The motion picture can affect the intellect, the emotion, and the very spirit of humanity.

In my room that night, I realized that God can use the motion picture as a means to speak to the masses, just as He used a burning bush to speak to Moses. I decided that I wanted to become a filmmaker and produce movies that say what God would have me say.

I began reading every book from the library concerning the art of motion-picture production. By the time I reached twelve years old, I began to say a nightly prayer to God.

I repeated this prayer every night for one year: "Oh God, whoever You are, I ask that You make me a great producer, director, writer, cameraman, editor, and I will make films that say only what You want me to say."

I didn't even know who God really was, nor did I understand how I would be able to hear His instructions. All I wanted was to be used by Him to bless others.

To this day I cannot understand why not even one Christian ever told me why I should believe in Jesus as my Messiah. It seemed as if they did not understand their own faith. The amazing thing is that not even my best friends tried to tell me about the Messiah of Israel. It is as if they assumed that my being a Jew meant that I wouldn't be interested in hearing about Him.

Could it be that today's church is repeating the same mistakes of Israel during the times of Jesus? Could it be that the very things that Jesus condemned in the Pharisees are being repeated by many in the church today—legalism and following of the doctrines of men, instead of living lives of obedience to God's commandments? Has following blind tradition become more important than seeking God's truth? Christian, please ask yourself the next time you are praying if you truly meant what you said, or are you like the Pharisees repeating meaningless prayers by rote? Next time you are worshiping God in song, check if your heart is truly in it. What about communion? Has it become as empty a traditional observance for you as the Passover Seder has become for many modern Jewish people? Is today's church so steeped in blind tradition and empty observances that it has become impotent in carrying out the great commission?

TEN

INVASION OF THE BODY SNATCHERS

God is constantly reaching out to each one of us with His reality. He will use people, events and circumstances to draw us closer to Himself. Sometimes, as with me, He will use extraordinary means. I often wonder why God took such effort to reach me. Certainly, there were easier and more noble targets. For whatever reason, it remains a mystery. When I was five years old, God had appeared to me in a dream. Then, years later, again He spoke to my heart, this time from the motion picture screen of our local theater.

However, God isn't the only one trying to get our attention. Satan, the enemy of God, will use every method at his disposal to capture our souls. As a child, I was confronted with the same temptations and lustful desires as anyone my age. While God was seeking, hounding, and wooing me by His Spirit—so, as the Bible declares, was the world, the flesh, and the devil trying to win my soul into a kingdom of slavery and bondage.

I remember growing up with a strong urge to question the world around me. Why am I here? What is the purpose of life? Why does God allow suffering in the world? These were a few of the questions that my little mind would ponder.

My closest childhood friend was my cousin Floyd. He lived one block from my house in the same suburban development. By the time I was nine years old, I would walk to his house and spend hours with him. In many ways, he was a great influence on me. Floyd was the only child of my Uncle Ben, Dad's brother.

I loved to spend time at Floyd's house. He always had the latest toys, and Uncle Ben always made me feel at home. He loved my father, the eldest brother of the family.

Uncle Ben was once a drummer with one of the big bands. It

was his twin brother, Uncle Sol, who had written such hit songs as "When the Lights Go on Again All Over the World," "I Don't Want to Set the World on Fire," "Till Then," and "Don't Let Me Be Misunderstood." Many times, I would stay late at Floyd's house, especially when Uncle Ben would sit at the vibraphones playing riffs on the vibes, while Uncle Sol would sit at the piano in one of their all-night jam sessions. Sometimes, Floyd would sit at the drums, then I'd switch off and play the drums, while Floyd picked up a guitar.

At twelve midnight the phone would always ring. My mother would call, annoyed that I was not home yet. I learned quickly that my best defense was to let Uncle Ben talk her into letting me spend the night, so I could be a part of the scene taking place at what I endearingly called: "Bennie's Bar & Grill."

"Oh, Pearl, let Warren stay over. Solly's over here and Floyd. You should hear your son play the drums," he would shmooze.

"But, Bennie, it's so late. I don't want him coming in so late," she would argue.

Ben kept up the pressure, "Pearl, what harm is there? Let the kid enjoy himself. I'll drive him home myself when we're done." I would often wander in at 3 A.M. or later, and Mom would lecture me the next morning. However, I continued to use Uncle Ben's pleading strategy until she relented and even gave me a key so I would not wake up my father when I sneaked into the house.

By the age of eleven, Floyd was convinced that he was going to have a career in the music industry. He told me about a movie he saw in school about Franklin Delano Roosevelt.

"Warren, do you realize that Franklin Roosevelt once said as a boy, 'I am going to be a famous man one day! I'm going to be the president of the United States!'" Floyd's eyes were wide with excitement.

I failed to see the significance. "So what?"

Floyd was amazed at the fact that one might actually be able to forge one's own destiny.

Floyd had big dreams and hopes. "Warren, he knew what he wanted at our age and he set out to accomplish the goal. He had a jump on his peers! I'm gonna do what Franklin Roosevelt did. I'm gonna tell you right now, Warren, that I'm gonna be a great rock star some day!"

As I walked home that day, it suddenly dawned on me what had influenced Floyd's decision to choose music as his career. It was seeing a motion picture. What power there is in the motion picture! Forceful enough to persuade someone to make decisions that would affect the rest of his life.

I could empathize with Floyd's dream, because I too had a lofty vision—to become the greatest filmmaker the world has ever seen.

"God, please let me make movies that help others make decisions to believe in You," I prayed with new fervor.

I tended to look up to Floyd because he dared to dream about the future and put his plans in motion. And, Floyd wanted me to be a part of it all. He even began teaching me how to sing.

We loved the Everly Brothers and practiced their songs. On Friday nights, when Uncle Ben and Sol would begin their jam sessions, Floyd and I would sing, and Uncle Ben would beg Sol to open up doors for Floyd and me in the music industry. Floyd began to write his own material and began to get ideas about forming a rock band.

I followed along in music. I fell in love with playing the drums and began taking lessons at school, but my heart was into making movies. And while Floyd decided at a very young age that he wanted to be a rock star, I was determined to be a filmmaker, a director, a cameraman, a producer, a writer, an editor—I wanted to do it all! Just by hanging out with one another, we encouraged one another to pursue our dreams.

Unknown to me at that time, Uncle Ben was an avowed atheist. I would never have guessed this since Ben would always bid everybody farewell by saying, "God love you." I learned that Floyd's mother, Stella, had suffered a serious bout with breast cancer. The radical mastectomy not only scarred Aunt Stella's body, but left indelible wounds on her marriage. Uncle Ben could never believe in a God who allowed such suffering, and the only comfort he could find was in a Seagram's 7 bottle.

Once I remarked to Floyd about the conversation I had with my Gentile neighbors when we sat on the grass staring up at the stars.

"Floyd," I asked, "did you ever look at the stars and realize the miracle of God's creation?"

Floyd laughed, "I don't believe in a god!"

I was dumbfounded.

"What do you mean you don't believe in God? How can you not believe?"

"All right, prove it to me! Prove to me that God exists!" he challenged me.

"All you have to do is gaze at the stars and you'll see that only God could have created them. Look at pictures of the Grand Canyon. Could anything man has created compare with that?" I retorted.

"That doesn't prove the existence of God. You can't show me definite proof that He exists, so He doesn't," Floyd continued.

I started telling him about my childhood dream. I could sense his interest. I described the way God looked and spoke. He seemed to hang on my every word.

A sudden obstinate look seemed to shadow his countenance.

"That still doesn't prove that there is a God. It was just a dream!"

I could see there was no way to communicate how real that dream was to me. How could Floyd sense what I was feeling? I never had another dream that ever could approach that life-changing experience. I gave up on trying to convince Floyd. He seemed set in his ways. It appeared to bother him that he couldn't convince me to reject God.

Fed up with his negativity, I put on my coat to leave.

"Floyd, maybe I can't prove to you that God exists, but you can't prove to me He doesn't!"

Floyd seemed to move backwards like some fighter who was hit with an unexpected left hook. Floyd was learning about life from his father's own atheistic viewpoints. He wasn't prepared for the challenge I had proposed.

As I was walking out the door, he aimed his gun one more time. "If God is real, then why doesn't He come right now into this room and reveal Himself to me?"

I couldn't answer his question, but I understood the difference between us. I had seen God in a miraculous dream, but Floyd had never experienced His reality.

This conversation did not hurt my friendship with Floyd. I loved to hang out with him. My other friends seemed to be so shallow in intellect. They would rather play baseball than exercise their minds.

I was ten years old when Floyd showed me my first *Playboy* magazine. It was the first time I had gazed on a picture of a naked woman. I found an unexplainable attraction in these pictures. Yet inside, I could not escape the feeling that I was doing something wrong. I couldn't remember anyone teaching me that I shouldn't look at *Playboy*. However, I felt uneasy about this newfound voyeurism. There was no one around to explain to me about what the Bible calls a "God-given conscience."

Floyd taught me about the *Playboy* philosophy:

"There is nothing wrong in looking at the naked body. Only, society has said it is wrong. Even the Bible says that Adam and Eve were naked!"

I assume that he was using the Bible to drive his point home, knowing that this might make an impression on me. And that it did.

When I got home that night, I remember blurting out to my mother, "What's wrong with looking at a naked woman?"

My mother was embarrassed and shaken by my question, "What do you mean *why* is it wrong? It is *just wrong* to expose ourselves to one another!"

"But who says it is wrong? Adam and Eve were naked, weren't they? Where did the concept of clothes come from, anyway? Aren't there nudist colonies where people don't wear clothes? Aren't there?" I rattled on.

My mother seemed puzzled, "Where did you hear such things?"

I was only ten years old, and in those days it must have been a shock to my mother to realize that her little boy was growing up so fast.

"At Floyd's house. He showed me some *Playboy* magazines," I answered.

"Where did he get his hands on that? Those things are disgusting!" Mom said in revulsion.

"Uncle Ben and Aunt Stella gave them to him to read," I told her.

"I think that's horrible! It's just wrong to be naked in front of others!" she contended.

Her explanation seemed to be exactly what Hugh Hefner explained it to be. Society put such restraints on mankind; it was tradition passed down by our ancestors, but there really was nothing wrong with being naked. On the contrary, the human body was beautiful. It was as if she were giving the usual Jewish response, "It's tradition! Just obey and shut up!"

As I discussed my new interest with my Gentile neighborhood friends, I found that they too were aware of *Playboy*. Furthermore, several of the older boys knew where their parents hid other books of this nature. I remember going into their homes just after school, when their parents were not yet home from work. A friend would open a closet, or some drawer in his parents' dresser and carefully sift through junk and pull out the buried treasure. We would sneak peeks at these naked women, while looking out the window in case the parents came home earlier than expected. We'd laugh at some of the pornographic photos, not quite understanding what they were all about. There was a sort of fascination. Still, I kept asking myself why I felt it was wrong to look at those magazines. Was the feeling coming from the fact that my friends' parents could be angry if we were caught? Why was it all right for the parents to have those books and not us?

Later that year, a horrible series of experiences with an older teenager would prove to be Satan's greatest effort to rob my youthful innocence. It is not important what relation he was to me, nor his actual name. For purposes of communication, I will refer to him as Ted. Sexual abuse is more common than the American public chooses to accept. Only children who have experienced the horror of this moral perversion can accurately comprehend how deeply the following events could effect my entire way of thinking. I warn you not to read the rest of this chapter if you are overly sensitive to sexual matters.

A friend named Ted began reading books to me on sexual encounters. I wasn't comfortable listening to the graphic descriptions. Furthermore, since I was not yet sexually active, I didn't quite understand his fascination with this matter. Little did I know that he was already involved with exploring his own sexual identity. To this day, I wonder whether or not, by sharing with me, he was laying a foundation to later involve me in his sexual experiments. I'd rather like to believe that we were both victims of the godless philosophies contained in the books on his father's shelves.

I would leave Ted's house with a queasy feeling, but I was

challenged by this young man's intellectual depth and intrigued with learning about the unknown.

I trusted and loved my mom and was never afraid to ask her anything, but my questions were becoming more and more difficult for her to answer. She would stop and stutter, but always answer my every inquiry the best she could. However, when it came to discussing the "facts of life" she would freeze.

"Where are you hearing about all this?"

"Some of the kids in school," I finally learned to lie, for fear that she would not allow me to play at my friend's house anymore.

She called to my sister for help. Fran was always great to talk with. She was twenty years old and seemed to know everything. We loved each other very much.

"What's the problem, Ma?" she asked as she came into the kitchen, grabbing an apple from the refrigerator. When my mother told her that I was asking questions about sex, Fran seemed as shocked as my mom that I was already aware of such things.

Fran tried her hand at explaining it the right way.

"Sex is a beautiful thing. That's how you were born." As she continued, it suddenly dawned on me that my parents had sex. My sweet mother was doing the type of things I had seen in some of my friends' porno books. I was now getting sick and very confused.

My sister went to the library and got a book entitled: *The Storks Don't Bring Babies*.

"Here, Warren. I think this will answer your questions," Fran said.

I read every word of it, but it didn't answer all my questions about sex. Without anyone to tell me the biblical answers to these questions, I began to visit Ted's house more frequently for the answers.

It was after school, and Ted's parents weren't home yet from work. As usual, Ted and I were sitting in his bedroom and he brought out his Playboy magazines. We began talking about sex. Ted began to tell me about his experimentation with his own body. He then told me to take off my clothes and said he would show me. He began to remove his clothing, but I resisted. I was quite uncomfortable with the situation.

"Come on! Take off your clothes!" he said, a bit angry. He was now standing naked in front of me.

"I don't want to!" I said.

"Why not?" he said angrily.

I tried to think of the right words to say.

"What about your parents? What if they come home?" I finally blurted out.

Ted stopped for a moment, then proceeded to take a baseball bat and wedge it between the bedroom door and the wall of the closet which jutted out causing a wedge.

"There, if they come, this will give us enough time to put on our clothes," he said, turning back to me.

Reluctantly, I took off my clothes. That day Ted began experimenting sexually with me. He threatened to beat me up if I didn't do exactly what he said. All I wanted to do was get home. I prayed to God that his parents would come home, but they didn't. I received no enjoyment from the experience, especially since I was not yet sexually mature. Ted warned me to tell no one.

When I got home that afternoon, I went to my room and cried. I felt sick and dirty inside. I didn't understand how I could let Ted talk me into doing such things with him. I felt there was nowhere I could turn for help. I cried out to God for His forgiveness, and I vowed to myself never to go over to Ted's house again.

I didn't go over to Ted's house for at least a week, nor did I call him. Finally, he called me. There was no discussion about the event. He asked me to come over and play.

I quickly made up an excuse.

"I can't Ted, I have to do my homework."

Ted seemed to know I was lying.

"No that's not why! You're lying to me!"

I did my best trying to convince him that I was telling him the truth. Yet, I could not get him off the phone without promising that I would see him the next day.

For the next several weeks, I would go outside and play with my other friends until it was too late to go over to Ted's house. I would not answer the phone, and when my mother told me he was on the phone, I would tell her to say I was out, or sleeping.

Finally, Ted came to my house. He demanded to speak to me. I went outside, and we sat on the front steps.

"Why don't you want to play with me anymore? Don't you like me anymore?" he confronted me.

"I still like you. I've just been busy!" I tried my best to lie.

Ted knew that what had happened at his house was the real reason I would not come over.

"Look, I'm sorry for what happened. If you come over, nothing will happen," he promised me.

He told me about a new toy he received for his birthday. It was a battery operated airplane with propellers that turned and would actually taxi. I went with Ted to his house. As he promised, nothing bad happened that day.

My routine of playing over at Ted's house continued without incident, until several weeks later. Ted's father had placed a new book about sex on Ted's shelf. He began to read to me a chapter on homosexual sex. The author treated the subject as if it was normal and proper for adults to engage in. Without saying anything more, Ted went to his bedroom door and took the baseball bat to secure it.

"Take off your clothes!" he ordered me.

I began to cry. At first, he had compassion on me and he began to cheer me up. He tried to convince me there was nothing wrong with what he wanted to do. I told him that I didn't want to take off my clothes. Then, suddenly, he became fed up with my resistance, and he became angry, threatening to beat me up. I got up off the bed and tried to leave, but Ted pushed me down back onto the bed. He was much stronger than me, since he had lifted weights since the age of seven. The specifics of what happened in Ted's bedroom that day are better left untold.

Almost as quickly as it happened, Ted's and my interests turned to girls and dating. Any conversations we would have about sex dealt with male/female relationships. To this day, I do not blame Ted. He was just as much a victim as I was. The books his parents gave him to read were a powerful influence over him.

Puberty is a difficult time for most young people, especially for those who lack sound counsel and wise guidance by understanding adults. My own sexual transition from childhood to adulthood was surely traumatic. The guilt and shame that I silently held deep within me robbed me of the joy God intended to have concerning a healthy sexual outlook—looking forward to a future day when I would marry. Satan had used others to introduce me to a habitual desire for pornography and perverted sex.

Even without any teaching from the *Tanakh* (Jewish Scriptures) or from the *B'rit Hadashah* (the New Covenant), there was something inside that told me that sex outside of marriage was wrong. I later learned that the Bible tells us that God puts in each one of our hearts a conscience. Yet, if we keep violating the conscience, it begins to become dull and ineffective. Paul the Apostle, in First Timothy, chapter 4, verses 1 and 2, puts it this way:

> Now the Spirit speaketh expressly, that in the latter times some shall depart from the faith, giving heed to seducing spirits, and doctrines of devils;
> Speaking lies in hypocrisy; having their conscience seared with a hot iron.

Had I been properly taught what the Scriptures say concerning sexuality, I might have made better choices. Leaving the child to his own conscience is a dangerous game. A child is very vulnerable without a biblical understanding of what is right and wrong and he is open to abuse. The conscience alone can never be enough to guide us in our decision making. A great fault of parents in the synagogue and the church today is that the subject of sex is seldom discussed with their children. This is one of the main failures that Satan can use to cause irreparable harm that will follow a child into his adult life. The Bible *does* have answers for what is right and wrong concerning sex. However, if parents don't discuss a correct view of sex with their children, they will learn it the wrong way from "the street." Had my dear mother known what the Jewish Scriptures had to say on the subject, perhaps I would have been spared the humiliation of sexual abuse, early on, even before it happened.

God is concerned about every aspect of our person: our minds, our bodies, our spirits, and even our sexuality. The Bible teaches that God blessed the act of sex for procreation and enjoyment in marriage. He told Adam and Eve to be fruitful and multiply. He gave Eve to be Adam's wife—to be flesh of his flesh and bone of his bone. In the book of Hebrews, chapter 13, verse 4, Paul states that in marriage sex is undefiled.

"Marriage is honorable in all, and the bed undefiled: but whoremongers and adulterers God will judge."

Had I been taught what God has to say about nakedness in the Torah, I would never have looked at that first issue of *Playboy* magazine. In appendix A at the rear of the book, I have listed a number of Scriptures that deal with sexual purity.

God has given the information in Scripture for each parent to explain to their children "the facts of life" in a way that guards them from the errors of the world and the attacks of Satan as they mature. The pleasure that one derives from sex is God-given, and the desire to want to satisfy oneself is also God-given. Yet, sex must be surrendered to God like any other appetite that we have. If we indulge ourselves whenever we are hungry, with any food in our refrigerator, we will almost certainly have a weight problem.

I thank God that He protected me from becoming a slave to sexual desires. Even though I sinned, He had mercy to keep me from plunging deeper into a life that could have led to an early death. Today, AIDS lurks in the darkness, looming over every sexual encounter outside of God's prescription for sex.

Were I a preteen today, how easy it would be for a sexual abuser to talk me into the idea that I was born to be a homosexual. With television, movies, politicians, and magazines declaring homosexuality as an acceptable lifestyle, I could have been easily persuaded into becoming a part of the modern-day gay movement. However, God in His mercy protected me.

How much easier it would have been if my dear mom or dad had known the appropriate Scriptures and taught them to me.

Homosexuality, heterosexual offense such as fornication or adultery, and self-gratification are all dealt with by God in His Holy Word.

No parents, Jewish or Gentile, can effectively share what the Bible says with their children while living in sexual sin themselves and then expect their children to remain holy before God. If they have pornography hidden in their closet, their children will find it. If they rent dirty movies from the video store, the children will feel they are condoning sexual sin by their actions.

In the Jewish Scriptures we read that the act of sexual sin is wrong in the eyes of God and calls for the perpetrator to repent. In the New Covenant, the Messiah clarified what true holiness demands. In the Sermon on the Mount, He said that the *thought* of adultery was already the sin. So too, we must realize that the thought of hate is in like manner the same as the act of murder. If we entertain the thought of stealing, we have already committed the sin of stealing. This strict call to holiness is hard to understand. It is simply impossible for us to be as holy as God has commanded us to be apart from the sacrificial Lamb, the Messiah, who died so we might have forgiveness.

How can a child ever lead a holy life, learning from the current moral trends of society or even from blind tradition, without understanding? Only through an education in the Word of God, learning what God expects of him, can a child even begin to understand what holiness is.

My wrong introduction to sex as a ten year old started me on a wrong view of women—primarily looking at them as sex objects, the way *Playboy* magazine categorized them. It was something that took root very early and continued into my adult years. What we learn as children often becomes a pattern in our lives. That is why Proverbs, chapter 22, verse 6, promises us:

Train up a child in the way he should go: and when he is old, he will not depart from it.

Likewise, if he learns the things of the world, these will carry on into the days of his adulthood. The only hope of breaking these patterns of sin is through the blood of the Messiah, and the forgiveness and freedom he offers.

Eleven

The Philadelphia Story

By the time I was in the seventh grade, my prayer life with God had intensified. Every night I prayed for God to bring peace and understanding on the earth. I asked Him for forgiveness over those areas in my life which were not pleasing to Him, and I continued to ask God to make me a great filmmaker.

My sister Fran was not the only sibling who had a good influence on me. My brother Stan also had a great effect. Fifteen years older than I, Stan was married and had two children, my nephew, Steven, and my niece, Sharon. I loved these two children as if they were my own brother and sister. There were times in the summer and around the holidays when I would go from Linden to Philadelphia for long visits with Stan. It was there that I met Marla, a Catholic girl whom I found quite cute. Her mother was divorced from her father, who was Jewish. By this time I was twelve, approaching my bar mitzvah.

Marla and I began seeing each other every time I visited Stan. She went to a Catholic school, and my public school closed down for the Christmas holidays one week earlier than Marla's. I begged my mother to allow me to go to my brother's house for the holidays. She finally gave in.

I enjoyed holding Marla's hand as I walked her to Catholic school. From across the street I heard the voice of someone yelling Marla's name. It was one of her classmates, an Irish boy named Patrick O'Sullivan. He was accompanied by a gang of his friends. Marla quietly told me to ignore them.

Patrick began to use abusive language as he crossed the street, making his way toward Marla and me, his friends following behind him. He didn't like the fact that I was dating Marla, because he liked her too. Suddenly, I was surrounded with his gang of friends. They were coaxing him on to beat me up.

Patrick was much taller than I. He stood on his toes and seemed to loom over me, his fists clenched as tight as his teeth.

"You want to fight, Jew boy?" he shouted.

Later, I found out that Marla was bragging about me to her entire class, saying that I was a "tough Jewish kid" from New Jersey who would beat the snot out of any guy in the class. She had shown them the picture I had sent her.

I remember feeling really scared seeing all those kids around me. Patrick began pushing me, trying to get me to fight. I felt like John Boy in *West Side Story* as he wandered onto the wrong side of town. All I could see in my mind was that movie and the gangs. I imagined one of Patrick's friends pulling a knife on me. Instead of fighting, I began crying. They laughed at me but left me alone.

I was really embarrassed by it all, especially in front of Marla. Yet, she still liked me. There was nothing at all sensual about our relationship. It was a very pure and clean friendship. Even if I tried to kiss her on the cheek, she wouldn't let me. It was Marla who took me for the first time ever into a church while a service was in progress. It was an old sanctuary, fully decorated with statues of the saints.

As I followed her down the aisle, I was scared and nervous. I couldn't understand why there were so many different statues, and I was too afraid to ask. In Hebrew school I was taught that to worship any statue is like worshiping an idol. To me, the people I saw kneeling by these statues with their rosary beads were practicing idolatry.

I tried to follow Marla in whatever she did. Before entering the pew, she genuflected and crossed herself. I also awkwardly bent my knees and tried to make the sign of the cross. Marla began to chuckle.

"You don't have to do that!"

"I want to!" I whispered back, wanting desperately to be like everybody else.

During the service, the priest kept crossing himself, and everybody else would do the same. I tried without success to follow the priest's actions, but it was like trying to read a book reflected in the mirror. I kept crossing myself in the opposite direction from everybody else.

Marla was watching me out of the corner of her eyes, getting a kick out of my antics. She couldn't hold back any longer. She started laughing and giggling at my attempts to be a Catholic.

We were instructed to sit down. The priest began talking about the Jews. He must have been referring to the Gospels. It didn't seem like I was in any condition to really understand the seemingly strange observances of the Catholic church. All I knew was that it didn't sound as if he was speaking about the Jews in a kind fashion.

As I looked at the statue of the crucified Christ, I was mesmerized.

Who was this man, Jesus, this man whom people worshiped as if He was God? I asked myself. As I sat there, I'd just get lost in looking at Jesus on the cross, trying to figure out what it all meant.

I thought to myself, Why would somebody nail a person to a cross? It's a horrible thing to think about. They shouldn't have done that to Him!

All of a sudden Marla got up to go to the altar to receive communion. She told me to stay where I was, but I quickly got up, following her. There was no way I was gonna let her leave me alone in that church. I went up with her to receive communion. I watched the people sticking their tongues out as the priest passed out this little wafer. I had no idea what I was doing, but at least I was kneeling next to my girlfriend.

As the priest placed the wafer on my tongue, Marla told me, "Don't chew it!"

I said, "What?"

She simply repeated her words, "Don't chew it! Let it dissolve in your mouth."

I followed her back to the seat, all the while the wafer just kept sticking on my tongue and hanging there. I had no concept of what Communion was all about. Everything practiced there seemed foreign to Judaism. I couldn't wait to get out of the church.

My first journey into a church was not one in which I consciously felt the presence of God. In fact, I felt intimidated because it was so different.

As I grew up, there were times when I was fascinated with the suffering of Christ on the cross. If I came across a painting in an encyclopedia, I would stare for awhile at Jesus hanging on the cross. I was trying to understand just what these Christians saw in it all.

That Christmas at the home of my brother, Stan, was very odd indeed. Stan and his wife, Rita, had a Christmas tree. It didn't mean anything to them; they just loved the custom. Christmas songs blared out from their record player. Sitting next to Marla, holding her hand, I flashed back to Susan Krietz as she sang in the elementary school choir. I was hearing the same words that had mystified me before.

How could Jesus Christ be King of the Jews? I wondered to myself, not daring to ask anyone!

I returned home from my stay at Stan and Rita's house and found my mother in the kitchen washing dishes.

"Can we get a Christmas tree?" I blurted out.

She reeled around, dropping a dish in the sink.

"What do you mean, get a Christmas tree?"

"Stan and Rita had one at their house," I declared.

Mom was so upset she called my brother to bawl him out. I heard poor Stan trying to explain that it meant nothing more than custom to them. In no uncertain terms she reminded him that we are Jewish, and Jews should be celebrating Chanukah, not Christmas!

That year in Hebrew school another unusual event took place— something that would change my life forever. It started as just another ordinary day in my Hebrew school classroom. The rabbi was teaching a lesson on the meaning of sacrifices. My mind was wandering as I thought how nice it would be if I were outside playing baseball with my friends on Lenape Road.

A fellow student named Aaron raised his hand to ask the rabbi a question.

"Why don't you ever teach us about Jesus Christ in this class?" Aaron asked innocently.

His question jarred me out of daydreaming.

"What do you mean, why don't we ever teach about Jesus Christ? Do the Catholics teach about Moses?" the rabbi responded angrily.

Aaron was undaunted.

"Well. Was Jesus a Jew?"

Jesus a Jew? I always thought he was a Catholic! I thought to myself.

The rabbi was now shouting.

"Of course he was a Jew!"

"But was he our messiah?" Aaron fired back.

My mind went into a spin.

Jesus is a Jew? I pondered, *What is a messiah?*

The word *messiah* was never mentioned in the synagogue. My parents never told me that the Jews were awaiting the coming of a messiah. None of my Jewish friends or relatives knew much about it.

By this time, the rabbi was fuming.

"He is not our messiah! Jesus was a Jew, a great reformer—a teacher—some rabbis say he was a prophet, but he was *not* our messiah!"

I hung onto every word as the rabbi drove home his point.

"When the messiah comes, the wolf will lie down with the lamb—perfect peace must come to the earth. He is not our messiah, and I never want to hear his name mentioned in this class again!"

I was dizzy with questions. *Jesus was a Jew? What is a messiah? If he was a Jew—a great reformer, a teacher, perhaps even a prophet—then why did the rabbi tell us to never mention his name again in class?* I had to find out. Immediately after dismissal, I rode my bicycle over to the public library and found a book entitled, simply enough, *Jesus Christ*.

To this day, I cannot find the exact book I read, but it was written specifically for a Jewish person. It talked about the Jewishness of Christ who came not to destroy the Law, but to fulfill it. I read that the name Jesus Christ is an English translation of the Greek *Yesus Christos*. I learned that his name in Hebrew is *Yeshua Hamashiach*. *Yeshua*, meaning *God Saves*, and *Hamashiach*, meaning the *Messiah* or the *Anointed One*.

After reading the book, I was convinced that Jesus was indeed the Jewish Messiah.

"Mom, you know what? Jesus Christ was Jewish," I told her excitedly.

She responded with a puzzled look.

"What do you mean he was Jewish? It's just a story. There was no real person named Jesus."

"No, Mom! The rabbi told us that he was real, and that he was a Jew. Not only that, I know that Jesus was our Messiah!" I shouted eagerly.

"What's a messiah?" she questioned.

I began to explain the fact that we Jews were awaiting a messiah and began imparting what I had read in the book. She was trying to get dinner ready and was becoming impatient with listening to my ranting.

Finally, she could bear no more.

"Warren, where did you hear all this? It couldn't be in Hebrew school."

I pulled out the book which I had been hiding behind my back. "No, it's all right here in this book!"

"You can't believe everything you read in a book," she said.

"But Mom, I got it from the library!" I shouted.

From that point on, no matter what I said to her, I could not convince her of what I believed. I felt disheartened and alone with this great truth that now burned in my heart.

Who would believe me? Who can I share this with that would understand how I feel? I asked myself.

I needed direction. I wanted to know what to do with this newfound knowledge. Suddenly, I remembered my Gentile friends, my neighborhood buddies. Surely they would understand.

Walking to junior high school the next day, I caught up with my old friend, Bob Pirigyi. I just couldn't get the words out quickly enough.

"Hey, Bobby! Guess what! I believe that Jesus is my Messiah!"

Bob stared at me with a puzzled look.

"I didn't realize that Jesus was a Jew! Why didn't you ever tell me?" I asked with a smile on my face.

"Jesus wasn't a Jew. He was a Catholic," Bob said, a bit irritated.

"You're wrong, Bobby. Jesus was a Jew. Ask your priest."

Bob didn't believe a word I told him. My confession of faith did not seem to impress him. I soon found out that the reaction was similar with all my Gentile friends. None of them seemed to understand about the Jewishness of Jesus. More tragic than that, not one of them realized the significance of my acceptance of Jesus as the Jewish Messiah. Without someone to tell me how to receive Him into my heart, this knowledge would remain dormant, deep in my spirit, for twelve more years.

There was another interesting aspect of seventh grade. It was in this class that I first met Donna Kustra. There was no romantic interest on my part. However, I later found out that she thought I was cute. Donna gained my attention when the teacher announced that Donna was leaving the class to have an operation—surgery to correct damage to her leg caused by a childhood bout with polio.

The entire class wished her well. Toward the end of the year, I heard my classmates talking about the phone call they had received from Donna. I was quite jealous and upset when I realized that I was the only one she did not call. Years later, I found out that the reason Donna never called me was because she had a secret crush on me and was afraid of rejection. However, in the seventh grade, neither Donna nor I had any idea that we would one day become husband and wife.

TWELVE

THE SUMMER PLACE

The school year, 1961, had ended, and seventh grade was over. Summer vacation had begun, and I was rejoicing. My mother had made arrangements for us to spend the entire summer at a cottage at White Lake in upstate New York. My expectations were quite high—new friends, perhaps some romance, swimming, and a nice dark tan were all a twelve-year old could fancy.

While Mom was busy packing, I had to go to the synagogue to meet with the cantor and review my bar mitzvah *haftorah* (a lesson from the Prophets, which is chanted). I would be thirteen years old in November, and at that time an entire morning service at the Suburban Jewish Center was reserved for my bar mitzvah. Unlike confirmation in many Christian churches which is usually performed with a group of young people all at once, the bar mitzvah includes only one Jewish boy at a time. I would be sitting on the *bema* (Hebrew for platform) with the rabbi and the cantor during the entire service.

Not only would I be responsible to read a portion of the Torah in Hebrew, but afterwards I would have to conduct the congregation in the rest of the songs of the service. The service would last several hours. My entire family, invited friends, and regular participants of the congregation would all be present for this important event. The bar mitzvah marked the day when a Jewish boy passed into manhood and no longer was under the covering of his parents, but rather, was now responsible for his own actions before God.

The cantor was about twenty years old. He was the one in charge of the worship parts of the service, since Scripture was not just recited in the synagogue, but sung. The rabbi taught the lesson, the cantor was under the rabbi, but without the cantor, the service would not be complete. It was also his job to make sure I was able to sing my *haftorah* and lead the congregation in song. He knew I was leaving for vacation, so he had recorded my *haftorah* on audio tape, so I could learn it over the summer. There was a prescribed melody that had to be sung. It sounded almost repetitious to the untrained ear. However, the elders of the synagogue would know if you were off one note.

"Wolf Mayer, I am very concerned that you are going away for the summer. You must learn your *haftorah,* and it must be perfect. I will not settle for anything less," the cantor cautioned.

Wolf Mayer was my name in Hebrew, a name which first belonged to my great grandfather. I felt extreme pressure to perform favorably, especially since my orthodox grandparents would be attending. I promised the cantor that I would do well.

My father drove us to White Lake, New York. The trip took several hours. Packed in Dad's Buick were my mom, grandfather, grandmother, and me. Dad was upset because the directions seemed rather confusing, and no one could talk to him when he was driving. Driving made him very nervous, and Mom's sideseat directions drove my dad nuts. "Pearl, will you just shut up! I know how to drive!" he would yell.

"Charlie, watch out for that car!" my mom would say, holding on tightly to the dashboard.

"Pearl, shut up! I'll turn the car around and go home if you don't keep your trap shut!" he'd carry on.

"Oy vey! I think I'm getting sick!" said Grandma to Grandpa in a whisper, afraid to let my dad hear.

"*Gey shluffin!*" (Yiddish for "Go to sleep!") my grandpa yelled back at her in the hopes of averting a conflict.

I had to listen to Mom and Dad argue all the way to White Lake. I did my best to shut it out by imagining the wonderful time I was going to have. I pictured the place to have a swimming pool and fancy Caribbean-like cottages. When we arrived, my father kept asking, "Are you sure this is the place?"

Kushner's Bungalows! Sure! Caribbean-like—after a hurricane, maybe! It was broken down, and it didn't have a pool. There was hardly any grass, just unmowed weeds. The cottages all needed painting. My father's blood was boiling. He hadn't gone with my mom when she went to look for a cottage to rent.

"Pearl, I can't believe you'd pick a dump like this! We're not staying here!" my dad yelled.

"But, Charlie, we already paid for it. I saw it in the winter, with snow on the ground. It looked good then," my mother said, tears flowing from her eyes.

My father always gave in to my mother's crying. He unloaded the bags, and by Sunday he was on his way back to Linden to work. He would only be there for the weekends. We were on our own for the rest of the week.

Daily, I took an hour to listen to my *haftorah* tape and tried to memorize the melody. The outside was too alluring to stay inside to study. The people staying at the bungalows seemed to be all Israelis. They were very friendly to me, since I was the only bona-fide American boy staying at Kushner's Bungalows. I met two girls who developed a crush on me. I couldn't make up my mind which one I liked best. Leah was from Israel. Her dark hair and complexion were exotic. Shelly was American-born.

Rather than choose between the two of them, I would ask my mom for money to take them *both* to the ice cream parlor. The adults would laugh at me, calling me a young Casanova.

The older kids of the group were heavily involved in dating. I would listen to the boys brag about their conquests.

Then, one day, Leah invited me into her bungalow when her parents weren't there. I sat with her on the bed. We were just talking, but I slowly started moving closer to her. She didn't seem to mind. I made a move to kiss her. She pushed me away and refused.

"Why won't you kiss me?" I asked, feeling very rejected.

"My mother told me never to kiss on a bed, or I would become pregnant," she said with a sincere gaze on her countenance.

"You're kidding me? Don't you know how babies are made?" I queried.

She had never been told the facts of life. I began to tell her. Then her older brother suddenly walked in the door.

"Hey you, get away from my sister," he said.

Boy! Did he look angry! I must have turned white with fear. He began to laugh, and so did I once I realized that he was just teasing me.

One day, I brought my tape recorder outside and began to record the conversations of the older guys in the group. They were laughing and having a good time, when suddenly one of the guys brightened up with an idea.

"Warren, how 'bout hiding and recording me and Sasha as we make out?" he said as the others agreed, laughing.

At first, I thought he was joking. However, he was not. I found myself with the tape recorder plugged in and the microphone carefully hidden near where they got together. It seemed to take forever for him to come back with Sasha, but finally I heard them arrive. Hidden, I recorded all of their intimate love talk. After Sasha left, I played the tape for the fellow. He laughed all the while. He called in the entire crowd, including Sasha, to hear the tape. I felt bad for Sasha, because she didn't have a clue as to what I was about to play. I watched her face closely as she heard her voice. The rest of the group, both boys and girls, began to giggle. Sasha was slow to realize that it was her on the tape.

"Is that us? You mean you recorded us?" she shouted angrily. "Warren was hidden the entire time," he said laughing.

Sasha turned toward me, tears in her eyes, "Warren, you did that?" I felt horrible. In no way did I want to be a part of hurting this girl. When I got back to my bungalow, I asked God to forgive me for hurting Sasha. I wanted no role in playing such dirty tricks on anyone ever again.

Every time I turned on the tape recorder to practice my *haftorah*, I would be convicted of the cruel joke I had been a part of. It was then that I realized that there are two ways to use the wonder of modern technologies. Whether it be a tape recorder or a movie camera, it could be used to help or to hurt people. I vowed before God to use technology and the gifts He had given me only to do His pleasure.

There was an older fellow named Perry who would try to hang out with our group. He was heavyset, and rather grotesque, and a bully. Just the sight of him gave me the creeps. The worst thing about this man was that he was a convicted pedophile and an avowed homosexual. One day when we were swimming at the lake, Perry sneaked up behind me and grabbed me in a bear hug.

"Let me go, Perry!" I yelled to no avail.

"I'm just showing you a wrestling hold," he said as he crushed me.

"Let me go!" I yelled loud enough for Leah's brother to hear and run to help.

I broke into tears as Leah's brother and the others pulled Perry away from me. Leah's brother punched him several times, ordering him to leave.

"Get out of here," he screamed at the bully. I was quite troubled by what Perry had done because it revived all the agony of the sexual abuse I had suffered at the hands of Ted.

One week later, Leah, Shelly, and I decided to explore the forest trails. Shelly knew them quite well. She told us of a cave once used by the Indians and thought we might be able to find some arrowheads.

I felt great holding the hands of these sweet girls. We stopped along the way to pick up rocks and turned over an old fallen beehive. Leah decided to go back. It seemed too far for her to walk alone. I insisted on all of us going back, but Leah would not let us. She said that she didn't want to ruin our good time.

Shelly and I went onward, making our way toward the cave. As we walked, holding hands all the way, I began to realize how beautiful Shelly was. Her shoulder-length blond hair was blowing gently in the warm summer breeze. We stopped for a moment to rest. I was standing by a large oak tree, leaning on it for support.

Shelly stared at me in a strange way as she slowly moved closer.

"Hold still. There's something on you," she said softly. I dared not move. She leaned against me as she plucked a caterpillar off my shoulder. She didn't pull away.

"Look, isn't he cute?" she said, toying with the insect.

The desire overcame me to kiss her, but I was frightened of being rejected.

"You're much cuter than that caterpillar," I heard myself say. She looked up and stared into my eyes. Ever so slowly, her lips met mine, and we kissed. It was my first kiss, and I was going to treasure it forever.

She pulled away and began to run.

"Come on, we've got a way to go!" she shouted.

I ran after her, hardly able to keep up. As we came to the cave, I heard a familiar voice but couldn't quite place it. As I drew closer, I saw it was Perry. He had a young boy with him who looked no more than ten years old. Perry was showing him the cave, when he spotted me.

"Hey, you, come here," Perry called out.

"Not me, you pervert!" I yelled back, taking Shelly's hand and yanking her hard.

The young boy beside him looked confused as Perry began to walk toward me.

"Run, run! He's a very dangerous man! Get away while you can!" I yelled to the boy.

Perry was angry as he pursued me. He cursed out loud, but he couldn't catch us as we ran quickly through the woods. He chased us all the way back to the bungalows, but stopped when we reached my mom and grandparents, who were sitting outside.

"What's wrong?" Mom asked, seeing the look of fear on my face.

"Nothing, Mom. Everything's just fine," I said as Shelly and I began laughing.

I never told Mom about Perry. I was too embarrassed about the past sexual abuse I had encountered. To this day, I hope and pray that the young boy made it back safely without ever experiencing the pain I had suffered.

My final confrontation with Perry came during our last week at White Lake. I had borrowed a bicycle from one of the older boys and was alone on a route that was several miles long. I had ridden it a number of times with a group. It was a road which took me up and down enormous hills and eventually led back to the bungalows. Suddenly, I saw Perry standing in the street. The minute he saw me, he began walking towards me.

"Hey, you! I want to talk to you," he said as he ran toward me. I began to pedal faster.

"Stop! I just want to talk!" he shouted as I tried to get away.

He grabbed the back fender of the bike and pulled me to a stop. I quickly jumped off and left him holding the bicycle.

"Leave me alone, Perry!" I said, keeping my distance.

He smiled and proceeded to look at the bicycle. "This is a nice bike you have." He began to squeeze the front tire.

"Give the bike back to me. It's not mine!" I demanded. He felt the front tire and said, "The tire's soft, but I can make it hard! I have a pump right in my bungalow over there," he said. Silently, I began to ask God for help. Mrs. Kushner's Bungalows were too far to walk to, and I just couldn't leave the bicycle with him.

"Oh God! Tell me what to say," I prayed. Then, like inspiration, the right words came to my mouth.

"That's not my bike! But I'm going back to Kushner's, and I'm gonna bring back my father. He's an ex-boxer. And now I know where you live."

Perry dropped the bicycle in anger. I refused to get on it until he walked far enough away for me to make an escape. He sadistically played a game, moving away and then advancing every time I moved toward the bike. Finally, he moved far enough away for me to grab the bike and make a getaway. On my journey back, I thanked God for His protection.

When the vacation ended, I had mixed feelings coming back home to Linden. On one hand I would miss the friendship of Leah and Shelly. On the other hand, I would never see Perry again.

The day after I returned, I had to go to the synagogue to meet with the cantor. I was not diligent in learning my *haftorah*. I cautiously entered the classroom. The cantor warmly greeted me.

"Wolf Mayer, welcome home!" he said as he hugged me and sat down to hear what I had learned.

I began to sing and watched as he nodded with pleasure at the part I knew. As I reached the uncharted territory, he began to frown as I tried to fake the melody. He grabbed the Hebrew book away from me.

"Wolf Mayer, I am very upset with you!" the cantor shouted as he slammed the *haftorah* book down on the table.

He was so mad that his *yarmulke* (prayer hat) fell off his head, and he had to stop to pick it up and kiss it, as was the custom when a Jew drops anything holy.

I couldn't hold back the tears as I whispered, "I'm sorry!"

The cantor composed himself and put his hand on my shoulder.

"Your bar mitzvah is not far away and you are not prepared. You don't want me to cancel it, do you?"

I shook my head no and promised to do better in my studies.

"I apologize for getting angry, but please don't disappoint me, Wolf Mayer," he said, more gently.

I applied myself daily and tried to learn the melodies to the best of my ability. However, I knew I wasn't fully prepared for my bar mitzvah—the most important day in the life of a Jewish boy.

THIRTEEN

YOU'RE A BIG BOY NOW

The day of my bar mitzvah was one week away, and I had not yet learned the entire *haftorah* melody. All the arrangements had been made. First, there would be the Saturday morning service in which all my family and friends, Jewish and Gentile, would witness the event. Then immediately following, there would be a brief gathering for the entire congregation to share in the *Oneg Shabbat*, a time of fellowship that followed the service with the eating of bread and drinking of wine.

I was extremely nervous. It seemed that even distant relatives would be flying in for the event. One fear after another consumed me. What if I can't memorize my *haftorah* by that day? How embarrassing it would be for my parents! I was feeling depressed as I sat Indian-style on the floor in front of the television set in our downstairs recreation room. While flipping the dial, I came across a Billy Graham Crusade. I tried to listen to every word. There were things shared which I couldn't understand.

"Jesus died for you to be saved," I heard Graham say. Suddenly, the upstairs door flung open as my dad tromped down the stairs, yelling to the police chief, who was visiting.

"Do you want a scotch or bourbon?"

The bar was in the recreation room and Dad would be running up and downstairs to get his guest more drinks. Quickly I switched off the set, not wanting him to see what I was watching. Over and over again the cycle was repeated. I'd be listening intently to the crusade, then my father would interrupt, getting more drinks. Quickly, I'd change the channel until he went back upstairs. However, I finally became so engrossed in what Billy Graham was preaching that I forgot to switch the set off when Dad came down for what seemed like the sixteenth time.

"What are you watching?" he said, stopping near me.

"Oh, I'm not really watching anything," I said, embarrassed.

"Don't watch that stuff! It will screw up your mind!" he said, continuing on to the bar to get more drinks for the other Linden policemen who had just arrived.

I changed the channel to appease him, but once he closed the door upstairs, I turned back to the crusade and turned the volume down to a whisper. Moving close to the set, I watched the conclusion of the show. When Billy asked all to bow their heads, I followed in obedience without quite understanding the prayer. I followed along with Billy Graham as I asked God to forgive me for my sins. I felt an amazing sense of the presence of God. It was a peaceful feeling. That night, I would turn back to God in prayer, begging Him to help me with my bar mitzvah and not let me look like a fool in front of my relatives.

The synagogue was packed on the day of my bar mitzvah. I was petrified as I sat dressed in my *talit* (prayer shawl) and yarmulke in a seat on the *bema* right between the rabbi and cantor. My father had invited all his Gentile police buddies. Also attending were my neighborhood friends. I couldn't believe my eyes as my friend Bob Pirigyi entered the sanctuary with a yarmulke on his head. The Jewish custom demanded that *anyone* who entered had to wear a prayer hat.

The Marcus family was sitting in the first few rows. I would try not to glance over at them, because they would all wave and try to get my attention. Floyd and my cousin, Sam Pomper, sat right in front of me. Floyd kept making faces to try to make me laugh. All stood as the Torah was removed from the ark. It was a holy moment, as sobering as communion was to Christians. It was my honor to carry the adorned scrolls from the altar through the aisles, so the congregation could pay respect to God's Holy Word. As I walked slowly with the Torah, the congregation sang in Hebrew. At every pew many would press forward to kiss the Torah, first kissing their hand or prayer shawls, and then touching them to the outside of the scrolls.

The adornments of the Torah were removed and the ancient scroll containing the Ten Commandments in Hebrew was uncovered. After reading a portion of the Torah, I opened my haftorah book to the selected area, and began to sing my *haftorah*. Everything was going wonderfully as I sang the portion I had memorized so well. I watched the elders of the synagogue as they bowed in reverent prayer following the words in Hebrew in the *haftorah* prayer books. I glanced at my mom as she and my grandparents proudly watched my every movement.

Then, I came to the portion of *haftorah* I didn't quite know. I had asked God in prayer while watching Billy Graham to keep me from looking like a fool in front of my parents, family, and friends. As I faked the melody, I began to hear groans and grunts of discontent from my cantor. The rabbi said a few oy veys as I confidently made up the melody. A few of the elders of the synagogue were now looking toward one another, shrugging their shoulders, appearing to recognize my charade. Yet, my relatives and friends looked impressed at my performance.

I was so relieved once I finished my *haftorah* reading that I was silently thanking God for His answer to my prayer. The rabbi and the president of the congregation presented me with an English translation of the *Tanakh*, the Jewish Scriptures, as a gift from Suburban Jewish Center.

The rabbi said, "This is given to you with the hope that you will study the Scriptures and continue attending Suburban Jewish Center, becoming an integral part of the congregation."

I knew that I would follow in the footsteps of the many bar mitzvah boys before me. This would be the last time I would deliberately set foot in the synagogue again, except for future weddings, bar mitzvahs, and funerals. I said to myself, "I am free!"

After the service, it was customary for the bar mitzvah boy, the rabbi, and cantor to leave the sanctuary first and position themselves at the door to shake hands with the congregation.

The first words out of the cantor's mouth were, "Thank God that is over!"

Everyone congratulated me for a wonderful job, except for the elders who seemed to gaze at me with apparent disgust.

At home, the party was in full swing—plenty of kosher food and liquor. The noise level was unbearable as family and friends jammed into our tiny home. People were everywhere, in the living room, kitchen, recreation room, bedrooms, and even the bathrooms. I couldn't walk one inch without being grabbed by an aunt and kissed, or by an uncle and hugged. My Gentile friends and neighbors seemed to enjoy themselves, too. Everyone was handing me envelopes with checks or cash enclosed. I sneaked into the garage with my cousin Floyd to count the money. My mom had given me some paper and a pen to record names and amounts of the gifts. The names were needed so I could send out thank-you cards, but the amount was noted so that my parents would know what to give when they had to reciprocate on future occasions. They would never want to be guilty of under-giving a relative or friend, nor would they want to over-give.

Thousands of dollars were received. According to my parents, my bar mitzvah was a success. The receipts were exceptional, and everybody kept saying that they had a wonderful time. I just couldn't wait for it all to end. I kept looking at the *Tanakh* that the Suburban Jewish Center had given me. I had a great desire to look up the portion of my *haftorah*, to read what it said in English, to see if there was some significance for my life. I was overcome with great expectations.

Perhaps God would reveal Himself to me in a special way, I thought to myself.

Late that night, I opened the Jewish Scriptures (according to the Masoretic text) to find the portion of Scripture I had sung in Hebrew. Before I ever found those verses, my eyes fell upon Leviticus, chapter 5, verses 20 through 26 (in the King James Bible it would be Leviticus 6:1–7):

> And the LORD spake unto Moses, saying,
> If a soul sin, and commit a trespass against the LORD, and lie unto his neighbor in that which was delivered him to keep, or in fellowship, or in a thing taken away by violence, or hath deceived his neighbor;
> Or have found that which was lost, and lieth concerning it, and sweareth falsely; in any of all these that a man doeth, sinning therein.

I read on to what God commanded as the way of forgiveness for committing these sins:

> And he shall bring his trespass offering unto the LORD for his sin which he hath sinned, a female from the flock, a lamb

or a kid of the goats, for a sin offering; and the priest shall make an atonement for him concerning his sin. (Lev. 5:6)

I asked myself, *What were the Jews doing with a priest?*
There was no way that I could understand why the sacrifice of an animal was required for us to receive forgiveness. I never heard this discussed in the synagogue services nor in Hebrew school. I was disappointed that I couldn't discern God's direction for my life. It seemed to have no significance for today. Little did I realize that God was indeed speaking to me. He was pointing again to the ultimate sacrifice which the Messiah would obediently perform for the forgiveness of many. I skipped through the rest of the book, stopping from time to time, reading the Scriptures before me. It seemed that God's demands were so harsh upon His people that rather than receiving edification, I was feeling condemnation. There seemed to be no love. I put the book away and would not pick it up until years later when confronted with the Gospel.

With the money received from my bar mitzvah securely placed in a new checking account, my dad drove my mom and me to New York City to a monster camera store named Peerless. It was here that I spent most of my bar mitzvah money to purchase a 16mm Bolex movie camera and a sound projector.

I was using the money from my bar mitzvah to purchase the tools which would allow me to practice God's calling for my life—the calling to make films that would, as in prayer, say what God wanted me to say. For years I had been praying to God to make me a really great filmmaker, and now that vision was beginning to come alive.

I couldn't wait to get home to begin filming my first footage. I began by filming home movies of my brother's children, Steven and Sharon. I would direct them in little fun sequences, until I mastered proper lighting techniques and exposure levels. Then, I concentrated on learning the use of different lenses. By the ninth grade, I was producing films in place of book reports. My first movie was *Smoking and Cancer*. It combined comical skits with facts about the dangers of smoking cigarettes. My biology teacher was so impressed that she showed it to all her classes. I was proudest of the satiric cigarette commercial I had filmed. A fellow classmate was crawling in the sand, weak from the heat and thirsty for water, as the narrator asked, "Do your cigarettes make you feel hot and dry?" The classmate looked up toward the camera with a pathetic expression and nodded yes. At that moment, I threw a pail of ice cold water at him. He was soaked! He got up laughing as a next-door neighbor watched the filming and began to applaud, laughing uncontrollably. In the finished piece, I cut in a product shot of a pack of cigarettes, sitting near flowing water. The skull and crossbones were pasted on the pack.

I went on to film another movie for the class on the subject of primates. Again, I used humor to break up the educational segments. This time I had several classmates, including myself, portray multiple roles. I would start the camera as we walked into the door of the class and then stop the camera after we passed by it. Without moving the camera, I would have the same students walk in again, dressed in a slightly different way, giving the illusion of twenty students coming into class. The movie ended with a whipped cream pie being thrown. Everyone in the class laughed at the right times. They applauded the productions, and I received A's for the projects. However, I was not content with creating these little movies for class. I wanted to film a dramatic movie, like the ones seen on the screens of our local movie theater. I began to write a script. I decided to be loyal to God and write a script for a film that He would want me to produce. I decided the theme would be about Jesus returning as a student at Linden High School.

Privately, I desired the reality of the return of the Messiah. I felt that the world was so filled with hypocrisy and hatred. The synagogue and church seemed devoid of God. I imagined what it would be like for the Messiah to come back again to Earth. I had no idea that the Bible spoke of the actual return of Jesus. I began to write the opening character description. All I wrote was:

There he sat alone, but unaffected by the solitude of his confinement. He exhibited no element of fear, hate, lust, nor any of the human weaknesses. He could be wise, compassionate, temperate, and authoritative all in one moment. His mind could function at a most rapid rate; his manner of speech suffered not one impediment. His face appeared completely unmarred and perfect in every way. His dark hair fell long upon his shoulders, and his beard covered most of his face. The most prodigious feature of his countenance was his large piercing eyes. Any person, reciprocally man or woman, once gazing at his visage, would become mesmerized with his supernatural splendor. His knowledge of the Torah and · life in general astounded everyone with whom he would engage in discourse. He was the Messiah, and he had returned.

I soon found that I could not formulate any further ideas on the story line. Without having read the New Covenant, I had no knowledge about Jesus, except for what I remembered from seeing the motion picture *Ben Hur*.

It frustrated me that I had made myself available to God to "let me make films that You want me to make," yet the words would not come. I would need to hear from God before I could ever impart His concepts.

• FOURTEEN •

GREAT EXPECTATIONS

It was nine P.M. The doorbell was ringing as I sat at the kitchen table trying to do my homework. I had a final exam in my eighth-grade English class the next day. My mother was at her usual place, washing the dishes at the kitchen sink.

"Oh no, who is that?" Mom asked as she made her way to the door.

It was my two uncles, Ben and Sol. They were looking for my father, who had retired upstairs.

"Charlie, Charlie, come down," Mom yelled.

Ben and Sol made their way into the kitchen, and I rose respect-fully to hug them. I loved my uncles, but I realized that my study-ing would now have to cease. Mom told me to go upstairs and let my dad know that he had company.

I obeyed her request. Slowly, I entered his bedroom. He was sound asleep and snoring loudly. He had already been to his favor-ite bar and grill for a few drinks before coming home from work, and had continued to have several "boilermakers" (scotch with a beer chaser) with his dinner. I hated having to wake him in that condition. I started out softly calling to him, "Dad? Dad?"

He merely rolled over and continued snoring louder than before. I gingerly touched his shoulder, and he jumped up from his sleep like a madman possessed.

"What happened?" he yelled.

"Dad, Uncle Ben and Sol are here," I told him.

"What time is it?" he asked.

"It's about 9:30!"

Dad reluctantly got out of bed, put on his robe and made his way downstairs, cursing under his breath. Amazingly, his whole manner changed as he reached the kitchen and welcomed his brothers with a big smile.

"Pearl, give them something to eat," he directed my mom.

"I'm sorry, the kitchen is closed," she replied, as my uncles swore they would only be staying for a little while.

"What will you have to drink?" my dad offered. The two tried to turn him down, but he dragged out the scotch, and before I knew it, they were drinking. Dad was able to drink anyone under the table. My uncles could hardly hold their heads up straight, and Dad would still be pouring them more. By eleven P.M. both my mother and I had retired to our rooms. But numerous times my poor mom would have to run downstairs to quiet my father's boisterous joking, and many times my uncles would begin raising their voices, arguing over some moot point.

"Warren has school tomorrow! Will you please keep it down?" I heard her say as she ran downstairs again.

"Pearl, I *am* keeping it down! I don't get sick when I drink! Now, Ben and Solly, they're the ones who get sick and can't keep it down! Oh look! Ben threw up on the floor again," my father would tease my mom, throwing my uncles into hysterical laughter.

As I drifted off to sleep I heard Mom yell at them for not listening. This was just a typical school night at my house. If it weren't my uncles, it was an off-duty policeman or a city councilman. They loved to hang out with my dad. He complained about them bothering Mom and me, but I truly believe he loved playing bartender. I couldn't fall asleep until they left at 2 to 3 A.M. many, many times.

The result was pretty obvious; the next day at school I wouldn't be able to focus on my lessons. My mind would wander and fantasize plots for movies which I would remember and write down after school. During my junior high school days, I had a reputation as the class clown. I remember my eighth-grade English teacher, Mrs. Bushinsky. She criticized every little thing I did, whether it was on purpose or unintentional. Even innocently, when I would click my ballpoint pen, she would get annoyed and yell that I was trying to disrupt her class. If I cracked my knuckles, she would come over to me and chastise me and make me stand in the corner for the rest of the period. She began giving me F's in the class because of my frivolity. She called my mother for a meeting at school.

"Your son is the class clown. And if he continues, I'm going to boot him out of the class," she told her.

My mom threatened to tell my father. I begged her not to tell him, and I promised to buckle down.

I remember Charles Dickens's *A Christmas Carol*. I really loved that story. When asked on a test to make a summary, I wrote a ten-page essay. When Mrs. Bushinsky saw it, she accused me of cheating because of the accuracy of some of the quotes. She called me to her desk.

"Warren, I know you cheated on this test."

"I didn't cheat! I swear to you!" I defended myself.

"I don't believe you," she said.

I asked if I could take the test again with her watching me every second. She assented to my challenge. To her amazement, I did even better than before. She sat me down for a serious talk.

"You're a much smarter boy than you appear to be. Why don't you use your brains and use your mind to write stories of your own?"

Mrs. Bushinsky actually played a part in helping spark in me an interest in creative writing.

In light of my problems at home, with an alcoholic father, I was not prepared when I took my first college entrance test. My guidance counselor had a meeting with my mom.

"Your son, Warren, is not college material," he told her. "Rather than take college prep courses, he should sign up for business or trade school."

Little did he know the potential that I had not yet tapped. Because of my problems at home, I was not applying myself in the best manner. I was eking my way through school with just passing grades. I began to pray to God. I would rely on Him for every test I took. Whenever I prayed, my test scores improved. I began to trust God to help me do better in school. During this time, there was another area in which I found a closer relationship with God. I noticed that when I became sick, as with a stomach virus, I could pray to Him to take away my illness. My greatest fear was that I might vomit. Yet, immediately after praying, my stomach cramps would vanish. My faith began to grow. I believe that God was protecting me even then and developing in me a reliance on Him for my every need.

My cousin Floyd's interest in rock and roll music became my obsession too. As a little boy, when I used to go to Bradley Beach, New Jersey, with my parents, there was a live band performing at the boardwalk pavilion. I would intently watch the drummer. When I attended those late-night jam sessions at Floyd's house, I would be invited to sit at the drums and play. It was in those early days that I fell in love with this instrument.

My drum lessons in elementary school were not enough to satisfy my curiosity about the instrument. By the time I was in the seventh grade I was taking drum lessons from a professional. That year my dad had bought me my first Ludwig drum set. The day they were to be delivered, I couldn't wait until I got home from school. I ran all the way home, only to find my mother crying. She hugged me the moment I came in the door.

"Warren, something happened to Dad. He's in the hospital," she said holding me.

"Is he dying?" I asked as I stared at the unopened boxes sitting on the living room floor.

"No, sweetie, but they say it could be his heart," she said as she got ready to leave for the hospital.

I had to stay home until my sister, Fran, came over to prepare my dinner. As my mother left, I got on my knees and prayed:

"Dear God, so many times when I was sick, you helped me. Please, help my dad. Don't let him die. And please, don't let it be anything serious."

That night the good news came. Dad had lost a large amount of blood from a bad case of hemorrhoids. He had ignored the bleeding, refusing to see a doctor. His blackout was due to the loss of blood. The doctor reported that the whole thing could be taken care of with an operation.

As my mom shared the good news, I silently thanked the Lord. From the moment I set up my first drum set, I was really hooked on playing. I became involved in a band with my cousins, Floyd and Sam. The band was called The Delphis. Floyd sang, Sam played the sax, and I, of course, played the drums. The Delphis began getting gigs, playing all the popular rock and roll songs of the day including the Beach Boys and some 1950s numbers. What revolutionized our lives and brought us into a whole new thrust in our appreciation of music was Beatlemania. We began to play every one of their songs in our band. I began wearing my hair in the Beatles' style and bought boots in the style of the Fab Four.

In those days in junior high school, when we walked the halls, the principal would grab us if our hair was over our ears. The assistant principal would pull us into his office if our clothes were too stylish. Whether it be bell-bottom or pegged pants, I would be lectured on my rebellious attitude. I began combing my hair with grease and tucked the long part of my hair in my collar. I avoided certain corridors the assistant principal or teachers monitored. When I got home, I would wash my hair and comb it down in the Beatles' style.

My cousin Sam not only played the saxophone but bought a folk guitar. He was into the early works of Bob Dylan. The times, they were "a changin'" all right, but my dad did not like the changes *he* was seeing. He would constantly criticize my hair style.

"Why don't you get a haircut? You look like a little girl," he would say between bites of dinner.

"This is the new style, Dad, and you better get used to it," I would insist.

But Dad would not let up in his objections. Usually, it would end up in a shouting match between us, and my mother would have to step in to break it up.

I loved performing with the band before a live audience. I could sense the approval immediately. There were many girls at the dances, and they'd gather around us. When I walked the halls of school, my peers would come over to me and commend my expertise as a drummer.

One of the better Linden bands was playing a CYO (Catholic Youth Organization) dance at Saint John's Catholic Church, and Floyd and I went to check out our main competition. I hated to dance, but enjoyed watching the girls shaking their bodies and secretly envied the guys they danced with. It was at this mixer where I spotted the ringleader of the Catholic gang that years ago threw me into the Rahway River when they found out I was Jewish. I began to see my chance for revenge.

I spotted two of my older cousins, Uncle Sol's sons, Steve and Fred Marcus. Their reputation in Linden Public School was one to be feared. If anyone looked at Fred or Steve in the wrong way, they would punch out his lights. Fred was known to bench-press 600 pounds in weight-lifting competition. I told them about the incident and pointed to the ringleader, who was across the dance floor, joking with some of his friends. Steve and Fred made their way over to him. I couldn't see what happened next, as the entire crowd seemed to smell blood and encircle them. I heard shouts and screams from the onlookers. By the time I was able to make my way through the crowd, I was shocked to find the wrong person lying on the ground. Steve and Fred had hit the wrong one.

"That's not him!" I said to them.

"What do you mean? I thought he was the guy," Steve said, quite upset.

Then, my eyes met with the eyes of the ringleader who now pressed forward to see what the commotion was. I lifted my finger, pointing right at him, "That's him!"

The fellow now recognized me. He started toward me as Steve and Fred moved between us. The ringleader, realizing their strength and reputation, ran away. Everyone laughed and called him a chicken! Steve and Fred apologized to the fellow they had decked and helped him to his feet. That was the last time I attended a CYO dance.

My mother was upset with my dating Gentiles instead of Jewish girls.

"Warren. Why can't you find a nice Jewish girl, instead of all these *shiksas*?" (Yiddish for non-Jew).

"I haven't found one yet that I liked," I said.

"I heard they have dances at Anshe Hesed," she said, referring to the Orthodox Synagogue.

I told Floyd about the dances there, and he booked our band to play. I went in with an open mind to meet a nice Jewish girl. As I played, I noticed a group of girls standing near the stage, watching my every move. I dared not look directly at them, since I felt it was uncool to be caught peeking.

Floyd's Catholic girlfriend, Barbara Jean, grabbed my arm when we broke for a brief intermission.

"There's a girl here that really likes you," she told me.

"Where is she?" I asked with high expectations.

"She's wearing a pink dress," she said, pointing across the room.

I recognized her as a girl who attended the same Hebrew classes I did.

Oh, that's Barbara Finstein, I thought to myself. My mother might be happy about my dating her, but she definitely was not the prize I was looking for.

"Oh, they must have switched dresses. It's the one wearing black and white," Barbara Jean said, pointing to another girl.

"You mean Donna Kustra? I was in her seventh-grade class. She's cute," I said, now excited. Then I thought, "How was I going to tell my mother that I met a nice Catholic girl at the synagogue?"

At first, I did not want to settle down with any one girl. Donna kept coming over to my house with Barbara Jean. My mother was getting angry at the calls and visits I was getting from this new *shiksa.* I thought she was a nice girl, but I just didn't want to get tied down. When I went to my cousin Floyd's house for band practice, Donna would be there with Barbara Jean. Our relationship grew over a period of several months. Donna won me over, and I finally asked her to go steady. I truly believe that God brought us together. In spite of my mixed-up view of sexuality, she was raised in a manner which protected me. She would allow kissing, but anything more was strictly off-base.

FIFTEEN

THE SOUND OF MUSIC

It was 1962, and I was in eighth grade when I heard the principal of our school make an announcement over the public address system: "The Supreme Court of the United States of America has ruled that it is illegal to have involuntary prayers in school."

As I walked down the hall, I heard some students cheering and others seemed upset. I couldn't understand all the fuss. I saw Bob Pirigyi as he passed me.

"Hey, Bobby! What is all the commotion?" I called out to him.

"The Supreme Court just killed saying prayers in school," he said, unhappy with the decision.

Looking at the others cheering, I blurted out, "That's good. No more prayers."

Bob looked at me strangely. I thought about my statement to him as I walked home from school with Donna.

Why was I so happy about the decision? I believed in God and surely there was nothing wrong with prayer, I said to myself. When I got home, the television news was full of commentary and man-on-the-street interviews about the decision. The newscaster said that many Jewish children felt uncomfortable with Christian prayers. He said that the Supreme Court was concerned about the issue of the separation of church and state.

Then, I heard the comment of a clergyman who was against the decision: "From the founding of this great nation, the primary book that was used in school was the Holy Bible. Prayer was an integral part of every school morning. Our founding fathers never meant for us to keep God out of the state, but rather, the state out of religion," the cleric stated.

I began to wonder what was happening in America. Were we turning our backs on God, like the Israelites did when they worshiped the golden calf in Moses' day? Would God judge America in the same manner? I prayed that God would have mercy on our country.

By the eleventh grade, our band, The Delphis, had broken up. My cousin Sam and I got mad at Floyd. He said we couldn't make it in music without him. Sam and I formed a group called the Felonious Monks. There were five members in the group, and we all wore monks' robes as a gimmick. Floyd formed a group called the Demons Five, obviously aimed at head-on competition with us. At a battle of the bands, our band was in competition against his. Thanks to God, neither of us won. Instead, it was a group from nearby Elizabeth, New Jersey, that took home the prize.

However, a guitarist heard me play the drums at the competition and asked if I'd play in his trio called Ocean on Friday and Saturday nights. He told me that I would be paid fifty to one hundred dollars per night. I accepted as long as I could also continue playing in the Felonious Monks.

The trio, Ocean, played at Club Hi-De-Ho bar and grill in Union City, New Jersey. Club Hi-De-Ho was a real dive, to say the least, and I was playing illegally because I was under the legal drinking age. The trio would pack the place, playing a lot of James Brown and other classic soul songs. There were other attractions as well. The club had a blond, bikini-clad go-go dancer, who would do her gyrations right in front of me and my drum set. Whenever she would turn away from the audience, she would be facing me, smiling and winking. I was so naive that I thought she did that to everybody.

The first night at the club she approached me during the break.

"Hey you? Want to get out of here and get some coffee?" she asked quietly so no one else could hear.

I thought she had a great idea, so I turned to the other guys in the group.

"Yeah! Hey guys, you want to go and get some coffee?"

When I turned back toward her, I saw her rolling her eyes in frustration. It was then that I realized that she was making a pass at me. Later that evening, Jack, the lead guitarist enlightened me.

"Hey, Warren. Natalie really likes you. You play it right, you can wind up going home with her tonight," Jack said as if he knew by experience.

All I can say is that I thank God that Donna was in my life. There was no way I'd cheat on her. If I did not have Donna, who knows what trouble I would have gotten into with this twenty-year-old dancer?

Eventually my father found out that I was coming in at three and four o'clock in the morning and he was very mad at Mom.

"Where the heck does Warren go that he comes in so late?" he demanded.

"He's playing a band job. I don't know where, but I'm sure it's okay. Why don't you ask him?" Mom replied.

As soon as I came downstairs that Sunday, my dad popped the question.

"Where does the band play?" he asked, his usual beer in hand.

"Which one? I'm in two," I commented in an offhanded way.

"I want to know where you were last night!" Dad raised his voice angrily.

"Some bar in Union City," I told him, not realizing the response it would elicit.

Dad spat out the beer that he had just sipped.

"Union City? Are you crazy? You could be knifed there!"

I would not believe him until he called his friend, the police chief of Linden. He came over to our house just to talk to me and convince me that Union City had one of the worst crime rates in the state. He also informed me that the club could lose its liquor license for letting me play there.

I knew it was over, but I begged my parents to let me play one last gig. Reluctantly, Mom consented, but kept the truth from Dad. The last weekend I played, Club Hi-De-Ho had a packed house. When I told the guys in the group that I couldn't play anymore, they hit the ceiling. Jack upped the amount he'd pay me. Buzzie, the bass player, said that I shouldn't listen to my parents, and should move in with him and his girlfriend.

"Think of the money you'd make! Where else can you meet babes like this?" he tempted me, kissing his girlfriend to show what I'd be missing.

"Hey, cutie! You could stay with me until you save up enough money to get a pad of your own," Natalie spoke up, getting into the act.

During the final set, a twenty-year-old man came forward from the bar and told me that I was the greatest drummer he had ever heard. He said he represented a group called the James Gang and wanted me to consider joining. He confided in me that they were ready to sign a recording contract. Jack seemed to know the agent and told me that the James Gang was a band that was going places. Jack's prediction proved to be correct, for the group went on to record several hits. For awhile, I wondered what it would have been like had I accepted this offer and remained in rock music.

Even though I had been tempted, deep inside I really knew rock music was not going to be my career. And even though I was a long way from becoming a messianic believer, I was convinced that God wanted me to be a filmmaker. Even hell—coming in the guise of a potential recording contract—could not thwart God's plan for my life. And, mercifully, the Lord had given me enough good sense to know that I would have to put all my efforts toward getting good grades my senior year if I was to get into film school.

I made the decision to leave the Felonious Monks also. My cousin Floyd's group, the Demons Five, had disbanded and he was available to take over my slot as drummer. The group changed its name to the Nineteen Ten Fruitgum Company. In time, it would receive a Gold Record for a hit single, "Simple Simon Says." Yet, as the poet Robert Frost said, I took a different road, and that's made all the difference.

My senior year had arrived. From first grade on through eleventh grade, I had not taken school seriously. Throughout most of my school years, my mind seemed to be in a fog. Today, I wonder how I even made it through to the twelfth grade without being held back.

I knew that the most important year, concerning college admissions, was the final year of high school. For that reason, I decided I would buckle down and get good grades. All my older friends as well as Floyd and Sam told me I had better pray, and pray hard, that I did not get Harold Voltz as my English teacher. They told me that he was the hardest teacher they had ever had and that he didn't give out an A easily.

Of course, guess who got Mr. Voltz for his senior English teacher? I asked God to help me get great marks, and I took an active interest in Mr. Voltz's literature class. Poets such as Shelley, Keats, and Byron were my favorites. I found that I loved studying

Shakespeare and even enjoyed reading such classic books as *Crime and Punishment*, and I actively participated in the classroom discussions. Mr. Voltz often called on me to answer questions and to give my opinions on topics. Sometimes, he called on me so often that I felt as if we were having a two-way conversation with nobody else in class.

Often I would be so inspired by the class I would stay afterward and continue to converse with Mr. Voltz. Another student would sometimes join us. His name was Courtland Buchanan. He claimed to be a Christian and was planning to go to seminary. When he expressed his ideas, I automatically took the opposite side. He was operating from a biblical basis, and I was expressing a humanistic viewpoint. One of our arguments was over whether it was ever warranted for a man to steal. I felt if a man was hungry enough, it was justified for him to steal bread. Courtland took the position that breaking God's commandments was never justified. It was the first time I had heard anyone proclaim biblical standards. I was drawn to his positions by a force beyond myself, yet I never gave him the satisfaction of knowing that he was raising my curiosity.

I received straight As in Harold Voltz's class, and at the end of the year, Mr. Voltz called me up to his desk. He spoke quietly, only loud enough for me to hear.

"Warren," he said sincerely, "I wanted you to know that it was wonderful having you in my class. You worked hard and did well. You have a *very* creative mind, although I feel that you are not as good in communicating as a writer as you may be in other ways. However, I must tell you that you are, by far, the most brilliant student I have ever had in my class."

I was stunned by his words. I thanked God for answering my prayers. In my other subjects I excelled, too, and was on the honor roll that year.

My search for the right film school led me to two choices: the School of Visual Arts in New York City and Eastman Kodak in Rochester. I had plans to marry Donna as soon as I graduated from college so I chose the School of Visual Arts. This way I could be close to her, living at home in Linden and commuting every day by bus or train.

When I visited the dean of the school, he asked me a very important question.

"Why do you want to come to this art school to study film?"

The words came to me without any real thought.

"I want to learn about film as art. I believe that movies are not just entertainment, but that the motion picture can be used to communicate philosophies and ideas."

The dean leaned back in his chair.

"What kind of philosophies are you talking about?"

I took a moment to think and then blurted out, "Philosophies like those in Shakespeare and the Bible!"

The dean liked what he heard and said I would be welcome at the school, provided my grades remained up to par with their requirements.

Just before I graduated from high school in 1967, I was in the dentist's office waiting room, reading an article in a national magazine that Satan would later use to plant seeds of destruction in my life. The article spoke of the experimentation with drugs on the campuses of America. It described the effects of LSD, speed, cocaine, hashish, and marijuana. The article seemed to endorse marijuana as a harmless substance. It described it as a drug that opened the senses to new sensations. It proclaimed that the drug was nonaddictive and was one that could be controlled. It was right there in the dentist's office that a great urge to try this drug welled up, a desire that would not be satisfied until my college years. That one article played a significant part in my later use of marijuana.

Sixteen

Reefer Madness

Mom attended the first day of orientation at the School Of Visual Arts (S.V.A.) in New York City. I was enrolled in the Film Arts program. When we went into the school for a tour, my mother was shocked by the what she saw. These were art students. The boys had very long hair and both the boys and girls wore "hippie" clothes. The school was housed in an old building on Twenty-third Street between Second and Third Avenues.

"If your father ever saw this place he'd have a fit," Mom whispered to me. "Are you sure you don't want to be a doctor or lawyer?"

For years, my mother had been trying to talk me into another career, ever since I told her that I wanted to be a filmmaker. Once she had her brother, Uncle Joe, talk to me about my future. Joe was an optometrist, and he warned me how competitive the motion picture industry is.

All of this, however, was nothing new to me. Every book I read on the subject warned about the rivalry and dog-eat-dog mentality of the business. I had attended the Hollywood pavilion at the New York World's Fair in 1965. The people there presented a mock filming of a dramatic scene, and I was in seventh heaven as I watched the event. Afterward, I talked with the director. He told me that he was a member of the Directors Guild of America. When I told him that I was considering a career in the industry, he tried to discourage me.

"Son, it's not as glamorous as it looks here! Frankly, you have to know someone to get anywhere."

I listened to his frank talk, but I felt I knew someone who could assure me a job in the industry. His name was the God of Israel.

As Mom and I sat in the auditorium at the School of Visual Arts,

Everett Aison, dean of the film school, took the microphone and delivered a sobering speech.

"There are almost five hundred students enrolled as freshmen in the film school this year. This is the highest enrollment in our history. By the end of the first year, only half of the students assembled in this room will enroll for the second year. Of those, only one hundred will continue into the third year. About fifty will actually graduate. Of the fifty, three to five will actually get jobs working as professional filmmakers."

"So you don't want to be a doctor or a lawyer? How about a dentist?" Mom whispered.

I told her not to worry. I had the faith that God would see me through and answer my prayers, because I had committed my work to Him.

Learning about film in an arts school gave me a totally different perspective than I would have received had I attended N.Y.U. or U.C.L.A. At S.V.A., film was not just considered entertainment. It had a higher purpose.

"Film is art, to be used to communicate the artist's heart and soul," I was taught by an S.V.A. professor.

I knew then that God had chosen the right school for me.

At S.V.A., I began producing films on super 8mm. My first S.V.A. film was entitled *The Messiah*. It was complete with sound, while the other films in class were silent. It was an experimental film that centered on a person who looked like Jesus. I shot it in Bridgeport, Connecticut, in a Catholic shrine. My main character walked among the statues of the saints, trying to learn his identity. At first, the audience would think that my main character was supposed to be Jesus Christ. As the film progresses, the audience learns that he was searching for the truth about God. On his journey, he was sidetracked by drugs, sex, and the loss of a girl-friend. The film ended as he climbed a hill and found a statue of Jesus, crucified on the cross. He bows his head in humility.

After I showed the film to my Experimental Film class, the teacher stood up and applauded. He said that it was the best movie any of his students had ever produced. Others in the class ripped it apart. One girl lambasted it for its male chauvinist viewpoint. It was 1968, and I had never even heard this term. However, S.V.A. was just beginning to expose me to many radical ideas and differences in culture. The liberals hated my film because of the religious overtones. Yet, there I was—a Jew, trying to make an honest film about my own search for the reality of God.

My teacher, Carl Linder, defended the movie and told the dean about my talents. I grew in my craft as a director, cameraman, writer, producer, and editor. I was beginning to realize the reality of my dream. God was being faithful in answering my prayers.

One day I sat at lunch with some of my fellow students and was surprised to hear their negativity. This particular group was slicing the school to pieces. I spoke up to defend it.

"I like the school. I feel that you will get from it what you put in," I declared.

The student with the biggest mouth laid into me. "Yea! What do you think this school is going to do for you? Do you think you're going to get a job in the industry after you graduate?"

"Yes! I believe if I do the best I can and have a positive attitude, I'll get a job!" I responded.

The other students laughed. He continued with a smirk on his face.

"You're so naive! I really feel sorry for you."

I was hesitant to tell them that my faith was based on a belief in God. I felt it was like "casting pearls before swine." Subsequently, none of those students enrolled for the second year.

My favorite class was Directing the Actor for Film, taught by Bob Brady. The class met at his Fourteenth Street studio. We learned acting and directing techniques, and had to write and direct various scenes using the acting pool that hung around the Brady Studios.

These were professional actors and actresses who ate, drank, and relished it all. Bob had black and white video cameras which he used to tape and play back our work for critique. I learned about the method actor, the quick-study actor, and how to elicit the best performance from a first-time actor.

Despite all that was good in this class, it was here that Satan began a new effort to pull me away from God. At the end of the class, a number of us would hang around. Someone would pull out a bag of marijuana and roll some joints. He would light them and pass them around to the students and actors. I was tempted to try one, but I was afraid of the effects of the drug. I remembered the article I had once read in the dentist's office in which the reporter claimed that this drug was harmless. I watched as the joint was passed and noted that everyone seemed to become very mellow. The group would then participate as Bob demonstrated more directing techniques.

However, it wasn't at the school that I actually tried the drug. During Christmas break, I got together with one of my cousins who was home from college. We were driving in his car when he pulled out a joint of marijuana and lit it.

"You want a hit?" he asked.

Figuring it must be okay if he was smoking it, I tried it. I expected something to happen immediately, but nothing did. We finished the joint.

"Man, this is good stuff! You stoned or what?" he inquired. "I don't feel anything," I said, disappointed.

"What do you mean you don't feel anything? Did you ever smoke before?" he queried. I lied to him that I smoked the stuff all the time. He lit another joint, and we smoked it all, but still I didn't feel anything.

"Wow, I'm really stoned! How do you feel now?" he asked.

"I still don't feel a . . ." Suddenly I burst out laughing. He was laughing too.

We went into his house, and his mom was home. Every time she asked us a question we'd just start laughing hysterically.

"What's wrong with the two of you?" she asked.

"Nothing, Mom. Warren just told me a funny joke," said my cousin. I fell laughing to the floor. I could not look my aunt in the eyes for fear she would know I was stoned.

From that point on, when I walked through the School of Visual Arts, I was aware of the smell of marijuana. It was everywhere! Students freely smoked joints in the bathrooms and hallways.

It was about this time, my second year at S.V.A., that I became good friends with another Jewish student. His dad worked in films. He had his own studio, and I would go there whenever I was invited. I also went to another friend's apartment. There, at lunch time we would smoke a few joints and go back to class.

Watching old films, stoned in Film History and Film Aesthetics class, was a trip I'll never forget. One of the movies shown was the classic Russian silent film, *Potemkin*, directed by the celebrated filmmaker, Sergei Eisenstein. In another classroom the teacher was playing the Beatles' newest album, "Sergeant Pepper's Lonely Heart Club Band." The music began to make perfect sense, as if it were scored to the silent movie. When the Beatles sang the words, "Lucy in the sky with diamonds," there was a sailor on a ship who picked up field glasses to look at the sky. He reacted as if he saw Lucy in the sky. All the students who were stoned laughed at the phenomenon, until the teacher stopped the film.

"We will watch the rest of the movie tomorrow, without the soundtrack by the Beatles," our teacher said caustically.

Marijuana was not the end of my drug experimentation. Sadly, it was the beginning. I started buying nickel and dime bags of the substance and brought it home with me to Linden. I was now smoking the drug each night. My dad was upstairs with his police friends getting drunk, while I went into the bathroom downstairs and got stoned on marijuana.

Everybody seemed to be using marijuana. The Beatles and other rock musicians openly talked about their experiences with drugs. Marijuana did not seem dangerous at all. I rationalized that it was far better than drinking. I told myself that I had complete control of my faculties and I could become sober anytime I wanted to. I figured that since marijuana was harmless, other drugs must be all right too.

Like the unacceptance of the *Playboy* philosophy, perhaps society has rejected the value of drug experimentation because of a closed mind, I told myself.

A group of us film students were at a friend's apartment when he began passing a pipe full of a new strain of "hash." It was a stronger form of marijuana. I watched patiently as they all inhaled deeply, holding the smoke in their lungs. Ever so slowly they would exhale and remark how good the stuff was.

The tiny apartment was quickly filling up with smoke as the pipe came to me. My friend put a fresh wad of hash in the pipe and lighted a match, telling me to smoke it. I inhaled as deeply as I could and tried to hold the substance in my lungs. However, it was so harsh that I began to cough. As the smoke flowed out of my mouth, an intense rush overcame me. My mind was clouded with dizziness while my entire body felt bathed in warm water. Everything around me seemed to move in slow motion.

"What is this stuff?" I asked.

"It's opiated hash! You love it?" my friend responded.

"Wow, it's heavy stuff!" I said, not too sure that I liked it.

We all left the apartment together to go to see the grand opening of Robert Altman's movie, M*A*S*H. We had to walk down eight flights of stairs in the tenement building. I felt as if my legs were becoming part of the stairs. Once outside, the buildings seemed to look small. I felt like I was Godzilla walking on a Japanese movie set. We saw one of our S.V.A. professors as he was getting into a cab.

"Hey, Mr. Martin!" a friend yelled. The teacher waved as he got into the cab. From my point of view it all seemed to happen in slow motion.

"Is everything in slow motion? Or is it just me?" I asked as we got on a city bus.

My friend laughed loudly, "You're really stoned, aren't you?"

At first there was standing room only on the bus. My eyes focused on a fat man who was talking out loud to himself. At first his words were incoherent, but as I continued to listen, I was beginning to understand what he was saying. It sounded like, "Satan has control of you now!"

Frightened, I turned to one of my pals, "What is that guy saying?"

He made me point him out. He observed him for a short time. "He ain't saying anything. He's just babbling," my friend said, looking at me strangely.

"I know, but what's scaring me is that I understand what he is saying!"

My friend began laughing loudly. His laughter was contagious, and I burst into hysterics.

Some people got off the bus, and I was happy to get a seat. The bus was so crowded that I had to press close to the older woman sitting next to me. I became quite uncomfortable. I felt as if the side of my body was becoming a part of hers. I tried to move away from her, but the more I moved, the more it seemed that my side was actually melting into her side. Finally, I could take it no more and jumped up.

Sadly, this incident didn't stop me from continuing to use drugs. I had heard about LSD from a number of friends at S.V.A. One friend had taken acid a number of times. He refused to sell me any, since he didn't want to be the one to turn me onto any drug for the first time. I would ask him all kinds of questions about the effects of taking the drug. When I felt confident enough, I bought a tab of Orange Sunshine from a dealer in school. I was too afraid to take it alone. I invited a friend to see Stanley Kubrick's 2001 on the big screen. We broke off tiny pieces of the LSD tablet and both swallowed them. I had seen the film before when I was straight, but it was nothing like seeing it on acid. I felt as if I were floating in space. The movie became too intense for me at times. I closed my eyes, but the movie was still playing in my mind. It was hard to tell where my fantasies began and the movie left off. Afterwards, my friend and I went to an Episcopal Church on Fifth Avenue. I had been there before to visit. It had a wall of carved sculptures of the saints. I sat down and watched the wall. It seemed to move. I prayed to God to help me through the trip I was experiencing, unharmed.

Walking through the Port Authority terminal to our bus was a nightmare. People looked garish and zombie-like. My pal began freaking out.

"Warren, I don't think I can handle this stuff," he admitted.

I realized that the less I looked at objects and concentrated on my thoughts, the more I could control them.

"Don't look at anything," was all the advice I could give him.

Somehow we made it home. I seemed to be coming down from the effects by the time I walked into my house. Both my parents were home. I went downstairs to watch television with my father. The nightly news was on, and there was a scenic painting of the skyline of New York City with a cloud pattern behind the anchorman. I noticed that the clouds were moving.

"Hey, Dad, since when did they have the clouds moving?" I blurted out to my father.

"What clouds are moving?" he said, looking at me strangely.

I realized that I was still hallucinating. I looked over at my old drum set. The marble finish on the drums seemed to be liquid. I went up to my room and got into bed, closing my eyes. I prayed to God to help me get through this, and I promised Him I would never use LSD again.

In spite of my drug use, my grades did not suffer. As a matter of fact, I received all A's and B's on my report cards. I produced and directed two more movies while at the school and helped others with their projects, serving in different capacities.

The further I strayed from God, the more He seemed to reach out to me. There were street witnesses everywhere in New York with signs, "Repent and be saved." There were people preaching the Gospel right on the street corners. I'd often stop and listen to what they had to say, especially when I was stoned. Many placed tracts in my hands, little religious booklets, which I read on the bus ride home. One in particular got my attention. It was a Chick Tract named "This Is Your Life." It was in a comic-book format about a man who is living a life of sin and dies. He is immediately transported to heaven before a silhouetted God who sits on a giant throne.

"I was a good person. I never hurt anyone," the man told God.

God began reviewing elements of his life on a giant movie screen. You can imagine how this story was affecting me, since I was studying to be a filmmaker and pledged to God to use films to communicate what He wanted to say!

Every terrible thing that man had done was recorded on film and projected on the cinemascopic movie screen. The man was confronted with the day he turned God down in church when an altar call was given. The sins of this man's entire life flashed before him in this supernatural movie of his life. He tried to make excuses, but ultimately was banished to hell. The tract told what would have happened if he had accepted Christ. I started weeping as I read this tract and cried all the way home. I asked God to forgive me and help me know what was the right thing to do. Yet, I fell short of receiving Yeshua into my heart as my Messiah.

SEVENTEEN

PATHS OF GLORY

During my high school days, I supported the war in Vietnam. President Kennedy had supported the war, and back then he was my favorite president. However, by the time I attended the School of Visual Arts, more and more Americans had begun to speak out against the war. More and more television shows were debating the U.S. involvement. The 1968 Democratic convention had provoked sentiment on the campuses of America for the peace movement. Network news reported on the trial of the Chicago Seven, and the rock musicians I admired were singing anti-war songs and speaking out for peace. The Beatles were singing "All You Need Is Love," while Country Joe and the Fish sang "I Feel Like I'm Fixin' To Die." Everybody at the school seemed to be anti-war.

I was safe from being drafted—thanks to a student deferment. Upon graduation, however, my name would be at the top of the list, and the way the war was escalating, I was certain I'd have to go. For safety's sake, I began buying into the rhetoric of the peaceniks.

On May Day, the entire School of Visual Arts canceled classes so students could march in the New York City peace rallies. The school allowed its facilities to be used for meetings before the march, and there were many anti-war speakers at the school that day. I remember one speaker in particular. "This war is immoral, but so is capitalism itself," he began. "We must rise up against the establishment, even if it takes a revolution!"

A student near me stood up and interrupted the speaker.

"What form of government do you see us replacing capitalism with?"

The speaker was surprised, but responded, "I believe that socialism is the perfect government."

The entire student body began to "boo" the speaker.

Another student stood and confronted the speaker. "Russia is a socialist country, but look at the repression there!"

"Russia is not the perfect socialist nation. They have corrupted socialism. I'd say that China, even Cuba, are prime examples of pure socialist nations," he said, defending his position.

The students began to leave the auditorium, upset with the speaker. For the most part, we did not march for peace because we were Communists, but rather, we were just against that particular war. It felt good as I marched in a crowd of my peers. I sensed an incredible power, raising my hand to make the peace sign as we yelled in unison, "Hell no, we won't go!"

There was a unity of purpose and a sense of commitment in the hearts of all of us in those days. I was serious in my desire to help end the war and use our tax money to help the poor. Anti-war was a movement in which caring and compassion were initially the main ingredients that attracted me. I identified with the liberals and their causes. Without a complete understanding of God and the Bible, I thought I saw the heart of the Messiah in the midst of the movement. I couldn't see how it was godly to kill others. After all, wasn't God love?

I applauded such religious men as the now defrocked Father Daniel Barrigan and religious denominations such as the Quakers and the Jehovah's Witnesses. For the most part, I thought that any Christian who supported the war was a hypocrite. Surely Jesus wouldn't be in uniform and fighting in the Vietnam War.

As the war continued to escalate and the liberal news media seemed to champion the peace movement, I began to read radical books such as the *Communist Manifesto*. Socialist literature was handed out freely at the peace rallies I attended. I began to believe the radical theories telling of plots by the wealthy to subject the middle class and poor to slavery. Karl Marx wrote that religion was the opiate of the masses. He further explained that under the banner of the church and, even in the name of Christ, killings and persecution were commonplace. It was religion that kept the poor suppressed so that the rich could remain in control and enslave the masses. Other literature I read highlighted the persecution of the Jews by the church—even in the name of Jesus!

Justin Martyr (A.D. 100-165) accused the Jewish people of incitement to kill Christians in order to build animosity between Christians and Jews.

Origen (185-254) accused the Jewish people of plotting in their meetings to murder Christians. Furthermore, he wrote that the Jews nailed Christ to the cross, which incited hatred by Christians against the Jewish people for many centuries.

Eusebius (260-339) spread the lie that the Jewish people, each year at the holiday of Purim, engaged in the killing of Christian children.

St. John Chrysostom (347-407) said in his homilies that Jews could never receive forgiveness because God always hated them. He urged all Christians to hate the Jews, because they were the assassins of Christ and worshipers of the devil.

St. Cyril (died 444) gave the Jewish people under his jurisdiction the choice of conversion, exile, or stoning.

St. Jerome (347-420), who translated the Latin Vulgate, tried to prove that the Jews were incapable of understanding the Scriptures and that they should be severely persecuted until they confessed belief in Christianity.

St. Augustine (354-430) said Judaism is a corruption and that the true image of the Jew was Judas Iscariot. He decided that the Jewish people should be relegated to the position of slaves for their own good and the good of society. He believed that like Cain, who murdered his brother, Abel, the Jewish people blamed for murdering Jesus are doomed to wander the earth as living proof that Christianity is the truth and belief in Judaism was a sin.

St. Thomas Aquinas (1224-1274) demanded that the Jewish people be called to perpetual servitude.

The Crusaders (1099) rounded up all Jewish people into the Great Synagogue in Jerusalem and locked the doors, setting the building on fire. All the Jews were burned to death. The Crusaders marched around the blazing building singing "Christ, We Adore Thee."

Martin Luther (1483-1546) wrote in his *Von den Juden und Ihren Luegen* the following:

"What then shall we Christians do with this damned, rejected race of Jews? Since they live among us and we do know about their lying and blasphemy and cursing, we cannot tolerate them if we do not wish to share in their lies, curses, and blasphemy. . . . We must prayerfully and reverently practice a merciful severity."

The literature further suggested that years of hatred and misguided preaching against the Jewish people paved the way for the Nazi Holocaust. Hitler wrote in his book *Mein Kampf* the following: "Hence today I believe that I am acting in accordance with the Almighty Creator: by defending myself against the JEW, I am fighting for the work of the Lord."

Today, I understand that the underlying premise behind such persecution was the tragic misconception taught by the Gentile church that the Jews were solely responsible for the crucifixion of Jesus. Did the Jewish people have a part in the crucifixion? The answer is yes, though the modern church has now swung to the extreme position of denial, understandably distancing itself from the German Holocaust against the Jews. The Bible reveals that it wasn't the Jews alone who killed Jesus, but rather the Romans under Pilate, Jewish leaders, Herod, a portion of the Jewish people, and a portion of the Gentiles as stated in Acts, chapter 4, verses 27 and 28:

For the truth against thy holy child Jesus, whom thou hast anointed, both Herod, and Pontius Pilate, with the Gentiles, and the people of Israel, were gathered together,
For to do whatsoever thy hand and thy counsel determined before to be done.

During the experience of my Vietnam days, as I read about the horrible acts of persecution the Jews suffered at the hands of the church, I suddenly saw the modern Christian church as the enemy of the common people and full of hypocrites. The writings that criticized Christianity seemed to make sense. I hadn't seen evidence of a church which was committed to reaching out to the poor and downtrodden. My Gentile neighbors were no different than I. There was no evidence of the reality of Jesus in their lives.

How can we expect the rich to ever help the poor? I thought to myself. "In a socialistic society, money from the rich would be redistributed to help the poor. No one would be hungry or without homes. Without the divisions of class, religion, and stature, the world would be one big happy family."

I bought the ideology, "Make love, not war!" I began to feel hatred toward those who did not agree with my viewpoint. I was becoming a different person. There could be no place for joy in my heart as long as people were dying in the war and the poor continued to suffer.

My dad couldn't figure out where my radical views were coming from. He would read the conservative *New York Daily News*, while I would read the liberal *New York Post*. We couldn't have dinner without arguing. Everything he said provoked me to protest. Mom tried to be the peacemaker, but to no avail. Adding fuel to the fire, my father was drunk, and I was stoned. It was like trying to mix oil and water.

I began to endorse radical political groups like the Yippies, the S.D.S (Students for a Democratic Society), and the Black Panthers. Jerry Rubin, Bobby Seale, and Abbie Hoffman became my heroes. In the summer between the spring and fall semesters, I worked at my father's jewelry factory. The business was jointly owned by my aunts and uncles on the Marcus side of the family. Most of my cousins worked there in the summers as well.

We would all get together for lunch in the final assembly room. My cousins and I would inevitably wind up arguing with the adults about the war in Vietnam and other political topics. It seemed that we opposed every conservative view they held. Not only did this happen at work, but also at bar mitzvahs, weddings, and even funerals. A true generation gap existed between the younger and older members of the Marcus family.

When I watched television and heard someone with a conservative view, I became incensed. I couldn't figure out what was happening to me. I identified with the hippies who espoused the "Make love, not war" philosophy. And yet, in the midst of my serious social concern, I couldn't help but feel that I was becoming a hypocrite, singing the Beatles' song, "All We Need Is Love," but incapable of loving others who disagreed with my views.

The pressure of school combined with my family strife and the tension created by the war, led me to use marijuana every day as a means of escape. Marijuana began to take the place of God in my life. I'd sit with my friends from school, and we'd pass around a joint—our communion wafer. We felt as if we were now on the same spiritual plane every time we got stoned. Without realizing it, I began to see God and the world around me in eastern religious terms.

Drugs influenced me to write the following (which reveals how eastern my thinking had become):

The Universe is a living organism, within an infinity of larger organisms. And this infinity, which transcends being, is God. Men who realize this esoteric knowledge are truly a special breed, for they know "the secret of the universe." They have come to the realization that man, animals, plants, the planets, and the stars are God.

The war is a living cancer destroying the organism from within. Man is part of God; therefore, he is God. Mankind holds the power to put an end to the cancer, or to let it destroy the entire cosmos.

War is the devil! Man must never fear war, but understand it. For in understanding war, he will transcend it. And those who comprehend actually are a new breed of human beings, an animal who uses his intellect to the fullest capacity, rather than using physical strength.

We are the next step in the evolutionary chain. We shall bring about change, without forcing our ideologies on others. We will be transmitting good vibes so that others will desire to be like us and follow in our footsteps.

Think positively at all times, even when you are down. We are God, not alone, but corporately. If we become paranoid, then all the world will seem to be against us.

Be happy and think positive and the world will catch the good vibes we beam out to others. This is how we can defeat the devil, that cancer, known as war.

God knew I needed something strong to break the hold Satan was gaining over my soul. He was about to introduce me to a man whom He would use to confront every radical idea I embraced.

In September of 1969, I was glad to get back to the School of Visual Arts after the summer break. I couldn't take working any longer at my father's jewelry factory. It was slow, tedious work. If anything prodded me onward to be successful at school, it was realizing that I could be stuck on a machine for the rest of my life, producing watch cases.

It was my second year at the School of Visual Arts and everyone had become more radical—in both their appearance and their thinking. It seemed like another world in comparison to Linden, New Jersey. Students were dressed in hippie garb, smoking joints in the hallway and lavatories. I was getting stoned every day before leaving the school. My senses were so disoriented that my daily walk from Third Avenue and Twenty-Third Street to the Port Authority terminal on Fortieth Street and Eighth Avenue became a blur. When stoned, I tuned out the world around me. Block after block I'd walk deep in thought about an idea for a movie script. The long walk to the terminal passed quickly, but once inside, I found myself walking over to the row of various booths set up in the main lobby. Here, individuals from sundry organizations were allowed to set up card tables and distribute their literature. While waiting for my bus, I killed time by debating the representatives at each table. I loved playing the devil's advocate, so I always took the opposing sides of the issues. At the tables sat representatives of the John Birch Society, the National Order to Make Marijuana Legal, the Black Muslims, and many more.

For me, none of these groups had the answer. The man at the John Birch Society gave me a book entitled *None Dare Call It Conspiracy*. It suggested that the world was being controlled by a conspiracy of wealthy individuals and corporations. The Trilateral Commission, the United Nations, the Rockefeller Foundation and the Rothschilds were the primary villains cited.

As I read the book, I realized that the right-wing and left-wing extremist organizations agreed on the conspiracy theory. Both believed secret organizations dictated world affairs. But the right and the left offered different solutions. The right-wingers believed in law and order as ultimately manifested in fascism, while the leftists believed in revolution and anarchy to install a socialist government of bleeding-heart liberals. I identified more with the liberals than the conservatives. To me, the right appeared heartless. In my eyes, the conservatives emulated Hitler and the Nazis—lacking compassion, but demanding law and order without mercy toward those who opposed their ideologies. I lumped all Christians into the right-wing category, and I had no understanding of the vast differences among the various denominations.

I spent most of my time at the anti-abortion stand. That is where I met Richard Gallagher, a Catholic activist committed to gathering millions of names on a petition against abortion. Because I had been indoctrinated by the liberal position on abortion, I began to argue with him.

"Why do you waste time with this, when so many Americans are dying in Vietnam?"

"More innocent lives are murdered by abortion than are killed in Vietnam. Why don't you protest that?" he challenged me.

I fired back, "I believe it's a woman's right to choose. It's her body!"

"What about the unborn babies' right to choose? They can't speak for themselves, but they deserve the right to live," countered Richard.

"But it's not a life until it's born," I claimed.

"It is life upon conception! God in the Bible said to David, 'I knew you in your mother's womb,'" he argued.

"Men wrote the Bible. I don't think you can use that to support your views," I fired back loudly.

A group of travelers crowded around the booth to listen.

Richard showed me gruesome photos of fetuses with tiny hands and feet. I didn't believe these were real. I thought the photos must be doctored. He explained how a suction device aborted the unborn babies—literally ripping the arms and legs off the fetus. I peered over a nauseating photo of a mutilated fetus, dumped in the bottom of a trash can with its arms and legs still in one piece. Then he gave me a lot of information to read concerning the pro-life stance.

Once home, I began to pour over the material. I couldn't believe what I read about the stages of fetal development.

I thought to myself, *If these pictures are real, then innocent babies are being murdered.*

Troubled by the literature, I went to the public library to check the veracity of the information from Richard. To my surprise, the library books confirmed the information. In good conscience, I now agreed that at least *some* restrictions should be applied to abortions. For instance, I now agreed that no abortions should be allowed after the first three months. This was a major concession on my part, a radical change from my original belief of absolutely no restrictions on abortion. The next day I confronted him, "Richard, perhaps there should be some restrictions on abortion. But what about when the mother's life is endangered?"

Richard replied, "Abortion is always wrong. There is nothing immoral about a doctor's treating a woman for a physical problem and the fetus dying as a result. But to attack the unborn child with the intent to abort it—that's murder."

I was puzzled.

"Sounds like semantics to me!" I shouted.

No matter how well he tried to explain his position, I couldn't see the difference. However, God had planted His messenger, Richard Gallagher, in the Port Authority Bus Terminal, a place I passed every day. I looked forward to talking with Richard as I traveled daily on my way back from New York to Linden.

EIGHTEEN

THE WAY WE WERE

My time at school slipped by quickly. I began worrying about graduating and facing the draft. A cousin was seeing a psychiatrist, who happened to be anti-war.

He told me, "Warren, you should start seeing her now and just tell her how you feel about the war. She will write a letter saying you are not army material."

I approached my parents about it.

"Dad, I need to start seeing a psychiatrist. It's the only way I can avoid the draft."

"I'm not sending you to any shrink. That stuff will be on your record forever. You won't get a job!" he shouted.

"But Dad, I'm going into the film business. Everybody in Hollywood is seeing a psychiatrist. They won't care! This is the only way I can get out. There's no way I'm going to Vietnam," I reasoned.

Despite his conservatism; my father finally agreed to the psychiatric consultations. The first visit was to determine whether Dr. Chun would take me as a patient. My cousin gave me tips on how I should act on my first visit.

"Act despondent. Tell her your deepest thoughts and don't be afraid to exaggerate. You need to convince her that you need her help, because she is very busy and won't take just anybody."

I found an outdated book on psychiatry at a garage sale. I began to read about various psychological disorders—paranoid schizophrenia, catatonia, depression, obsessions, and more. I prepared myself physically by staying up late hours and smoking inordinate amounts of hash and marijuana the week prior to my first session.

As I drove to see Dr. Chun, I lit a joint and smoked it. I hid it in my hand so I would not be seen by other motorists. I kept my eyes out for cops, ready to pop the joint into my mouth and eat it in case a police officer pulled me over. Once inside the office, I sat in a chair as she took notes at her desk. I told her my problems, exaggerating them as my cousin had directed. Nothing seemed to faze her as I talked until I mentioned that I used drugs.

"What kind of drugs are you using?" she asked.

"Marijuana, hash, LSD, speed, cocaine!" I answered, speaking slowly.

She put down her pad and began to speak solemnly, "Warren, some of those drugs are very dangerous. Why do you feel you need to take them?"

I sat for awhile, contemplating her question. Finally, I replied, "I feel good when I'm high. I forget all about the world around me. I mean, what is life all about, anyway? Is this all there is? Or, is there another reality, greater than the one we see with our physical eyes?"

She nodded slightly.

"Warren, I would like to see you some more. Would Tuesday evenings at 6:30 be good for you?"

"That would be fine," I answered, trying to remain subdued and look depressed. Inside however, I was rejoicing. Once inside my car, I began shouting excitedly, "Thank you, God!"

I hurried home and told my cousin that I was *in*.

When my parents went to sleep at about 11:30 P.M., a couple of friends would sneak over to my house. I'd let them in through the back door, and we would smoke some joints of marijuana, or smoke some hash in a pipe and get stoned. Often, I turned on the television and muted the audio. I'd play some of the latest rock music and turn the channels until I found suitable video which seemed to sync with the music. We would sit and sometimes laugh at how remarkably the music fit the pictures on the tube. My favorite thing was to turn the television to a non-broadcast station and turn off all the lights in the room. I would turn various combinations of the horizontal, vertical, and brightness controls in sync to the soundtrack of the movie *2001*. As the orchestra would build, I'd bring up the intensity of brightness. When the orchestra would diminish, I'd dim the television picture to complete darkness. For the final crescendo, I would bring up the intensity of brightness to its maximum. My friends and I would freak out at the new reality that was created in the room. To us, it was like a religious experience.

One night, I tried opening up to them about my views on God. I asked them what they thought about Jesus.

"Oh, Warren, don't talk about God now. You're bringing us down," one friend said.

"But what if Jesus is who the Christians claim He is? What if He is our Messiah?" I asked.

"Come on, Warren! You're bringing me down. Light up another joint!" my other friend insisted.

I refused to smoke any more dope, unless they let me speak my mind. This resulted in an argument. One of the fellows walked out. The other stayed and we smoked some more grass. Suddenly, he began to hold his chest. He said he thought it was a heart attack. I tried to convince him it was all in his mind. He asked me to wake up my father immediately. I told him that I couldn't do that, because he would know that we were using drugs. My friend was completely unreasonable. He was totally freaking out. All I could think about was how horrible it would be if my dad found out about my using drugs. The fellow started upstairs to wake my dad.

"Please don't do this. You'll get us both in trouble! Look, I'll go upstairs and get my sister. Okay?"

My words comforted him because he knew Fran was a registered nurse. I went upstairs to her room and woke her up, telling her what was going on. She hurried downstairs and took his pulse, then told us that he was not having any heart attack symptoms. At her advice, I drove him home, and he seemed to be all right as I helped him inside.

However, the next day I found out that he was in the hospital. He had experienced severe anxiety attacks. Later, he was admitted into a private psychological hospital for further treatment.

At my session with Dr. Chun, she told me that my friend, who was also a patient of hers, should never have used marijuana.

"He already has suffered from mild chronic anxiety, but the drug has brought on a more serious case," she explained. "He will have to live with this illness for the rest of his life."

I was shocked. This was the first time I heard that marijuana could have harmful effects.

I was tormented with the thought of whether I should stop using the drug. Finally, however, I rationalized that perhaps my friend's problem had nothing to do with the drug. Instead, I told myself that it was a weakness in his character. After all, nobody else I knew suffered from this problem. Thanks to this brilliant exercise in reasoning, I continued to use marijuana.

For a long time, I did not experience any bad side effects. Then, one night when I was up late working on a project for school, everything changed. I was painting cells for an animation project. I went to the kitchen sink to clean my paintbrushes and on my way back downstairs to the recreation room, I inhaled as deeply as I could on a pipe full of marijuana resin. I stood on the stairs, holding in the smoke as long as I could. Suddenly, I felt very dizzy, as if I were going to faint. I tried to continue down the stairs. It felt as if I were walking in slow motion. I saw the paintbrushes as they fell out of my hand. I seemed to make it to the bottom of the stairs. Then, everything went black, and I felt as if I were falling. The next thing I remember was feeling an intense coldness on the left side of my head. I opened my eyes and realized I was lying on the floor. Slowly I sat up and remembered what had happened.

"Wow, now that was some rush!" I said to myself.

As I walked over to the couch, a splitting headache began to pound on the left side of my head. I knew then that I had passed out and hit my head on the cold tile floor of the recreation room. But, even this incident did not stop me from using marijuana.

My third and final year at the School of Visual Arts was my most productive. I produced a short theatrical film for my cinematography class called *The Editor*. It was a satiric look at the life of a film editor who gets carried away with his work. Fantasy soon became reality as the outtakes of film on the floor of the editing room came to life and attacked the editor. With the room full of film from ceiling to floor, the camera revealed that the editor was still relentlessly cutting film, oblivious to what had happened. *The Editor* was well received by my teachers and the dean.

Another movie I produced and directed was *Visions of Johanna*, a one-hour dramatic short. It was about a rock musician depressed over losing his girlfriend to another man. Little does he realize that she and her new boyfriend were part of a plot to drive him insane. This bizarre film reflected my innermost feelings from heavy drug use. The students responded favorably to the premiere screening of this film. Also, during my last year at the arts school, I helped with several friends' productions, including a short film directed by Irv Goodnoff who would later become a director of photography for independent feature films in Hollywood.

At S.V.A., I learned from professionals that the message we were conveying was the single most important aspect of any movie we would produce. Every aesthetic and technical aspect of film-making was to be subject to the "theme and conflict of the script." Everything the actors did—the way they moved and how they delivered their lines—must corroborate the message conveyed in the script. The technical aspects of camera, lighting, and sound must all orchestrate the actor's motivations and inner monologue.

In the Directing the Actor class, I learned how to work with quick-study and method-actors. I was taught the various techniques needed to elicit the greatest performance.

In the Cinematography class, I learned that the type of lighting, be it hard or soft, high key or silhouette, was carefully manipulated to support the overall intent of the message. The lighting also can set the atmosphere and mood of the entire scene. Every camera angle and subject size must be adroitly chosen for what is best for each particular "beat" in a scene. The height of the camera affects how the audience will view a particular character at any given time. A low angle makes the actor look dominant or high in stature, while a high angle suggests a diminutive quality. The movement of the camera can affect the emotion of the audience as it dollies into a close-up of a character as he delivers a key line, or it can take the audience's breath away as the camera helicopters up and sweeps back leaving a character alone in the midst of his dilemma.

In the Sound for Film class, we were taught that the sound effects and music chosen for a movie can change the entire meaning of the scene.

In the Film Aesthetics class, I watched thousands of classic movies and analyzed them to comprehend what makes them work. I soon realized that many movies and television shows were often uninspired in the way they were produced.

I fell in love with one particular step in filmmaking—editing. I discovered that it was in editing that new life can be breathed into a production. The editor was like a miracle worker, taking the various filmed takes and literally creating the movie, cut by cut, bringing it to life. I decided that if God would allow me to get my first job in the industry, I hoped it would be in film editing.

The height of my graduation was the screening of the films my class had produced. My mother and my girlfriend, Donna, came to the school for the event. When my films were screened I could see how proud both of them were as the audience broke into applause.

Upon graduation, I kept a promise to marry Donna. We had been going out since 1965, and it was now May, 1970. We planned our wedding for December 12. My Jewish mother and father had come to think the world of Donna. I had great rapport with Donna's father, Joe, and her mother, Josephine. However, when it came to announcing our engagement, the one question asked by both sets of parents was, where would we get married—in the synagogue or the church? Finally, Donna and I had to talk about it. Up to that point, neither of us talked much about our religious views.

"Warren, Mom and Dad want us to get married in the church," Donna blurted out one day while we were riding in my car.

"The church! No way! My mother would be heartbroken! Look, I think it's best if we keep religion out of the wedding. I mean, I never go to the synagogue and you don't go to church. That's how we'll keep the peace," I responded as carefully as I could.

"So, where will we get married?"

"How about at a good restaurant! And my father can get the mayor of Linden to marry us," I answered.

My wife loved the idea, but seriously wondered if her parents could be sold on it. We first told my mom and dad, and they bought in with excitement.

Dad said he could definitely get the mayor. Then, Donna and I drove over to her house. She asked her mother and father to sit down, and we told them the idea.

"No way! We want our daughter married in the church," her father said.

"Dad, it's not fair to Warren's side of the family. I mean, Pearl isn't demanding that we get married in the synagogue," Donna argued.

They were stubborn, but finally agreed that we could get married by the mayor. However, they wanted us to be married again later—in the eyes of God. So, I went with Donna to Saint John's Catholic Church where we had an appointment with the pastor, Father Eilit. I felt very uneasy about being there, but we told him our plans to get married by the mayor of Linden and that we hoped he would then marry us in the Church.

"What religion are you, Warren?" the priest asked.

"I'm Jewish," I said.

The priest started telling us that the only way he could marry us was if I'd sign papers promising to rear our children as Catholics. I was shocked that this was what the Catholic Church demanded.

"No offense, but I couldn't, in good conscience, sign any papers promising that," I said offended.

The priest was nice but firm in defending the demand of the church. I told him I would think about it. Once in the car with Donna, I insisted that I would never sign such papers. She totally agreed. We told her parents what the priest was asking us to do. They weren't ready to give up on the idea of a wedding in the church.

"You have to bring your children up with some kind of religion," Donna's mom said.

"Donna and I want to raise our children without dictating our religious views. We will let them decide what they want to be when they grow up," I stated.

Donna's parents began yelling at me, upset that we weren't going to give our children a religious education. Finally, Donna couldn't take anymore:

"Look, I don't even go to church! What Warren and I want to do with our children is up to us! Besides, who says we'll have kids anyway?"

To keep the peace, I told her parents that we would get married by the priest at a later date. I made them promise not to mention this to my parents, or they would want us to get married by the rabbi.

Our wedding took place at the Town and Campus Restaurant in Elizabeth. Dad paid for half the wedding so he could invite all the Jewish relatives and his many friends. Donna's Italian and Polish relatives all came to the wedding as well. Mayor Gregorio performed the service in the same hall where the banquet was, and both sides of the family got along wonderfully. The band played Italian, Polish, and Jewish songs. Everybody had a wonderful time. By keeping religion out of the wedding, we avoided controversy. We moved into an apartment in Linden. We had been going steady for six years and marriage didn't seem to be any different from when we were dating, except for the delights of the marriage bed. We had not had sexual relations before the wedding.

I was working at my dad's factory while I was looking for a job in the film industry. The work was hard, but at least I was bringing home a salary. Donna continued working as a secretary for a manufacturing company. I bought a publication which listed all the production companies in New York City and made up index cards for each film company listed in the book. Twice weekly, with my resume and sample reel in hand, I'd take a bus into the city and systematically visit one company after another. I didn't care if all I got was a job as a janitor for one of these companies. I was willing to start at the bottom if need be. My promise to God in prayer to produce films that said what God wanted me to say made me feel confident He would get me a job somewhere in the industry.

Several months went by—not a single offer was made. Even when a job was available, I was always asked the same question: "Are you in the union?"

"No, but I just need a break. I know I could do the work," I would repeat over and over again.

"We are a union shop. You can't get a job here unless you are in the union," they'd always reply.

"But how do you get into the union?" I asked.

"You have to get a union job; then you can get into the union," they would answer.

It was a Catch-22 situation. I began to earnestly pray to God, asking Him to please get me a job. One of the companies I went to see was called The Editor's Pad. As I stood outside the door ready to knock, I heard an argument going on inside. Two men were shouting loudly at each other. I stood at the door, waiting for the argument to subside. It continued for at least twenty minutes, and I finally decided to leave. It was the only place I walked away from without soliciting a job. I wrote on the index card: "Forget about this place. Yelling and screaming!"

I became discouraged. As I worked in my dad's factory, I wondered whether Donna and I should move somewhere else. Lost in my thoughts, I didn't see Dad standing right behind me. When he called my name, I jumped in fright.

"Warren, I want you to meet someone," Dad said, smiling. I followed him into the office, and we walked up to a man who was going over the Margrove Manufacturing books.

"Howard, this is my son, Warren," Dad said.

Howard Bookbinder was the company accountant. He rose to shake my hand.

"Warren, glad to meet you. I understand that you are looking for a job in film," he said.

We talked for some time as I shared my desire to work in any capacity for a film company.

"Warren, I have a friend who owns an editing company in the city. He just fired one of his workers. He may be willing to hire you. I'll call him first. Then, if things look good, I'll tell you to call this number," he explained.

Howard gave me a piece of paper with his friend's name on it; made the call; and gave me the go-ahead. I prayed a brief prayer as I called the man whose name was on the paper, Norman Goldstein.

"Norman, this is Warren Marcus. Howard Bookbinder suggested I call you," I began.

Norman asked what my plans were, and I told him that I just wanted a job in the industry, that I would do anything.

"The timing of your call couldn't be better. I just fired one of my workers last week. Are you in the union?" he asked.

"No, I'm not," I answered, expecting to hear the inevitable. "That's all right. We can always get you in later, after a six-month trial," Norman said.

Could this truly be happening to me? Elated, I was to start my first day of work the following Monday. When I went home, I looked up the name of the company on my index cards. It was The Editor's Pad, the company that I had written off because of the arguing I heard. I later found out that what I was hearing that day was the actual firing of the man I was replacing. I felt that God had clearly answered my prayers and gave me a sign that it was indeed He who opened the door. There was no way this could be merely a coincidence!

I was hired to be an apprentice editor. The job entailed keeping the editing room clean, logging the outtakes, and taking film to the labs for developing. I watched the editors work and asked why they chose one cut over another. I was amazed at how much I had learned at school concerning editing. One of the editors was breaking the rules of editing without realizing it. This gave me confidence that I could definitely handle a more difficult job if it were offered. Still, I was not impatient because I was so glad to have the break—to actually be working in the film industry! I found out that the dean's prophecy on orientation day came true. Only fifty of the original five hundred students graduated. Of the fifty, only five of us were actually working in the field!

The Editor's Pad serviced some of Madison Avenue's top film production houses, especially in animation. Initially, only three of us worked at the company. Norman Goldstein was the president and chief editor. Al Strauss was the assistant editor, and in less than six months, I was brought into the IATSE Local 771 Editors Union as an apprentice editor. The advantages of working for this small company were numerous. I moved up quickly from apprentice to assistant. Because the other two trusted me, they gave me their work to do, and I gladly did anything they put in my hands. Everything was going well. Then, I received my draft notice in the mail!

I was still seeing Dr. Chun. I begged her to help me get out of the draft. I told her that I would kill myself before I would ever go to Vietnam. She wrote a letter which she sealed in an envelope. When they asked for letters from our doctors, I was to hand this envelope to the officer in charge. She cautioned me to be despondent and slow to speak, or they would feel the letter was a sham.

Several days before my scheduled induction, I stayed up late. I snorted some speed which I had bought from a dealer in New York in a deliberate attempt to mess up my mind. I smoked joint after joint, hoping to look the part of a despondent psycho case. At the same time, I kept a vigil of prayer to God, asking Him to forgive me for my sins, but begging Him to get me out of the draft. My hair was near shoulder length. After washing it the morning of my appointment with the draft board, I teased it with a brush. It stood out like Bob Dylan's. I wore a torn blue jeans jacket, denim pants, and a large swastika around my neck. I finished my costume by donning beat-up cowboy boots and a pair of psychedelic shades.

My mother was upset that I was dressed so radically, but she still went with Donna and me to the selective service center in Elizabeth. I kissed Donna as I made my way into the building. The army transported us in a bus to Newark. I saw many of my old high-school classmates on the bus. At first, they didn't recognize me with my costume. They freaked out when they realized it was me. I wanted to talk with them and catch up on their lives. However, I knew I might be watched by the sergeant who was in the front of the bus, so I remained low key and despondent.

Once at the center, they ushered our group into a classroom. A mean sergeant shouted orders as if we were already enlisted privates.

"I want you to turn over the papers that are on your desk and put your name and selective-service number on the top with the pencils we have supplied," he shouted loudly.

"You are to answer every question on every page. Let me warn you about the consequences of answering these questions falsely, or trying to be funny. You will face heavy fines and imprisonment. Do you understand?"

I was petrified. The sergeant looked directly at me as he talked. Silently, I asked God's mercy as I began to answer the questions. I had been advised by friends that I should answer the questions as if I were "out of my mind."

"Do you wet your bed?" I read in a whisper. As I marked yes, I said to myself, "Of course, but only on Sundays!"

The list continued, "Did you ever use any kind of drugs?" Without hesitation I marked off the types I used: Marijuana? Yes! LSD? Yes! Cocaine? Yes! Heroin? Of course not, do you think I'm stupid or something? No!"

I was interrupted by the sergeant's "sweet, melodious" voice.

"If any of you have any excuses, they must be in the form of a letter from your doctor. You must give it to me right now, or forever hold your peace!"

The group began leaving the classroom. I lagged behind, timidly giving the sergeant the sealed envelope. He glared at me as I lowered my head, afraid to look him in the eye.

At the physical exam, I must have looked quite comical, stripped down to my wild-colored boxer shorts with a swastika hanging around my neck, the old battered cowboy boots, and my psychedelic glasses. An overweight boy fainted in front of me as the doctor tried to take a sample of his blood. A number of people around me began to laugh as the boy hit the ground. However, I kept a straight face, remembering to play the part of a withdrawn and depressed psychological reject.

The doctor couldn't find my vein and wound up jabbing my right arm several times without success to get blood. For each jab, a Band-Aid was placed on the arm. Finally, he found a vein on my left arm and placed a Band-Aid over the needle mark. I was told to keep my arms up and fists clenched until the blood had a chance to coagulate. Imagine how outrageous I looked. I was sitting opposite a black teenager, and he burst into laughter, pointing at me with his finger right in my face. I felt like punching him in the nose, but I continued to play the part and stared into space like a catatonic.

"I can't take this, I know I'm gonna crack. Please God, help me," I prayed silently.

A medical officer began to ask me about the questionnaire I had filled out earlier. "You have some real problems, son. Do you actually still wet your bed?"

I shook my head in the affirmative as I heard several giggles from the boys standing in line behind me.

"You say here that you used every single drug in existence. Is there anything you haven't tried?" he asked sarcastically.

"I never used heroin," I said quietly.

"Why not? You did everything else!" he shouted back.

I couldn't resist answering.

"To tell you the truth, I tried it once, but I didn't want it to go on my record!"

The mean sergeant was standing nearby. He spat out his soda in a fit of laughter at my remark. I looked up toward him briefly as his eyes met mine. Suddenly, he stopped laughing, staring at me with contempt. A flash of fear overcame me. What if they find drugs in my blood? They could prosecute me and put me in prison.

"This is a loony bin. Oh God, please get me out of here," I prayed again and again to myself.

Next, they ushered a group of us into another examining room. The doctor was waving a pencil-like instrument as he gave instructions.

"When I put my hand under your crotch, I will ask you to cough. If I hear any jokes, my fist and your nose will have a collision. I'm checking for hernias! You better not fake it, or Sergeant Davis will cart your asteroid off to Fort Dix!"

As the doctor moved down the line toward me, the mean sergeant came into the room with a letter in his hand.

"Where is Warren Marcus? Is Warren Marcus in this room?"

I raised my hand and quietly called out to him.

"I'm over here!"

My mind raced with the various scenarios of why I was being summoned. Perhaps they had found traces of drugs in my blood and he was going to take me to jail, I worried.

"Get over here, now! You get your clothes on and get out of here!" he shouted for all to hear. "You're a nut! You're a psycho case, and we don't have room in the army for people like you!"

I felt as if my entire face was flushed with red. I was so angry it took all my resolve to keep from hitting him. I told myself, *Be cool. Don't blow it now! Calm down.* Tears came into my eyes as I dropped my head in embarrassment. Everyone looked at me

I walked away as I heard the sergeant's angry voice.

"Hey you, take this to Room 101," he said, giving me the letter. "Now, get out of my sight."

As I walked to Room 101, I felt unclean. He humiliated me, and I realized this masquerade was a criminal act. I was tempted to read the letter from Doctor Chun, which I held tightly in my hand. There was no way I could go to Vietnam, I rationalized. I would be a real basket case if I went there! At the same time, I felt bad about what I had done.

Upon entering the room, I saw three medical men sitting at a desk playing cards.

"Yeah, can I help you?" one of them asked.

I gave him the letter, and he proceeded to open it.

"Hey, this is heavy. You're a paranoid schizophrenic, huh? Hey guys! Look at this."

I couldn't believe my ears. They had little regard for me as a human being. They all read the letter and laughed, making sarcastic remarks.

Finally, the one who originally took the letter turned to address me.

"Hey, why are you still here? Get out of here—you're classified 4-F."

I remained expressionless until I left the building. My mother was waiting for me in her car. I jumped in and greeted Mom. Donna's mother had also come along for the ride. Shocked at the way I looked, she almost didn't recognize me.

My mom was the first to address me, "What happened?"

A smile broke out on my face for the first time.

"I'm 4-F. I'm free!"

Mom and Josephine were, of course, happy. We all agreed to keep this quiet, since Donna's father, Joe, was a veteran of World War II. Little did they know the personal anguish I suffered. Whether the Vietnam War was a righteous conflict or not, young men were sacrificing their lives for me so I could have freedom. So many people my age were going into the army and dying for their country. I said a silent prayer for them as my mother drove me home, and I asked God to forgive my cowardice.

NINETEEN

WEST SIDE STORY

Every morning, I'd sleep while riding the transit bus from Linden to the Port Authority bus terminal, then walk from the terminal to The Editor's Pad.

I loved my job as an apprentice editor and gladly did every task given to me by my boss, Norman Goldstein. However, he was not the easiest man to work for. He never called for me respectfully.

"Warren, get in here right now!" he demanded.

Running into his office, I responded humbly like a good soldier, "Yes, sir. What do you need?"

"Didn't I tell you to deliver those film elements to Young and Rubicam?" he asked, covering the phone receiver with his hand.

"Yes, Norman, and I did," I assured him.

"Well, they don't have them," he said angrily.

Pulling a signed document out of my pocket, I produced the evidence of a signature.

"It was Helen Byrd who signed for it," I responded.

Norman smiled at me for doing my job right and then gleefully told the client that the problem was with the agency—not with The Editor's Pad.

Eventually, Norman rewarded me for my thoroughness by allowing me to edit my first television commercial. Of course, neither the editor's union nor the client knew it. Norman took the spot to the client and showed it to him, as if he were the one who created it.

From that point on, Norman let me do the work of a full editor until I performed most of his work for the business. This enabled him to solicit more customers. However, there was a down side. If he visited a client, and a problem surfaced with the editing of the commercial, he angrily called me on the phone—in front of the client—and blamed me for the mistake.

Later, I heard that he would tell the client, "Oh, that Warren! I let him edit a little bit, and he messes up again!"

I always had an answer for Norman when he called.

"Norman, I cut it that way because there's going to be a dissolve added and then a burn-in title!" I explained on one particular project.

Norman, in turn, communicated what I had just told him to the client, and invariably, the client accepted the job. Then, Norman thanked me with the client standing beside him.

Norman's assistant editor, Al Strauss, questioned me about Norman's treatment.

"Warren, I don't understand how you are so nice to Norman after he screams at you like that."

"Well, Norman gave me the break I needed, so I'm grateful to him. He's my boss and I respect his authority," I replied.

Often, I heard the two of them argue, but I never nosed into anything that was not my business. I became good friends with Al.

Once during my lunch break, a friend took me to the porno district of Times Square. I had never been to a sex peep show, so the friend decided to indoctrinate me. Once inside, he gave me some quarters to watch porno movies on old arcade-like viewing machines and showed me the racks and racks of pornographic magazines.

"Over here are the S & M magazines, and here are the ones I like, lesbians making love," he said, opening the magazines for me to see.

Never before had I seen such explicit photographs. These made the *Playboy* magazines I saw as a child look like a comic book by comparison. Then, he ushered me into one of a dozen curtained booths at the back of the store. He put a quarter in the slot and told me to look through the small, opening peep hole. A naked woman posed on a rotating platform, massaging her entire body. I couldn't believe this was legal. I noticed pairs of eyes looking through dozens of peep holes along the walls. I felt sick inside as I realized how perverted this was.

Somebody left a handful of porno magazines in the bathroom

at The Editor's Pad. Whenever I was alone in the office, I went in the bathroom to look at the dirty photos and developed a habit as bad as the daily use of marijuana. Satan was really gaining ground in his attempt to control my soul. Every day the urge to smoke a joint and look at the pornographic magazines in the office bathroom would overtake me. It was a horrible feeling that came from deep inside me. I seemed to have no will power over this heinous carnality. Yet, when I gave into the lust, I always felt a deep sorrow. Many times, I prayed for forgiveness and the strength to overcome this bondage.

Drugs were everywhere. One of our major clients was having a Christmas party. People from the ad agencies, as well as other producers, were invited. Everyone at The Editor's Pad was in attendance. Here, I met the client's son. He was my age and the apparent heir to his father's company. He invited me into an office. At least a dozen of us crowded in as he lighted up an electric pipe full of marijuana. Everyone was smoking the stuff, including me.

A week later, I was in the office, editing a documentary. Al picked up the phone and yelled that it was for me. I picked up the blinking line. I was stunned when I found out who was calling me. It was the son of the client who threw the Christmas party.

"What can I do for you? Norman is out at a mix with another client," I said, figuring that he wanted to speak with my boss.

"I don't want him, Warren, I want you!" he laughed. "Can you join me for lunch today? I want to talk to you!"

"I guess so. What's up?" I asked.

"I just want to get to know you better. Oh, by the way, please don't tell Al and Normie that we are having lunch," he said.

I agreed reluctantly to meet with him, and I hung up the phone. I immediately went into Al's editing room.

"Al, can I talk with you?" I said as I sat down near him.

"Of course," he responded with a air of curiosity.

I told him that the client had invited me to go to lunch with him and told me not to say anything to anyone.

"He probably wants to offer you a job! I have a feeling that he hasn't been happy with the prices Norman's been charging," Al said.

"No way! I'm an apprentice editor. What would he want with me?" I asked.

"I'm telling you that he's going to offer you a job." Al looked me straight in the eyes as if he were reading my mind.

"If that's true, then I'm not going to meet him for lunch. There's no way that I would ever hurt you and Norman," I stated.

Al told me that this client was 80 percent of The Editor's Pad's business, and if he pulled out on us, it would destroy our company. He told me to at least go and hear what he had to say.

I met the client at a posh Italian restaurant. He was quite friendly. My heart pounded with anticipation.

"Warren, let me get straight to the point! I talked with my dad and we have made a decision to end our business relationship with The Editor's Pad. This is something that will happen and nobody can stop it. Dad and I feel that we need an on-staff editor, and we want you," he said, smiling broadly.

"Me? You want me? Why?" I asked, impressed by Al's discernment.

"You're the one editing our commercials, not Norman. Every time we ask a question about an edit, he calls you on the phone to explain. You're the editor, not him," he said, sipping his wine.

"Even if that was true, and I'm not saying it is, I can't be your editor. I'm only an apprentice as far as the union is concerned," I said, hoping I could talk him out of it.

"Look, my dad is powerful in the business," he responded. "He will get your status with the union changed immediately. And, we're prepared to pay you seven hundred dollars a week, plus overtime."

I was only making one hundred and fifty dollars a week. I was flattered that the offer was made. However, I had deep reservations about it.

I tried to answer him tactfully.

"Thanks for the generous offer, but can't you keep using The Editor's Pad? Your company provides 80 percent of their work. They'll go out of business if you stop using their services!"

He tried to convince me that nothing I said would change his decision about ending his relationship with The Editor's Pad. I asked if I could think about the offer and give him an answer in the morning. He said that would be no problem.

When I returned to The Editor's Pad, Al was sitting on a couch in the waiting room, like some father awaiting his daughter's return on her first date. Norman was not in the office. I paused to find the right words to say.

"Al, you were right! He offered me a job, but there's no way I can take it—not after Norman gave me my first break. I'd rather quit the business than hurt you and Norm."

Again, Al tried to convince me to take the job. I told him no, but that I had until morning to think it over. In the meantime, I asked him not to tell Norman, until I talked with him first.

I started walking to the film lab with some dailies that needed to be developed. As I walked, I began talking silently to God.

If this is the way the film business works, then I don't want to be a part of it. Oh God, help me do the right thing. I don't want to hurt Norman and Al. I don't want to see The Editor's Pad ruined.

I started to think about how far I had strayed from God. I didn't pray to Him every day as I did when I was a child. A deep conviction came over me. I felt ashamed of my addiction to pornography and marijuana. I asked God to forgive me and help me.

I began to immediately feel as if I should go back, without delay, to The Editor's Pad. I felt as if it was God Himself saying softly, "Go back!" I obeyed.

As I walked into the office, I saw Norman with his coat on, standing over Al who was sitting on the couch in the waiting room. Al looked as if he was "the cat who swallowed the canary" as his eyes met mine. I pretended not to notice them as I made my way into one of the editing rooms. I listened closely to their conversation.

Norman was shouting angrily at Al.

"What do you mean, you think they are going to dump us? How do you know this?"

Al responded quietly, "I just know it, okay?"

"What do you mean, you just know it? You must have heard something! What did you hear?" Norm demanded.

"Nothing, I heard nothing! It's just a feeling!" Al stammered.

"Well, don't assume anything like that! We'd be dead in the water if they ever pulled out on us!" Norm said as he left for the day, slamming the front door behind him.

I began thanking God for telling me to return to the office. I believe that God helped prevent Al from telling Norman before I did. I didn't embarrass Al as I waited a while before entering his room. Once inside, I told Al there was no way I was taking the job. He began to apologize for trying to tell Norman before I did.

I told him I understood and proceeded to convey my thinking.

"Al, if the client could do such a thing behind Norman's back, then what would prevent him from later doing such a thing to me? I'm going to tell Norman tonight, in person at his home."

That night, I called Norman at home.

"Norm, could I come over tonight to talk with you? It's something I must tell you, face to face!"

When I arrived at Norman's house, he was anxious to hear what I had to say. I asked if he would take a ride in his car with me. As we drove, I proceeded to tell him what had transpired. I told him that I was offered the job, but I was going to turn it down in the morning. He was puzzled why I would turn it down. I proceeded to tell him.

"Norm, you gave me my first break in the business. I would never do anything to hurt you. If you don't know by now that I am loyal to you, I don't think you'll ever know."

Because I told Norman about the son's offer, he was able to confront the father and keep The Editor's Pad from losing the account. From that day on, Norman never yelled at me again. Instead, he became a great friend and boss. He told me that if I needed or wanted anything, he would love to help me in any way he could.

"Warren, what is the one thing you would want, if you could have anything?" Norman later asked me.

"I want to be a great director and cinematographer some day," I told him.

Norman had been trying to broaden the company from just performing editing services to including full production capabilities. His efforts finally paid off. We landed a big educational contract with the State of New Jersey to produce a fifteen-minute bicycle safety film. Norman asked if I would like to take a shot as the director and cinematographer. I happily took on the challenge. The film was my first professional piece, and the client was pleased with my work. Norman was too.

"Warren, you have great talent. Not only can you edit, but you are a good director and cameraman. I want you to direct all the films that Editor's Pad and Goldway Productions produce," Norman said as he took me to lunch.

The job offer episode taught me a great lesson which I follow to this day. Never let personal gain take precedence over doing that which is right in the eyes of God and your neighbor. Finally, unlike my shameful avoidance of the draft, I had taken the right path, and God had rewarded me. My childhood dream was becoming a reality.

At this time, I also completed writing my first full-length screenplay, *Yesterday is Only a Dream*. It was about an atheist who, before he dies at the end of the movie, turns his life over to God. I was inspired to write the script out of personal experience from an event that deeply touched my heart. Time and again, I had witnessed the homeless wandering the streets of New York and was deeply moved by their plight. One day on my way back to the bus terminal, I had seen a wino as he fell outside a liquor store. I saw that he had cut his forehead open; it was bleeding profusely. I rushed over to him and helped him get up. I gave him my handkerchief to wipe the blood as the liquor store manager ran outside and tried to chase the man away.

"Mister, he fell and is bleeding. Please get some help," I pleaded.

"Get him out of here! Next thing ya know, he'll say he cut his head at my door and he'll sue," the owner shouted, waving his hands in excitement.

"I saw him fall right outside your store and cut his head. Now, please call an ambulance. Look, this is a human being! He isn't some animal. Please help him!" I begged.

"If you care so much about him, you help him," he said, going back into his store.

I couldn't believe what I was hearing. I stayed with the man until I got the attention of a police officer and heard him promise that the wino would get some help.

This real-life experience became the climactic scene of my motion picture script. In the final scene, the main character stumbles down a flight of stairs in a drunken stupor, splitting open his head as the pedestrians walk past him.

"Oh God, please help me!" cries out the dying atheist.

In an answer to his prayer, a Good Samaritan stops to help him. As he bends down, the atheist imagines the Samaritan to be

Jesus himself. The script ends with the nail-scarred hands of Jesus anointing the atheist's head with oil, set against the backdrop of heaven.

I remember writing the end scene and sensing the reality of God's presence in the room with me. I felt like the words coming out of my pen were from God Himself. It was as if God were answering my childhood prayer—that if He would make me a really good filmmaker, I would produce films that said what He wanted me to say.

Today, as I look back at the old script, I can only shake my head in amazement. For this script—illustrating the final encounter of a man with Jesus Christ—was written by a drug-addicted, draft-dodging, unsaved Jew from Brooklyn! Friends who read the script questioned where my inspiration had come from. They said it touched them deeply. God was indeed beginning to use me, in spite of my unbelief and the sin in my life.

TWENTY

BROTHER SUN, SISTER MOON

God used a rock musical to point me back toward the person of Jesus the Messiah. Remarkably, this rock opera was not written by a Christian, but rather, by two unbelieving Jews. From the moment I heard the music from *Jesus Christ Superstar* on the radio, I knew I had to immediately purchase the two-volume album. Listening over and over again, I learned the rock opera by heart. The person of Jesus the Messiah became so real to me, my heart was broken as He died on the cross. However, I had no idea why it affected me this way—*every* time I listened to it!

I went with Donna to see the Broadway production of the musical. The actor playing Jesus radiated warmth and compassion unlike any person I had ever met. The church community was upset by this musical, saying it was unscriptural. However, I didn't understand the intricacies of their doctrinal concerns. I only knew that every time I listened to the music and contemplated the words, I was transported back into the times of the Messiah. I beheld Him healing and helping the hopeless. I empathized with the suffering He must have felt during His inquisition and crucifixion. At the end of the play, Jesus was left hanging on a triangular cross, as the orchestra played the symphonic finale.

I left the theater in complete silence. The musical had given me a new appreciation for this man the Christians called Jesus. His death on the cursed tree remained a compelling mystery to me. I asked myself, *What is it about His death that keeps tearing at my heart?*

Often, during my lunch breaks while working at The Editor's Pad, I'd walk several blocks to Saint Patrick's Cathedral. I strolled through the ornate sanctuary, past the Catholics who were on their knees before statues of the various saints. To me, it appeared as if these parishioners were praying to the stone statues, committing some form of idolatry. This was something that a Jew could never do. However, I was impressed with their lack of concern for what others might think and for their sincerity of faith. I had never experienced this type of commitment in the synagogue.

I came primarily to view the carved pictures that lined both sides of the cathedral, what the Catholic Church calls the Stations of the Cross. These tell the story of the passion of the Messiah. Each picture depicts a different aspect of His trial, flogging, cross bearing, and crucifixion. Enthralled, I stood at each picture, meditating on the unfolding story before me and wondering, *Why did they do this to Him?* He committed no crime. He merely loved others and ministered to the poor, always meeting their needs. More importantly, I asked myself what His crucifixion meant for me today.

Obviously, to each of the people gathered in Saint Patrick's, Jesus had to mean something very important. I stood the longest at the final picture—the crucified Messiah. I studied every detail: the crown of thorns, the nails in His hands and feet, and the blood which flowed down His bruised and beaten body.

Ever since the first time I had looked at a statue of the crucified Christ (when my ex-girlfriend Marla took me into her Catholic Church) I had been drawn to try to understand the power behind this Person on the cross.

Mesmerized, I asked God, *Who is this man who turned the world upside down? A man who was a Jew, yet was rejected by his own people? Tell me, God. Please—tell me! Who is Jesus of Nazareth, and what does His life have to do with me today?*

Then I asked God to forgive the Jewish people.

"Oh God, please forgive my people for any part they might have played in crucifying this innocent man." Sometimes, to get home from New York City, I took the train at Penn Station instead of the bus. As I walked to the station, I'd always visit a Franciscan Catholic Church. The humble decor and poor people inside represented a different spirit—one of life and celebration, as opposed to the opulence of Saint Patrick's. I loved to look upon the life-sized, carved, painted wooden statue of Jesus on the cross. What intrigued me most was that His eyes were not closed, as in Saint Patrick's, but rather, His eyes were wide open. Compassionately, they seemed to peer into the deepest part of my soul. Tears welled up in my eyes and flowed down my cheeks as I stood staring into the eyes of the statue

Oh, how I wished I knew Him when He was alive, my soul would cry out.

And then, something very significant occurred. A feature film was being distributed in the movie theaters in 1973 entitled *Brother Sun, Sister Moon.* It was the story of Saint Francis of Assisi. I took Donna to see this movie, which was directed by Franco Zefferelli and had music by the folk-rock singer Donovan. Both Donna and I were captivated by the motion picture as the character of Saint Francis became preoccupied with the image of the crucified Christ.

In the beginning of the movie, Francis stared at the statue of the crucified Jesus, bothered by his closed eyes. It was just like the statue I had seen in Marla's church and like the one in Saint Patrick's Cathedral. However, at a pivotal moment in the film, Francis beheld a different statue—this time the image of the crucified Jesus Christ had its eyes wide open. As I sat in that movie theater, I no longer saw Francis. Instead, he was me. I completely identified with him as I watched him give up all his earthly possessions to follow the man on the cross. In a dramatic way, this movie underscored my own questions concerning the Christian church, which appeared to have amassed such great wealth—building ornate cathedrals while the poor, hungry, and homeless continued to wander the streets without anyone reaching out to them.

In the film, Saint Francis began rebuilding an old church that was destroyed in the crusades—stone by stone. Many of the young men in the city left their wealth behind and joined him in his quest to live simply as Jesus Himself had lived with His disciples. The city fathers and the pharisaical church leaders then joined forces to burn down the church that Saint Francis and his friends had built. They did this out of jealousy, for in their minds he stole their sons and rallied the poor from the cathedral in the city. After the fire, Francis and his followers trekked to Rome to meet the pope and ask him a simple question, one I had asked many times: "Why?"

The scene in Rome shocked Francis and his friends. They had given up all their earthly possessions to follow God, yet the church in Rome appeared to have amassed an enormous fortune. In a very dramatic moment, he and his shoeless friends walked down the aisle of the ornate Cathedral of Rome.

Finally, Francis confronts the pope with these words of Jesus from the Bible: "Take no thought for your life, what you shall eat, or drink; nor yet for your body, what you shall put on. Is not life more than meat, and the body more than raiment?"

The ornately arrayed bishops and other religious men of power surrounding the pope called for the guards to eject this motley crew. As Francis was carried out of the cathedral, he continued to shout the words of Jesus for the pope to hear:

> Lay not up for yourselves treasures upon earth, where moth and rust doth corrupt, and where thieves break through and steal.
>
> But lay up for yourselves treasures in heaven, where neither moth nor rust doth corrupt, and where thieves do not break through nor steal:
>
> For where your treasure is, there will your heart be also.

Later, the pope awakens from a catatonic-like trance and orders the guards to bring Francis back into the cathedral. In a symbolic stroke, directorial genius Franco Zefferelli has the pope step out of his ostentatious outer robes. Then, clothed in a simple white garment, he walks down from his throne—shocking all the Pharisees around him as he approaches Francis. The pope is so touched by the reality of Jesus manifested in the person of Francis that he kisses his hand, then kneels before him and kisses his feet, sanctioning his ministry—a ministry based on living a life of biblical simplicity.

As I sat in that movie theater, I felt God calling to me from the screen as if He were saying, "This is the truth, walk ye in it!" As if a sign to me, the camera then craned up to reveal an enormous painting of the crucified Christ *with his eyes wide open*. It was the same face I had seen on the statue of the crucified Christ in the Franciscan Church in New York City. Now, I was looking into the compassionate eyes of the crucified Christ on the movie screen. I was stunned and moved beyond anything I could describe in words.

Donna and I left the theater without saying a word. Once in the car, I automatically turned the radio on. Suddenly Donna shut off the radio.

"I don't want to hear anything! Not now, please?" she said quietly.

I agreed with her, and we rode all the way home in silence. My vision was renewed to use motion pictures for what God wanted to say. I realized again how powerfully this medium can be used to reach millions with the reality of God. More than ever, I determined to know Jesus and what His death on the cross meant for me personally.

The next day, I couldn't wait to see Richard Gallagher at the anti-abortion stand in the bus terminal.

"Richard, I just saw a movie that you *must* see. It really got me thinking about God," I said excitedly.

"What film was that?" he asked skeptically.

"*Brother Sun, Sister Moon!*" I said enthusiastically.

Unlike many Catholics I have met since, Richard claimed the film was an abomination and full of errors concerning Saint Francis and the Catholic Church.

I was crushed. Instead of reinforcing my religious experience, he continued to downgrade the film. I argued with him about the hypocrisy I saw in the church of the twentieth century, especially the Catholic Church. I believe that much of what I said was out of anger for Richard's insensitivity. Another man walked up and listened to us argue. He supported my arguments against the Catholic Church, and I suddenly found myself listening to the two of them as they shouted angrily. Finally, I couldn't take any more.

I spoke up in frustration. "Here you guys are supposed to be Christians, but you can't agree with one another. How do you expect me, a Jew, to ever follow this man called Jesus when His church is in such a mess? You two are perfect examples of the whole mess, and I don't want any part of it." I walked away from the two as they stared at me in silence. Suddenly, I felt a light touch on my shoulder. I turned around, and it was the man who had been arguing with Richard. He was teary-eyed as he began to speak.

"I'm a born-again Christian, and I want to apologize to you for what I did. If I had known you were searching, I would have never argued doctrine with that other fellow."

"His name is Richard, and he's okay," I said, touched by this man's sincerity.

"You were totally right to say what you did to us," he continued, "but please, don't judge my Lord and Savior Jesus by the way we acted. He's the only one who is perfect. There is nobody like Him. And without Jesus in my life, I would not be alive today, standing in front of you."

Sadly, I was never able to give that man the satisfaction of knowing the full extent of what his apology meant to me.

This man seems to really care, I thought to myself. *I shouldn't be so harsh on these people. They're just human beings like me.*

I vowed to myself that I would not take no for an answer anymore. I was going to have my questions answered, one way or another, even if it meant visiting the pope, a rabbi, or some eastern guru!

My spiritual pursuit escalated. My mind was preoccupied with finding out the truth concerning Jesus. I didn't want what I thought I saw the church offering. I wanted the real thing—the true reality of the living God in my life. I prayed that God would lead me in the right direction. I felt the uncontrollable urge to buy a Bible. I wanted to read it for myself. I remembered what I had once heard on a religious radio broadcast: "The Bible contains a wonderful plan for your life." I wanted to know what that plan was.

There were so many different Bibles in the book store, I didn't know which version to buy. I spotted a paperback copy in King James English, but what made me want this particular version was the phrase on its cover: "All the words of Jesus are in red print."

I started reading it from chapter 1, verse 1, of the book of Genesis. Soon, I started getting confused about how the Scriptures applied to me personally. I skimmed through what this version of the Bible called the Old Testament and read passages at random. Everything I read dealt with condemnation and judgment. Then, I turned to the Gospels. All the words spoken by Jesus were printed in red. I chose to read only the words of Jesus to see what He purportedly said. In the Gospel of Matthew, chapter 5, in the Sermon on the Mount, I sensed the power and authority in His words. The Beatitudes promised blessings to all the "have nots" in the world. And Jesus made some revolutionary statements—that rewards were not given by God to those who have succeeded in business, nor the wealthy, nor the powerful leaders and politicians of the world.

Rather, those who are blessed . . .

   . . . are the poor in spirit
   . . . are they that mourn
   . . . are the meek
   . . . are they which do hunger and thirst after righteous-
       ness
   . . . are the merciful
   . . . are the pure in heart
   . . . are the peacemakers
   . . . are they which are persecuted for righteousness' sake
   . . . are ye, when men revile you, and persecute you, and
       say all manner of evil against you falsely, for my sake.

I searched the list for a category that I might fit into and was thrilled when I saw the part about the peacemakers: "for they shall be called the children of God." At that moment, I was convinced that those involved in the anti-war movement were the "peacemakers" Jesus was referring to. I felt like I was one of them.

This Jesus is a revolutionary, I thought to myself. Why was today's church so far removed from practicing on a daily basis the words that Jesus taught?

I read what Jesus said of himself: "Think not that I am come to destroy the law (the Torah), or the prophets: I am not come to destroy, but to fulfill" (Matt. 5:17). This communicated to me that Jesus had not rejected His Jewishness, but rather came to live an obedient and perfect life, fulfilling all the Mosaic laws written in the Torah. I couldn't figure out why the Jews would reject a man who lived such a holy life.

I digested one revolutionary concept after another. Jesus gave a new, deeper meaning to the Ten Commandments as He said, "Ye have heard that it was said of them of old time, Thou shalt not kill. . . . But I say unto you, That whosoever is angry with his brother without a cause shall be in danger of the judgment. . ." (Matt. 5:21–22).

In the same vein, I read his words, "Ye have heard that it was said by them of old time, Thou shalt not commit adultery: But I say unto you, That whosoever looketh on a woman to lust after her hath committed adultery with her already in his heart" (Matt. 5:27–28).

I learned that the God of Israel was concerned not only with our actions but our thought life. He seemed to be saying that the thought of doing evil was the sin already. This was the most radical idea I had ever read. Jesus wasn't just talking about physically changing society, He was saying that the very heart and mind of mankind must undergo a change. I marveled at the call to purity that He was preaching. There was no hypocrisy in His words. His words were like a sword cutting into my heart. Nothing I had read by Karl Marx could ever compare with the pure vision I heard Jesus talking about. Karl Marx preached a revolution with the sword to overthrow the wealthy and impose a new system of government. Jesus was not calling for a revolution with swords, but one of the heart and mind. As I read on through the book of Matthew, chapter 6, I found the words quoted by Saint Francis of Assisi depicted in the movie, *Brother Sun, Sister Moon*. Jesus talked about learning to trust God in a way the birds and flowers of the field trust. He was saying, don't put your heart and trust in power and wealth, but rather in God.

Jesus said, ". . . Take no thought for your life, what you shall eat, or what you shall drink; nor yet for your body, what you shall put on. . . . Behold the fowls of the air: for they sow not, neither do they reap, nor gather into barns; yet your heavenly Father feedeth them. Are ye not much better than they? . . . Wherefore, if God so clothe the grass of the field, which to day is, and to morrow is cast into the oven, shall he not much more clothe you, O ye of little faith?" (Matt. 6:25, 26, 30).

I thought to myself, *Was Jesus saying that we can actually trust God to provide the food we eat and even the clothes we wear? How can this be?*

I knew of hippie communes where they tried to live off the land. I asked myself, *Is this what Jesus was talking about?*

As I read the last verses in the chapter, I received the answer: "But seek ye first the kingdom of God, and his righteousness; and all these things shall be added unto you" (Matt. 6:33).

I was transported into a new reality of being. It was beyond the feeling I had sitting in the movie theater and getting lost in a film. I felt as if Jesus were speaking these words directly to me, transcending time and space.

I wondered if His words should be taken so literally. How could He truly tell us, "If thy right eye offend thee, pluck it out, and cast it from thee: for it is profitable for thee that one of thy members should perish, and not that thy whole body should be cast into hell?" (Matt. 5:29). Did He mean I was to actually maim myself, or was he just calling me to a holiness that demanded complete obedience to God's commandments? I didn't understand how I could ever be as holy as Jesus was asking me to be. How could any of us live up to all 613 laws contained in the Torah? I could never do that. I would have to pluck out both eyes, so as not to look upon evil. Both of my hands would have to be severed so I would never do or touch anything unholy. Both my feet would have to be removed, so I wouldn't be able to go to any unholy place!

When I saw Richard Gallagher in the terminal the next day, I told him I had bought a Bible, and I had finished reading all four Gospels.

"What translation is it?" he asked.

Not understanding, I pulled out the Bible to show him.

"Oh, this is the King James Version. There are some serious errors in this version of the Bible," he said, leaving me with a puzzled look on my face.

I waited for sometime, then said.

"You know, Richard, I really feel Jesus was a revolutionary. There was no one ever like Him in history! But, I never read where Jesus ever directly claimed Himself to be the Messiah."

Richard became quite upset.

"Are you blind? Throughout the New Testament, Jesus is referred to as the Christ. *Christ* is not his name! It is an English translation of the Greek word *Cristos*. In Hebrew this word is *Ha Mashiach*, meaning the Anointed One or the Messiah. So when you read *Jesus Christ*, it actually is Jesus the Messiah!"

As he spoke, I suddenly remembered the library book that I had read about Jesus when I was only twelve years old. Richard was reinforcing the very things I had read in that book. Yet, I continued to play the devil's advocate.

"That doesn't prove anything. The writers of the Gospels called

Him Messiah, but He never referred to Himself as being the Messiah."

By this time Richard was raising his voice in frustration.

"Give me your Bible!" He turned the pages briskly to the Gospel of John, chapter 4, verses 25–26. "Now read from here!"

I began reading the following text:

"The woman saith unto him, I know that *Messias* cometh, which is called Christ: when he is come, he will tell us all things. Jesus saith unto her, I that speak unto thee am He."

Richard was right. It was as clear as the print on the pages of my King James Bible. Jesus *did* clearly state that He was the Messiah. However, I was not going to allow Richard Gallagher to get away with just one Scripture reference.

"That's fine, but is there any other place in the Bible that Jesus directly refers to himself as the Messiah?" I challenged him.

Richard grabbed the Bible and turned to the Gospel of Matthew, chapter 16, verses 15–20. He pointed to the verses.

"Now remember, the name 'Christ' means Messiah!" he reminded me.

I read the text with great interest:

He saith unto them, But whom say ye that I am? And Simon Peter answered and said, Thou art the Christ, the Son of the living God. And Jesus answered and said unto him, Blessed art thou Simon Barjona: for flesh and blood hath not revealed it unto thee, but my Father which is in heaven. And I say also unto thee, That thou art Peter, and upon this rock I will build my church; and the gates of hell shall not prevail against it. And I will give unto thee the keys of the kingdom of heaven: and whatsoever thou shalt bind on earth shall be bound in heaven: whatsoever thou shalt loose on earth shall be loosed in heaven. Then charged he his disciples that they should tell no man that He was Jesus the Christ.

I still was not satisfied with Richard's explanation that the word *Christ* was actually *The Messiah*. Richard was determined to prove his point as he turned to John, chapter 1, verses 41 and 42.

He first findeth his own brother Simon, and saith unto
him, We have found the Messias, which is, being interpreted,
the Christ. And he brought him to Jesus. . . .

There it was, but something inside me was still doubting as I
looked up at Richard.

"This doesn't prove anything. Why can't I just believe that Jesus
was a great man?" I asked.

"Warren, if I was not a Christian, I'd be a Jew, because at least
I'd have the right God, the God of Israel! But Jesus said to the
Jewish people, '. . . I am the way, the truth and the life, no man
cometh unto the Father, but by me' (John 14:6). That means that
if you don't believe in Jesus as the promised Messiah, the Son of
God, you are going to hell!"

I became infuriated.

"You mean to tell me that there is no other way to God? What
about the Hindus who worship Krishna and the Buddhists who
worship Buddha? Aren't these just other names for the same God?
God is love, and He wouldn't reject their sincerity. When they
pray to their god, they are reaching the ears of the God of Israel.
There is only one God, and when we pray, He hears our prayers
no matter what religion we are."

"No, Warren," argued Richard, "The one and only true God
chose to reveal Himself to Father Abraham and his descendants.
Over and over again, you will read in the Scriptures how God
dealt with Israel and judged them when they turned to strange
gods (idols). He allowed Israel to be taken into slavery. If all gods
were the same, then why would God get angry if they worshiped
another god? It is written in the Torah that God said to Israel, 'You
only have I known of all the families of the earth: therefore I will
punish you for all your iniquities'" (Amos 3:2).

"You're telling me that all the other nations of the world are
following false gods and that only the tiny nation of Israel worshiped the one true God?" I said in disbelief.

"Absolutely! That's why the Jews are known as the chosen people. Not only did God promise Abraham that He would make of
him a great nation, the nation of Israel, but, He also promised that
in him all the families of the earth will be blessed. That second

promise is what Jesus told His disciples to carry out in the great commission found in Saint Mark, chapter 16, verses 15 and 16, 'Go ye into all the world, and preach the gospel to every creature. He that believeth and is baptized shall be saved; but he that believeth not shall be damned.'"

The scripture Richard quoted frightened me. I reacted in anger, yelling loudly.

"I don't believe in hell! It's just a word used by the church to make people feel guilty. God is love. He wouldn't condemn people to hell."

"If you don't believe in hell," Richard countered, "then why do you get so upset when the Scriptures tell you that this is where you will go if you do not accept Jesus? God obviously has put the reality of hell into your conscience."

A middle-aged man came up to the anti-abortion stand to sign Richard's petition. This gave me time to open my Bible and look at the Great Commission for myself. It was exactly as Richard had stated. Now, for the first time, I understood why there were people on the street carrying signs that read, "Repent and be saved!" Jesus had commanded His church to preach the Gospel to every creature. Yet, what about my Christian neighbors and friends in Linden, New Jersey? Why didn't they ever try to tell me about Jesus if they were commanded by Him to do so?

I watched as Richard gave the man some anti-abortion literature. I appreciated his commitment to his cause. I thought to myself: This man is a good example of what a Christian should be like. I watched as Richard reached into a bag beside his stand and pulled out a book. He handed it to me.

"Warren, read this book. It should answer any questions you have about Jesus."

I thanked him and left for my bus.

During my ride home, I read some of the book. It was written by a Jewish Catholic. It was simply his answers to questions about religion that were asked in meetings on the streets, squares, and parks all over America. The front of the book indexed hundreds of questions and answers contained in its pages.

The questions were divided into categories: God the First Cause, Creation, Man, Soul-immortality, Salvation, Adam and Eve, The

Jews, Jesus Christ, Christ's Church, The Bible, and many more. God had provided through His servant Richard the perfect book for me. I didn't have to read it from cover to cover. I could choose the questions I was most interested in and look up the answers immediately. It was like taking Richard Gallagher home with me to answer my religious questions whenever I needed an answer.

The category that interested me most dealt with Jesus. The question in the front of the book asked: "What are the Old Testament prophecies concerning Messiah?" These were passages of Scripture contained in the Torah (Five Books of Moses) and in the Psalms, Proverbs, and the Prophets. Some dated back to the book of Genesis and others were written 400 years before the birth of Jesus. I was never told in Hebrew school that these prophecies existed.

I began reading this section with great interest. It stated that the Orthodox Jews still accept these prophecies today as being messianic. I couldn't believe my eyes as I read them. I couldn't believe how specific they were, the details they gave about the Messiah to come.

Messiah was to be the "Seed of a Woman"

And I will put enmity between thee (Satan) and the woman (Eve), and between thy seed and her seed (Messiah); it (Messiah) shall bruise thy head (Satan critically wounded), and thou shalt bruise his heel (Messiah crucified) (Gen. 3:15).

Promised Seed of Abraham

Seeing that Abraham shall surely become a great and mighty nation (Israel), and all the nations of the earth (Gentiles) shall be blessed in him (Messiah)? (Gen. 18:18).

Promised Seed of Isaac

And God said, Sarah thy wife shall bear thee a son indeed; and thou shalt call his name Isaac: and I will establish my covenant with him for an everlasting covenant, and with his seed after him (Covenant to be finalized in Messiah) (Gen. 17:19).

Promised Seed of Jacob

I shall see him (Messiah), but not now: I shall behold him, but not nigh: there shall come a Star out of Jacob, and a Sceptre (symbol of rulership) shall rise out of Israel, and shall smite the corners of Moab, and destroy all the children of Sheth (Num. 24:17).

Will Descend from the Tribe of Judah

The sceptre (symbol of rulership) shall not depart from Judah, nor a lawgiver from between his feet, until Shiloh (Messiah) come; and unto him shall the gathering of the people be (Gen. 49:10).

The Heir to the Throne of David

Of the increase of his (Messiah's) government and peace there shall be no end, upon the throne of David, and upon his kingdom, to order it, and to establish it with judgment and with justice from henceforth even for ever. The zeal of the LORD of hosts will perform this (Isa. 9:7).

Place of Birth

But thou, Bethlehem Ephratah, though thou be little among the thousands of Judah, yet out of thee shall he (Messiah) come forth unto me that is to be ruler in Israel; whose goings forth have been from of old, from everlasting (Mic. 5:2).

Time of Birth

Know therefore and understand, that from the going forth of the commandment to restore and to build Jerusalem unto the Messiah the Prince shall be seven weeks, and threescore and two weeks: the street shall be built again, and the wall, even in troublous times (Dan. 9:25).

Born of a Virgin

Therefore the Lord himself shall give you a sign; Behold, a virgin (or young maiden) shall conceive, and bear a son, and shall call his name Immanuel (meaning: "God with us") (Isa. 7:14).

Massacre of Infants

Thus saith the Lord; A voice was heard in Ramah, lamentation, and bitter weeping; Rachel weeping for her children refused to be comforted for her children, because they were not (prophesying Herod's slaying of all the infants in Bethlehem to try to kill the Messiah) (Jer. 31:15).

Messiah's Flight into Egypt

When Israel was a child, then I loved him, and called my son out of Egypt (Hos. 11:1).

Ministry in Galilee

Nevertheless the dimness shall not be such as was in her vexation, when at the first he lightly afflicted the land of Zebulun and the land of Naphtali, and afterward did more grievously afflict her by the way of the sea, beyond Jordan, in Galilee of the nations.

The people that walked in darkness have seen a great light (Messiah): they that dwell in the land of the shadow of death, upon them hath the light shined (Isa. 9:1–2).

As a Prophet

The Lord thy God will raise up unto thee (Israel) a Prophet (Messiah) from the midst of thee, of thy brethren, like unto me; unto him ye shall hearken (Deut. 18:15).

Like unto Moses

I will raise them up a Prophet (Messiah) from among their brethren, like unto thee (Moses), and I will put my (God's) words in his mouth; and he shall speak unto them all I shall command him.

And it shall come to pass, that whosoever will not hearken unto my words which he shall speak in my name, I will require it of him (Deut. 18:18–19).

As a Priest, like Melchizedek

The Lord hath sworn, and will not repent, Thou (the Messiah) art a priest for ever after the order of Melchizedek (Ps. 110:4).

His Rejection by the Jewish People

He (Messiah) is despised and rejected of men; a man of sorrows, and acquainted with grief: and we (Israel) hid as it were our faces from him; he was despised, and we esteemed him not (Isa. 53:3).

Some of Messiah's Characteristics

And the spirit of the Lord shall rest upon him (Messiah), the spirit of wisdom and understanding, the spirit of counsel and might, the spirit of knowledge and of the fear of the Lord (Isa. 11:2).

His Triumphal Entry on a Donkey

Rejoice greatly, O daughter of Zion; shout, O daughter of Jerusalem: behold, thy King (Messiah) cometh unto thee: he is just, and having salvation; lowly, and riding upon an ass, and upon a colt the foal of an ass (Zech. 9:9).

Betrayed by a Friend: Judas

Yea, mine own familiar friend, in whom I trusted, which did eat of my bread, hath lifted up his heel against me (Ps. 41:9).

Sold for Thirty Pieces of Silver

And I said unto them, If ye think good, give me my price; and if not, forbear. So they weighed for my price thirty pieces of silver.

And the LORD said unto me, Cast it unto the potter: a goodly price that I was prised at of them. And I took the thirty pieces of silver, and cast them to the potter in the house of the Lord (concerning the thirty pieces of silver that Judas was paid to betray Jesus) (Zech. 11:12–13).

Judas' Office to be Taken by Another

When he (Messiah) shall be judged, let him (Judas) be condemned: and let his prayer become sin. Let his days be few; and let another take his office (Ps. 109:7–8).

False Witnesses Accuse Him

Deliver me (Messiah talking of himself) not over unto the will of mine enemies: for false witnesses are risen up against me, and such as breathe out cruelty (Ps. 27:12).

Silent When Accused

He (Messiah) was oppressed, and he was afflicted, yet he opened not his mouth: he is brought as a lamb to the slaughter, and as a sheep before her shearers is dumb, so he openeth not his mouth (Isa. 53:7).

Smitten and Spat Upon

I (Messiah talking of himself) gave my back to the smiters,

and my cheeks to them that plucked off the hair: I hid not my face from shame and spitting (Isa. 50:6).

Was Hated Without A Cause

They (Jewish people and Gentiles who rejected Messiah) that hate me (Messiah talking of himself) without a cause are more than the hairs of mine head: they that would destroy me, being mine enemies wrongfully, are mighty: then I restored that which I took not away (Ps. 69:4).

Suffered Vicariously

Surely he (Messiah) hath borne our (Israel's) griefs, and carried our sorrows: yet we (Israel) did esteem him stricken, smitten of God, and afflicted.
But he (Messiah) was wounded for our (Israel's) transgressions, he was bruised for our iniquities: the chastisement of our peace was upon him; and with his stripes (Messiah's bruises) we are healed (Isa. 53:4–5).

Crucified with Sinners

Therefore will I (God of Israel) divide him (Messiah) a portion with the great, and he shall divide the spoil with the strong; because he hath poured out his soul unto death: and he was numbered with the transgressors (two criminals crucified with him); and he bare the sin of many, and made intercession for the transgressors (Isa. 53:12).

Hands and Feet Pierced

For dogs have compassed me (Messiah talking of himself): the assembly of the wicked have inclosed me: they pierced my hands and my feet (crucifixion) (Ps. 22:16).

Mocked and Insulted

But I (Messiah talking about himself) am a worm, and no

man; a reproach of men, and despised of the people (people of Israel).

All they that see me laugh me to scorn: they shoot out the lip, they shake the head, saying,

He trusted on the LORD that he would deliver him: let him deliver him, seeing he delighted in him (Ps. 22:6–8).

Given Gall and Vinegar

They gave me (Messiah speaking of myself) also gall for my meat; and in my thirst they gave me vinegar to drink (Ps. 69:21).

Hears Prophetic Words Repeated in Mockery

He (Messiah) trusted on the LORD that he would deliver him: let him deliver him, seeing he delighted in him (Ps. 22:8).

Prays for His Enemies

For my love (Messiah's love) they (Israel) are my adversaries: but I give myself unto prayer (Ps. 109:4).

His Side to be Pierced

And I (Messiah speaking of himself) will pour upon the house of David, and upon the inhabitants of Jerusalem, the spirit of grace and of supplications: and they shall look upon me whom they have pierced (crucified), and they shall mourn for him, as one mourneth for his only son, and shall be in bitterness for him, as one that is in bitterness for his firstborn (Zech. 12:10).

Soldiers Cast Lots for His Coat

They part my (Messiah speaking of himself) garments among them, and cast lots upon my vesture (Ps. 22:18).

Not a Bone to be Broken

He (Messiah) keepeth all his bones: not one of them is broken (Ps. 34:20). (It was a custom to break the bones of the crucified and ensure that they would die before the Sabbath or a Jewish High Holy Day. John 19:33 explains: "But when they came to Jesus, and saw that he was dead already, they brake not his legs.")

To Be Buried with the Rich

And he (Messiah) made his grave with the wicked, and with the rich in his death; because he had done no violence, neither was any deceit in his mouth (Isa. 53:9).

His Resurrection

For thou wilt not leave my (Messiah's) soul in hell; neither wilt thou suffer thine Holy One to see corruption (Ps. 16:10).

His Ascension

Thou (Messiah) hast ascended on high, thou hast led captivity captive; thou hast received gifts for men: yea, for the rebellious also, that the LORD God might dwell among them (Ps. 68:18).

After stepping off the bus, I couldn't wait to get home. I wanted to find the *Tanakh* (Jewish Scriptures) given to me by the Suburban Jewish Center on the day of my bar mitzvah.

These prophecies can't be in the Jewish Holy Scriptures. Surely, the rabbis would have accepted Jesus as Messiah if these were in there. The Gentiles must have changed the words, I thought.

Once home, I immediately grabbed the Tanakh and opened it to compare the text with the book Richard had given me. As I looked up prophecy after prophecy, I was amazed to find that though there were slight variances between the translations and some of the numbering of verses, the essence of the prophecy remained intact.

I screamed in an angry outburst at my religious upbringing.

"Why did they hide this from me? I had a right to know!"

The tension of this moment cut straight to the core of my heart, and I tasted the bitter salt of my tears as I cried out to God—begging Him to forgive me for doubting. Yet, I wanted to be absolutely sure that Jesus was Messiah. I was again reminded of the book I had read about Jesus when I was twelve years old. I thought to myself: *That book must have been true.*

I had two questions remaining, and I confronted Richard the next day:

"When I read the prophet Isaiah, chapter 7, verse 14, the Jewish version read: 'Behold a *young woman* shall conceive, and bear a son, and shall call his name Immanuel.' In the King James Version it reads: 'Behold a *virgin* shall conceive!' Richard, why is there a discrepancy?"

What I didn't tell him was that my real problem was in accepting this business of people praying to statues of the Virgin Mary in the Catholic church.

Richard was surprised to hear of the difference, but answered.

"The original word used in the Hebrew is *Almah*, meaning a young maiden. This could be interpreted as merely a young woman, or specifically, as a virgin. God is telling us in this Scripture that He Himself was going to give us a sign, or a miracle. What kind of miracle would it be if the child was just born of a young woman and not of a virgin?"

"Yeah, I understand what you are saying. But, it's hard to believe this Virgin Mary stuff," I confessed.

"Well, look at how God answered his promise to Abraham," Richard responded. "Sarah was over 90 years old when she gave birth to Isaac, the son of the promise. Was that miracle any harder than a virgin birth? Besides, in order for Jesus to have been the Messiah, he must have been born without the stain of original sin. The Bible said he was perfect in the Law and never sinned."

I accepted his explanation, but then launched into the next problem area.

"In Isaiah chapter 11, verses 6 through 12, I read of a time when the wolf shall dwell with the lamb, and the leopard shall lie down with the kid. My rabbi once told me that until there is perfect peace on the earth, Messiah could not come. Furthermore, as I continued reading this chapter, it talked about the regathering of Israel from the four corners of the earth. How could Jesus be the Messiah when all these prophecies did not come to pass?"

My challenge did not seem to shake Richard.

"Jesus came as the suffering servant in His first advent, to bring sin under his subjection," he answered. "Yet, He told us that He would come again, this time as King of kings and Lord of lords in his second advent. At that time, He will fulfill those prophecies."

I was stunned.

"Wait a minute. What do you mean, when He comes back?"

Seeing the dizzy look on my face, Richard started laughing as he spoke.

"Just before He ascended into heaven, Jesus told his disciples that He would return in the clouds. He is now seated at the right hand of the Father. When the Father is ready, He will send His Son back to Earth."

I thought to myself, *If Jesus is coming back, then He is alive!* Somehow, I hadn't understood the full meaning of the Resurrection. I thought that He arose from the dead, but I had no idea that He physically rose into the heavens. I remembered my attempts in high school to try and write a screenplay about Jesus returning to the earth. Somehow, I knew his work was not completed, but I wasn't able to finish writing the screenplay, because I didn't know what God would have me say. This was the most exciting news I had ever heard!

Turning to Richard, I said, "I could accept that he might, indeed, be the promised Jewish Messiah, but this Son of God business, I could never accept. How could a man become God?" Richard rolled his eyes.

"No! God became man!"

I couldn't understand the difference.

"That's what I said, how can a man become God?"

Richard tried to explain it to me the best way he could: "Look, let's pretend that you are God, and that ant crawling on the floor is a man. What is the best way for you to communicate with that insect? If you became an ant, then you could tell him all about yourself in a language that he understood. That's why God sent his only begotten Son."

I responded, "Richard, I was raised as a Jew to never bow before an idol, nor before any man. I could accept that perhaps Jesus was the Messiah, a new leader like Moses who came to tell us about God. But I can *never* bow down and worship a man, acknowledging him as God!" I said passionately.

Richard huffed in frustration. Finally, regaining his composure, he responded.

"Warren, you are trying to understand something spiritual, but with your intellect. You can never understand this with your mind. Only the Holy Spirit can make it real to you. You need to ask Jesus into your heart. Then He will come in, and you will understand."

"Invite Him in? What are you talking about?" I asked, thinking that Richard had to be crazy.

"Jesus is like a man, knocking on the door of your house, every day. He tells you he has a great vacuum cleaner to demonstrate. The vacuum cleaner is the Holy Spirit, and you are the house the Lord wants to clean. He wants to remove all your sin and make you clean. All you need to do is let Him in to plug in the vacuum cleaner, and He will demonstrate its power. But you keep turning him away. So, He comes back, day after day, until you ask Him into your heart. He is a gentleman, and He will never force His way in. He says: 'Behold I stand at the door, and knock: if any man hear my voice, and open the door, I will come in to him, and will sup with him, and he with me'" (Rev. 3:20).

I felt deep inside that he was speaking the truth. Still, something was holding me back.

"Richard, I just can't do that."

"Warren, nothing I can do or say will make you believe. You have to invite Him in. What do you have to lose?" Richard asked as several people stepped up to sign his anti-abortion petition.

As I left to go home, I was in deep turmoil over what he had said. I knew it made sense. However, everything in my Jewish upbringing stressed that it was the unpardonable sin to bow down, even before a king. In my imagination, I saw those Catholics in Saint Patrick's Cathedral kneeling before the statues of the saints, praying to what appeared to be idols. I wanted no part of that.

How could God ever be in favor of such practices? I asked myself. If this was what the church practiced, how could I ever be a part of it? This all seemed so far removed from Judaism. How did Christianity ever stray so far from what Jesus Himself practiced? He was bar mitzvahed, and He celebrated Passover. I never read of such practices by the early church in the Bible. Throughout the next several weeks, I continued an internal dialogue. I argued silently with a voice inside me. It kept reminding me of what Richard had told me: "Jesus is knocking on the door of your heart." I wondered whether this voice was my conscience or what Christians referred to as the Holy Spirit of God.

It was late one night, and Donna had already fallen asleep. Again, I cried out to God for some answers.

"Oh God, am I going crazy, arguing with this voice in my head? Or, are You trying to get through to me?"

I felt a strong urge to open the Bible to any page and start reading. I turned to the Gospel of John, chapter 6, verses 41 through 47:

> The Jews then murmured at him, because he said, I am the bread which came down from heaven.
>
> And they said, Is not this Jesus, the son of Joseph, whose father and mother we know? how is it then that he saith, I came down from heaven?
>
> Jesus therefore answered and said unto them, Murmur not among yourselves.
>
> No man can come to me, except the Father which hath sent me draw him: and I will raise him up at the last day.
>
> It is written in the prophets, And they shall be all taught of God. Every man therefore that hath heard, and hath learned of the Father, cometh unto me.
>
> Not that any man hath seen the Father, save he which is of God, he hath seen the Father.
>
> Verily, verily, I say unto you, He that believeth on me hath everlasting life.

I wept as I read these words of Jesus. This was not something that happened long ago. It had relevance to me the very moment I was reading it. I was one of the Jewish people murmuring at Jesus. I knew He had an earthly mother, and I couldn't believe in the virgin birth. As far as I was concerned, Jesus had an earthly father. Yet, it was as if Jesus Himself was talking to me. Again, He was knocking at the door of my heart, saying: "Let Me in!"

Over and over again I kept thinking about what I had just read, especially the part where Jesus said: "No man can come to me, except the Father (the God of Israel) which sent me draw him." If nothing else, I knew that this was beyond my own reasoning, God was indeed drawing me. He had been reaching out to me ever since I was a little boy.

I fell to my knees and began praying, "I will bow my knees to you, oh Lord God of Israel, and to You alone. Are You trying to tell me that Jesus is the Messiah and, as the Christians claim, the Son of God? Please have patience with me, until I can truly believe."

It was an honest prayer from my innermost self, yet the turmoil did not end. If anything, it intensified.

TWENTY-ONE

YOU LIGHT UP MY LIFE

In early 1974, things at work were not going well. Our major client finally severed his relations with The Editor's Pad, so Norman Goldstein was busy trying to solicit new business. However, there was a slowdown that year in advertising, and conditions worsened until the company couldn't make payroll. Norman decided to leave the company and join a competitor. He wanted me to come with him, but I felt an obligation to finish a project for the New York State Department of Education. It was a thirty-minute film which I directed, photographed, and helped write. The subject dealt with school bus safety and included animation and live action. It also included drama and comedy, and I felt it would be an excellent springboard to greater projects if I would see the movie through to completion with Al Strauss as editor. After several weeks of late hours in the editing room, we completed the film. The New York Education people loved it.

During this time, Al was angry at Norman's sudden departure from the company. When Norman returned to pick up some of his personal belongings, Al tried to stop him. A loud shouting match ensued.

"You *goniff!*" (Yiddish for thief) Al shouted at Norman. To put it mildly, it was a horrible situation. A silent partner of The Editor's Pad, Ted Kholl, came to the organization as its new president. He had a reserve of cash from his other company, Elisar Research, an educational foundation which had landed the State of New York Department of Education account for The Editor's Pad.

Ted subsidized The Editor's Pad for several months, and I turned down a salary from the company until it could recover, remaining on the staff and retaining the freedom to solicit freelance work and use the company's equipment during off hours. I began to make inroads into some of Madison Avenue's best advertising agencies, including the world's biggest at this time, J. Walter Thompson.

I also helped Al and Ted with any work they had at The Editor's Pad, but things continued to get worse. One day, Ted called Al and me into his office for a chat.

He began speaking slowly.

"Guys, I need to be up-front with you. I don't know what to do. Things are so bad I haven't been able to pay our taxes."

I spoke up.

"Look, Ted, why don't you give Al and me some of the editing equipment in lieu of the past salary you owe us. That way the equipment will be protected, and we can all start a new business!"

Ted replied, "No, I believe if we pull together we can make it through the storm."

"Look Ted, the IRS could walk in at any moment and shut this place down," I continued. "You must protect the assets. It's the only thing we have left!"

Just as I was finishing my sentence, two men walked into the office and interrupted, "Doctor Ted Kholl? We're from the Internal Revenue Service."

Al and I couldn't get out of Ted's office quickly enough. I turned to Al.

"Hey, let's get the equipment out of here before it's too late."

One side door led to another hallway. Al and I moved the moviola editing machine out the door and into the hall, while Ted and the IRS agents were talking in his front office.

"Where do we put this thing?" Al asked.

"How about Lenny's place?" I added.

We pushed through the door of Lenny's Productions, Incorporated, a TV commercial production company directly across from The Editor's Pad. As we pushed the moviola into Lenny's office, he looked at us as if we were crazy, because we were intruding on him as he entertained some clients. Al and I were out of breath.

"Please, just keep this here for a little while," Al told him.

"Why, what is happening?" Lenny said, seeing the despondent look on our faces.

"You don't want to know!" Al and I gasped, both at the same time, as we ran back out of his office to The Editor's Pad to save more equipment.

We must have made at least twenty trips, carrying film equipment out the door, down the hall, hiding it next to a cove by the public rest room. When Al and I returned to get more equipment, the IRS agents and Dr. Kholl were now making their way into the editing rooms. Al and I sat down on the couch in the screening room, pretending to be reading magazines.

"Now in here, we have a moviola editing machine, worth a lot of money!" we heard Ted telling the agents.

There was a silence as Ted came into the screening room, looking for the moviola.

Ted yelled at us, "Where is the moviola? What did you do with it?"

Al and I were stunned at his ranting. I was frozen in fear as the two IRS agents came into our room staring at us.

Without flinching, Al spoke up calmly, "Keep your shirt on! Just calm down. We took the machine over to Lenny's. He needed it to show his client a commercial."

"Al, bring them over to Lenny's to show them," Ted ordered. Thinking quickly, Al responded, "No, we can't interrupt him in the middle of a client presentation. Why don't you continue your tour, and Warren and I will get it back as soon as his clients leave."

Ten minutes later, we had the moviola back. Al and I debated whether or not to bring the rest of the equipment back too.

"What if one of these IRS guys goes to the men's room and sees the equipment lying there?" I asked Al.

He agreed, but as long as they were there with Ted going over the books, we didn't dare get the equipment for fear of being caught. I prayed to God that He would have mercy on us.

Apparently, God answered my prayer. Once the IRS agents left, we sneaked the equipment back into the offices and left it there. We both decided the equipment wasn't worth risking trouble with the government. I didn't return to work for a few weeks. Neither did I call. Al contacted me at home and told me that The Editor's Pad was under lock and key by the IRS. We couldn't get in if we wanted to.

I had plenty of freelance work to keep me busy, so I incorporated and formed Sunrise Productions. I started working out of my apartment in Linden. I never had to look for work. My reputation as a filmmaker brought referrals and new challenges.

I began writing my second full-length screenplay entitled *Chaser!* It was based on a true story about an alcoholic whose life was coming apart at the seams. Much of the material for the screenplay was drawn from my childhood and my dad's own bout with alcohol.

One day, I traveled into New York City by bus to meet with a possible investor for *Chaser!* While in the bus terminal, I met an Orthodox Jewish rabbi and introduced myself.

"Rabbi, my name is Warren Marcus. Could you answer a few questions for me?" I offered him my hand in friendship.

The rabbi smiled, shaking my hand.

"Of course, I'll gladly help you if I can."

Without identifying my search for whether Jesus was the promised Messiah or not, I asked, "Do we Jews still believe that the Messiah will come?"

"Oh yes! We believe that he will come!" the rabbi said.

"Are there prophecies in the Tanakh concerning Messiah?" I asked in a humble manner.

"The Torah, the Psalms, and the Prophets contain many, many prophecies. Why do you ask?" the rabbi insisted.

"Oh, I was just wondering. You see, I was raised in a conservative synagogue, where they never talked about the Messiah," I explained, then asked, "What are some of these prophecies?"

"You want me to give you yeshiva lessons for free?" he said in a joking manner.

"I'd pay you to know just one!" I said fervently.

"You don't have to pay. I was only joking. Let's see, in Genesis, Moses is promised by the Lord God of Israel that He will raise up a prophet in the midst of them, and God will put His words in His mouth. He will be wise and we must listen to His every word."

"Is there a new covenant promised when Messiah comes?" I asked, continuing my investigation.

"The prophet Jeremiah speaks prophetically of a new covenant with the house of Israel, not like the one He made with Moses in the wilderness, when God wrote His law on stone. But, in this new covenant, He shall write His laws on our hearts, and we shall know them," the rabbi concluded.

"When do you think He will come?" I inquired passionately.

"No man knows the time, but I pray it will be soon. Some of

the ancient rabbis say He already came before the temple in Jerusalem was destroyed in 70 C.E. They say He is in hiding, waiting to reveal himself when we Jews are truly repentant and diligently obeying the Law," he explained.

He apologized that he couldn't stay and talk more. I was satisfied that the prophecies I had read in Richard's book were the same which the Orthodox Jewish people still believe refer to Messiah.

That night, Donna and I went to see the movie *The Exorcist*. An inordinate amount of Madison Avenue hype promoted the movie so I just had to see it. Everyone talked about the "green-pea soup" scene. The reality of evil permeated the movie theater as I sat watching the film. It was as if Satan himself were sitting right beside us.

The movies *Ben Hur* and *The Ten Commandments* both imparted a feeling of peace. However, *The Exorcist* transmitted deep feelings of anxiety. The gross language and the voice of the demon which emerged from the mouth of an innocent twelve-year-old girl were so terrifying that I couldn't wait for the film to end. As Donna and I left the movie theater, I ran into an old high school acquaintance, Gary King. In high school, I had drummed briefly in a rock band, and Gary had played the saxophone.

I was surprised to see him handing out Christian tracts which dealt with the film we had just seen, *The Exorcist*. He introduced the girl next to him as his wife, Debbie. Donna and I were surprised that he had a new wife, and that we had not heard of his divorce from Carol, his high school sweetheart. After all, they had dated for a longer period of time than Donna and I. Once inside the car, I took a peek at the tract he had given me. It explained that *The Exorcist* was just a movie, but that the devil was real and that without Jesus, people cannot overcome evil in their lives.

"It looks like Gary's into Jesus or something. He could be a Jehovah's Witness," I said to Donna.

"If he's so religious, how come he's married to another wife? What happened to him and Carol?" she asked.

I was perplexed by this chance meeting. I had no idea of the part Gary and his new wife, Debbie, would play in God's plan for my life. I gave the tract to Donna to read. She looked at it briefly, then gave it back to me without comment.

When we arrived at our apartment, I could still feel the lingering presence of evil all around me from the movie. Its demonic talons gripped the foundation of my spirit like a tornado ripping the deepest roots from an enormous tree. It didn't help any when Donna asked me to go through the apartment and turn on all the lights. She sensed the same demonic presence. Quivering inside, I pretended to be Mr. Macho Man as I went through the house, checking every closet. I had never sensed such apprehension before, except when I was a child and became frightened of lightning and thunder. I lit up a joint of marijuana and smoked it, hoping it would calm me down and help me forget the movie. It only intensified my fears.

In the middle of the night, Donna was sleeping, but my mind kept seeing the evil demon from the movie. Here I was, a grown man sleeping with my wife, yet afraid of the darkness! Turning on the night table lamp, I saw the tract on *The Exorcist* which Gary had given me. I was reluctant to read it, wary that it might conjure up more of the evil from the movie. Again, I was reminded of the different frame of mind I now possessed as a result of seeing *The Exorcist* compared to how I felt after seeing *Ben Hur*. This reinforced my belief that the motion picture is the most powerful medium for communication in existence today. My earlier conviction that movies could be used wrongly to promote evil, as well as rightly to promote God, was reinforced.

Unable to sleep, I went downstairs and rolled another joint. As I smoked it, I asked myself, *Is this all there is to life? Smoking a joint whenever I can't deal with my problems? There has to be more to it than this!*

I randomly opened my Bible and began reading. My eyes fell upon the prophet Isaiah, chapter 9, verses 6 and 7.

> For unto us a child is born, unto us a son is given: and the government shall be upon his shoulder: and his name shall be called Wonderful, Counsellor, The mighty God, The everlasting Father, The Prince of Peace.
>
> Of the increase of his government and peace there shall be no end, upon the throne of David, and upon his kingdom, to order it, and to establish it with judgment and with justice from henceforth even for ever. The zeal of the LORD of hosts will perform this.

Instantly, I accepted this verse as a prophecy concerning the Jewish Messiah. What amazed me most was that his name shall be called "Wonderful, Counsellor, The mighty God, The everlasting Father, The Prince of Peace."

Could this business about Jesus being the Son of God really be true? I asked myself, since these verses were right from the Tanakh. They certainly indicated this was the case.

I began to pour my heart out to God: "Oh God, whoever You are, please help me. There has to be more than all this. Oh God of Israel, if Jesus is indeed the Messiah and the Son of God, then I want Him in my heart. If He is not the Messiah, then I don't want Him in my life. I don't want to do anything to offend You, oh Lord God of Israel. You'll have to let me know the truth about Jesus. Amen!"

After praying this prayer, I immediately experienced a peace inside. It was like the feeling I had after seeing God in my childhood dream. The fear was completely gone. My mind was no longer flooded with the thoughts of the film we had seen that day. Now, I was immersed with thoughts about God and the excitement that somehow, I would know for sure if Jesus was truly the promised Jewish Messiah.

TWENTY-TWO

THE GREATEST STORY EVER TOLD

Several days later, I was leaving my apartment to do some shopping when I was surprised to see Gary and his new wife, Debbie, crossing the street and walking toward me. I ran over to greet them.

"Hey, Gary! What are you doing here?" I asked excitedly, wanting to know why he remarried and what his beliefs were.

"Do you live here?" he asked.

"Yeah, I live in that apartment over there," I answered.

"Well, I guess we're going to be neighbors. We're moving in just three doors down," Gary said, smiling.

I watched as the couple went to check out the new apartment. I couldn't wait to have an in-depth conversation. I knew he was somehow connected to God, but I didn't know if he was involved in some cult, or if he had the answer I was seeking.

Several days later, Donna invited them over to our apartment. Gary and his new wife, Debbie, came with Debbie's four-year-old son, Christopher. He was a cute little boy, who sat quietly as we adults talked. Assuming that Gary indulged, I pulled out a joint of marijuana.

Seeing an uncomfortable look on their faces, I asked, "Don't you guys smoke?"

Debbie laughed as Gary answered, "No, we don't do drugs anymore. We get high on Jesus!" I put the marijuana away and began to probe them about their faith.

"Gary, why were you handing out those pamphlets? You know, the ones about *The Exorcist?*"

"Didn't you read it?" he questioned.

"Well, I tried reading it, but I didn't quite understand the point. Are you guys Jehovah's Witnesses?" I queried.

"Oh no! We're born-again Christians," they responded.

I was perplexed.

"What is a born-again Christian?"

"It's a person who has accepted Jesus as Lord and Savior," Debbie explained.

"Well, I'm not into religion," Donna interjected as she got up from her chair to get the coffee.

"We're not into religion either. Religion is just tradition. We are into a relationship with Jesus. I mean, Jesus is alive and dwells within us," Gary said as he shifted in his chair.

I looked at Donna as she went into the kitchen. I knew that she thought they were crazy.

"How did you get into this born-again stuff? I never heard of it before," I asked Gary.

Donna returned and placed the coffee on the coffee table. We sat on the floor around the table, engrossed as Gary began his story.

"As you know, I was married to Carol for over four years. I mean, we were high-school sweethearts like you and Donna. But I think we were dating longer than the two of you."

We agreed and Gary continued.

"Debbie and her husband, Ken, moved next door. We all became good friends and did everything together, including a lot of things we shouldn't have done—you know, sexually—swapping partners!

"Debbie's husband, Ken, and my wife, Carol, fell in love. Neither Debbie nor I realized it until it was too late. The two of them broke the news to us, and they told us they wanted a divorce so they could get married."

"Did you and Debbie love each other?" I asked timidly.

"Not at first. In the beginning we were sort of thrown together because of the situation," Debbie answered.

Gary nodded and then proceeded to tell the rest of the story.

"The divorce went through, and Carol and Ken got married. Debbie and I decided to get married, too."

"Gary, did you have any children from your first marriage?" I queried.

"No," he answered. "Carol and Ken started going to Evangel

Church in Elizabeth. After hearing a sermon from Pastor Tate, both of them committed their lives to Jesus and made him their Lord and Savior. I can still remember the day they came over and told us that they had become born-again Christians. They told us that God revealed to them their sinful ways and has forgiven them, and their lives will never be the same again."

Gulping down a mouthful of coffee, I asked the obvious, "How did you respond to that?" Gary and Debbie looked at one another and started to laugh. Donna's eyes and my mouth were wide open.

"Well, let's put it this way. Debbie was not exactly happy with their visit. She wasn't as forgiving as I," Gary admitted.

Donna spoke up, "I wouldn't be either! I don't think I'd ever be able to forgive Warren if something like that happened!"

With prodding from me, Gary went on with the story.

"My ex-wife, Carol, invited us to come to church to hear Pastor Tate preach. Debbie refused to go with them, but I went. Pastor Tate did something I had never heard in a church before. He taught from the Bible, verse by verse, word by word. The Holy Spirit convicted me of my sinful ways. That day I gave my heart to Jesus Christ."

Donna turned to Debbie and asked, "What happened to you Debbie?"

Debbie then shared her story.

"When Gary came home from the church, I was angry. I was especially mad at my ex-husband and Carol. I mean, the two of them dumped us and divorced us, and then had the nerve to tell us they found God. Gary kept bugging me, but I refused to go to church with him, week after week. Then, finally just to get him to shut up, I decided to go to Evangel Church."

Donna and I were laughing as Debbie told her story. It was easy to imagine ourselves in her shoes. We hung onto her every word as she continued.

"I was very skeptical as we entered the church. I didn't want to sit anywhere near our ex-spouses. However, as Pastor Tate taught from the Bible, something happened in my heart. I began to cry. I found myself going up to the altar and falling on my knees. I gave my heart to Jesus. Pastor Tate was so nice to us, and the people in the church were hugging us and praising God for my salvation. I felt such love from everybody there."

I was moved by their story. I thought to myself, *Pastor Tate must be a great man of God to have such an effect on Gary and Debbie.*

I couldn't ask enough questions about Evangel Church and Pastor Tate. Debbie and Gary said many wonderful things about the people at the church and their pastor.

Gary, realizing my sincere interest, asked, "Warren, why don't you come with us to see the church for yourself?"

"Maybe I will. But sometime in the future," I said, trying to put them off. Deep inside, I was afraid of the powerful story I had heard.

Gary and Debbie became my close friends. Debbie brought over some literature for me to read, including magazines aimed at Jewish people and published by the Jews for Jesus and Chosen People Ministries. I was amazed that other Jews had proclaimed Jesus as the promised Jewish Messiah. Furthermore, these Jewish publications explained that a Jew does not convert to another religion when receiving Yeshua (Jesus) as his Messiah, but actually becomes a better Jewish believer, observing the Jewish holidays by understanding the full meaning as explained in and through the Messiah.

Gary brought me a copy of Hal Lindsey's book, *The Late Great Planet Earth*. I couldn't put the book down until I had read every page. It demonstrated the fact that God wasn't finished with Israel. Hal Lindsey wrote, using Scripture, that God would once again turn to the Jewish people after the fullness of the Gentiles comes in. I read with immense interest about the second coming of Jesus.

Donna told me that she wanted no part of Gary and Debbie's religious obsession, and she became jealous of my spending so much time with them. For me, there was something burning in my heart. It was a deep desire to know if they had found the truth I had been searching for. I observed them closely to see if their faith was real. I watched as they prayed before every meal. They abstained from drinking alcohol, even wine. Their conversation always centered on Jesus and the Bible. I felt so good being around them.

Gary worked at a factory weekdays and played in a Christian

rock band on weekends. He no longer listened to secular rock. He played me some of his collection of Christian contemporary music and gave me an album by a man named Phil Keaggy. He was one of the greatest guitarists I had ever heard, but more importantly, the songs he wrote touched my heart with his praise of God. Gary gave me some of his other Christian rock music. As I listened, I sensed an incredible peace. It was as if God was all around me.

After listening to these Christian albums, I no longer enjoyed hearing my old rock-and-roll music. The lyrics were confusing and depressing. Something was happening inside of me. I wondered— had Jesus truly come into my heart? I just couldn't stop thinking about God.

Gary asked Donna and me if we would like to hear his contemporary rock band play at a Christian retreat in Pennsylvania. Donna told Gary that she would think about it, but when he left our apartment, she told me that she didn't want any part of it.

"But Donna, I want to hear his band play. Please come," I begged her.

"Warren, if you want to go, then go!" she said.

I knew Donna was angry at me for even considering going. Yet I knew that I had to experience for myself what this Christian rock music was all about.

The next day, I drove with Gary and Debbie in their car to Pennsylvania. The band was set up to perform outside. I sat with Debbie and her little boy on a blanket spread out on a grassy field and enjoyed the music. I hung onto every word they sang. The six-member band included Gary on the saxophone, a bass player, lead guitarist, and a drummer. The other two members were Pastor Tate's sons. Wayne Tate played keyboards and sang harmony with his brother, Ray. The two ministered the Gospel between songs. Each band member shared his personal story—how Jesus came into his life. Gary introduced me to Ray and Wayne during the break.

"This is my old Jewish friend, Warren. We used to play in a group together. He was a great drummer," Gary briefed them. Ray broke into a huge smile.

"Praise God! It's great to meet you, Warren. Did you ever come to Evangel Church?"

"No, but I'd like to," I replied.

"Hey, please come. We could always use another musician," Wayne said.

I was overwhelmed with the love I felt from these people. This was the kind of Christianity I had read about in the Bible. The character of Yeshua was truly flowing from everyone I met.

At the end of the concert, Ray Tate asked everyone to bow their heads. He asked if there was anyone in the audience who would like to receive Jesus as Lord and Savior. I wanted to raise my hand badly, but I was embarrassed.

Ray talked in an amplified whisper, holding the microphone close to his lips.

"Christians, please pray out loud. Ask God to move on the hearts of individuals who need to make a decision to receive Jesus, right now."

I heard the voices of the hundreds gathered there, as they interceded aloud. The sound of their prayerful voices became louder and louder. Many were shouting to God; others could be heard weeping. I felt an incredible brokenness in my heart, and I started weeping. I realized a force, greater than anything I had ever felt before, present inside me. I began to shake uncontrollably. I didn't understand what was happening. I knew it was from God, yet I stubbornly refused to raise my hand.

Ray began to pray for those who raised their hands. I thought I had blown it. I missed the opportunity to get things right with God and to accept the Messiah into my heart.

On the way home to Linden, I was feeling depressed. I had failed God, and I felt as if there would never be an opportunity to know Him again. Donna was angry at me for the entire week for going to the retreat without her. After all, before Debbie and Gary came into my life, Donna and I did everything together. I couldn't explain to her in adequate terms what this search for lasting peace really meant to me. No matter how I tried to reason with her, she would become upset.

The following Saturday, Gary and Debbie stopped by the apartment. Donna was very polite to them. There was no sign of the frustration and anger she had expressed to me.

After some time, Gary popped the question.

"Donna, how about you and Warren coming to church with us tomorrow?"

I spun around on my heels, looking toward Donna, prepared for an atomic bomb to drop.

Instead, to my surprise, Donna smiled and said, "Let me think about it."

I got excited that Donna would even consider going to Evangel, but my hopes were dashed when Gary and Debbie left.

"There's just no way I'm going to church with them. If I wanted to go back to church, I'd go to Saint John's Catholic Church," she said angrily.

"Donna, please come with me. This is something I feel I must do. I might hate the place. What do you have to lose? I'd rather do this thing with you," I pleaded.

"If you want to go, you go! I'm not going!" she insisted.

I pleaded and begged; Donna didn't want to hear it. She said that I could go, but I knew she would hold it against me if I went without her. I went over to Gary and Debbie's apartment to ask their advice.

Addressing the two of them, I confessed, "Donna said I could go, but she refuses to go with me. What shall I do?"

Debbie spoke first.

"If she is uncomfortable, don't force her. I was sort of the same way. You need to do what Gary did. Let nothing stand in the way between you and God. It may take a while, but Donna will come around, just like me."

Gary then spoke, "This is how Satan works. I believe he's using Donna to keep you from truly knowing God."

"Let me see what I can do. I'll talk with her," Debbie said, trying to comfort me.

That night while watching television, Debbie called to speak with Donna. Donna took the call in the kitchen. She paced the floor as she talked. All the while, she would glance over at me, rolling her eyes and shaking her head in anger for putting her in this awkward situation. Upon hanging up the phone, she confronted me.

"I don't like you talking to them about me! What else did you tell them about our marriage?"

"Donna, I only told them that I felt badly that you didn't want to go. I love you. I have nothing bad to say about our marriage to anyone," I reasoned.

"You don't love me! If you did, you wouldn't go with them. Whatever you do, don't you ever talk with them about me again," she yelled.

I was devastated. I wanted to go to the church, but I also didn't want to hurt Donna. I sneaked back over to Gary and Debbie's apartment to talk with them.

"I want to go to church tomorrow, but Donna doesn't want me to go. She was very angry that you called, Debbie. She wasn't angry with you, but rather with me. Please don't tell her we talked about this, or she'll kill me," I implored.

"If Donna doesn't want to go, let her be," Gary said firmly. "God will deal with her later. But Warren, don't let *anybody* keep you from seeking God. The Lord will bless you for your obedience."

"I don't know. Donna will hold a grudge forever," I muttered.

"Warren, I was just like Donna. I didn't want Gary to go to church, either. I put guilt trips on Gary to try to keep him home, but everyone was praying for me, and believe me, God answers prayer," Debbie offered, trying to lift my spirits.

They both agreed that we should pray to God about the situation and leave it in His capable hands. We stood in a circle and held hands. Gary prayed:

"Father God, we come before You in Jesus' name. We ask that You will give Warren the strength to go to church tomorrow with us. Let him be assured that You will take care of Donna. If it be Your will, give her a change of heart and let her come too. However, please let nothing stop Warren from doing Your will for his life. We bind Satan in the mighty name of Jesus from interfering with Donna and Warren. Let Satan have no power over this situation. Thank You for hearing our prayer. In Jesus' name we pray. Amen."

As soon as we finished praying, Donna called. Debbie answered the phone, and I told her to tell Donna I had just left. I waved to both of them, thanking them for the prayer and immediately went home. Donna was still on the phone with Debbie when I walked in the door. She glared at me angrily. When she hung up, she confronted me.

"Were you and your friends talking about me again? Or, maybe you were praying for me?" she asked sarcastically.

A chill ran down my spine as I wondered how she knew about

the prayer. I was in no mood for her probing further. All I wanted to do was go to church. I knew there was absolutely nothing wrong with that. However, Donna was acting as if I were having an adulterous affair.

Angrily, I shouted at her.

"What is wrong with you? Look, I'm going tomorrow whether you like it or not! All we prayed for was that God might soften your heart."

"Oh, you did pray for me! Well, great! You and your new friends can pray all you want, but I will never set foot in that church," she insisted. Donna was still asleep when the alarm rang Sunday morning. I had mixed feelings about going to church. On one hand, I wanted to meet Pastor Tate. Still, I didn't look forward to the grief Donna would give me upon returning home.

I was dressed in my best suit as Gary and Debbie picked me up. Christopher sat on my lap as we drove. I had been to their apartment so much, Christopher called me Uncle Warren.

As we pulled up to Evangel Church, I first noticed the simplicity of the building. In fact, it didn't even look like a church. I followed them into the building and watched as they brought Christopher to his Sunday school classroom. The hallways reminded me of the Suburban Jewish Center where I had attended Hebrew school. It was in the hall outside the sanctuary that I first met Pastor Tate.

"Pastor, I want you to meet a friend of ours," said Gary.

Pastor Tate came over to us smiling. He was much younger than I had expected. I was twenty-four, and he appeared to be about thirty-six years old.

"Hey, brother and sister, give me a hug," Pastor Tate said as he embraced the two.

"Pastor, this is my Jewish friend, Warren Marcus," Gary said as the pastor released him from the hug.

"Warren Marcus! Shalom. I love the Jewish people. You know, we have a number of messianic believers at Evangel," Pastor Tate said. Then he switched gears, "Okay, come on, give me a hug!"

The Pastor hugged me like a father would embrace a son. I could see why Gary and Debbie liked him. He was so outgoing and friendly. He seemed to embody the compassionate heart of the Messiah as conveyed in the Bible.

I followed Gary and Debbie into the sanctuary. I was surprised that there were no statues or Christian symbols. It actually felt more like a synagogue than a church. We sat down in the middle row. The pews were filled to capacity when the service started. At least seven hundred people had gathered to worship God in the small sanctuary. In the front of the church was a raised platform with a simple pulpit. I watched as the choir filled the risers behind the pulpit. A band with guitar, bass, keyboards, drums, and horns tuned up their instruments. I recognized the Pastor's son Wayne at the piano.

Pastor Tate walked up to the pulpit. I noticed the words emblazoned in brass on the walls behind him reading: Thy word is a lamp unto my feet and Thy word is the truth.

The band played an upbeat rendition of "Power in the Blood" as the entire congregation stood up, singing and clapping. I couldn't get over the smiles on their faces as Pastor Tate stood at the pulpit leading them. I joined in with the infectious spirit, clapping and trying to catch the words to sing along. Gary slipped me a hymnal, opened to the right page. I took it and sang, "There is power, power, wonder working power in the blood of the Lamb." I understood the Lamb to be the Messiah.

At the end of the song, the entire congregation broke out in thunderous applause. This was not the conventional kudos heard at the end of some worldly performance, but rather, this praise was directed toward the heavens.

Pastor Tate led the pack, shouting, "Hallelujah! Praise God! Praise His holy name!"

Others in the assemblage shouted, "Precious is the name of the Lord!" and "Praise you, Jesus. Thank you, Lord!"

After several minutes of praise, the worship calmed down to silence. The air was charged with static electricity, as if everyone was waiting to hear the voice of God.

Then, one voice from the midst of the crowd groaned, "Oh God."

Other members began to cry and groan words of praise to God. I saw many of the group now lifting their hands upward toward the heavens. This congregation was so unlike the synagogue I attended. Neither was it like any church I had ever seen. I had never before witnessed such a moving display of power in worship.

Pastor Tate began to sing a slow worshipful song as the entire crowd joined in, repeating over and over again the word, "Hallelujah!" Then in the same melody, "Praise you, Jesus."

I participated in singing the words, at first uncomfortable with singing outloud the name of Jesus. However, the more I sang the name, the more I felt a powerful force moving inside me and all around me. I wondered if this was what the Gentiles called the Holy Spirit. I wept, and my body began to shake. My knees grew weak, and I was worried that everyone could see what was happening to me. As I looked around the room, every eye appeared closed. Some had their heads bowed, while others faced the heavens, stretching forth uplifted hands.

I heard Pastor Tate whisper into the microphone, "Everyone, lift your hands in praise to the God of Israel."

I lifted my arms in obedience. The ecstasy I felt was higher than anything I experienced from using drugs. It was beyond euphoria. I knew I was sensing the presence of Almighty God Himself.

After this period of worship and praise, we sat down as Pastor Tate began to give the message out of the Bible. He was not speaking on a subject, like we hear so many clergy do, but rather, he was reading Scriptures, verse by verse, and expounding on their meaning and relevance for our lives today.

His style was completely engrossing. I could have listened for hours. He would leave the main text often, asking us to turn to other areas of the Bible to prove his interpretation. He contended that the Bible never contradicted itself, and that we should never base our assessments on just one Scripture without the support of other verses. Everything he shared that day made so much sense.

At the end of the chapter, he closed his Bible and asked, "Will everyone please bow your head and close your eyes in prayer? I don't want one eye opened."

I felt my heart pounding as I knew what was coming. Pastor Tate continued, "If you want to receive Jesus Christ into your heart as Lord and Savior, please raise your hand high, so I can see it. No one else is looking, just God and me. His acknowledgement is much more important than mine."

A struggle raged inside of me. I thought, *What about Donna? What would she say? My mother will be so upset! How will I tell her?*

Just then, Pastor Tate spoke up, "Christians, please pray. Lives hang in the balance. If you feel a tug at your heart, please don't delay. God is speaking to you. You won't regret asking Jesus into your heart. God wants you to have real peace. I see that hand. And that one too. Any more? Please obey the Spirit."

I could hold back no longer. I lifted my hand high for him to see. It felt like an electric current charging through me when Pastor Tate acknowledged my desire to accept Jesus as my Messiah. "I see that hand. Another one of Israel has found his Messiah. You can put it down," Pastor Tate said in a reverent voice.

Instantly, I felt a calm that was indescribable. I felt pure and clean, like I had entered into the very gates of heaven.

Pastor Tate continued, "With all eyes closed and all heads still bowed, I want all who raised their hands to come down to the altar and kneel. Come on, everyone who lifted his hand."

I was stunned. I had no idea that he would ask us to come forward. But as soon as I saw others walking forward, I got out of my seat and went too. A counselor came over to me as I knelt at the altar. I told him that I was a Jew who now believed, without a doubt, that Jesus was my Messiah and Lord.

The counselor hugged me and told me to repeat a prayer with him, "Forgive me, oh God of Israel, for all my sins against You. I realize that only the blood of the Lamb can cleanse me of my sins. I confess my belief in Jesus as my Lord and Messiah. Come into my heart, Lord Jesus, and make me a brand new person. Amen."

The man hugged me a second time—tears flooding his eyes. Pastor Tate had ended the service while we were praying. He came down from the pulpit and gave me a hug.

"You realize that as a Jew, you have not changed your religion? You are now a Messianic believer. He was your Messiah all the time. You just didn't know it."

I was so happy as others in the congregation hugged me and welcomed me into the kingdom. Gary and Debbie were exuberant as they embraced me, too.

On the way home, I asked them to pray for me that I might have wisdom on how to share this with Donna and the rest of my family. They both prayed for me. When I walked into the door of my apartment, I couldn't help smiling. I felt so good inside. I went over to Donna and tried to kiss her. She pushed me away.

"Donna, I love you," I told her.

"Yeah? So what happened at the church?" she asked.

"Well, I received Jesus as my Messiah and Lord," I said softly, trying not to upset her.

"Oh, good! Now you can go to church every week with Debbie and Gary. You're part of their little family now," Donna said angrily.

I tried to reason with her, but there was no way she would listen. "And what will you tell your mother and father? They better not blame this on me," Donna warned.

"I'll take care of that. Don't worry!" I assured her.

Donna was watching television. I found the show quite boring. I picked up my Bible and began reading.

Donna jumped down my throat, "I can't believe you're into this. It's like a cult. You're a different person now!"

I smiled at her, "Yes, Donna. I am a different person. Jesus came into my life, and I'll never be the same again."

She became so angry that we got into an argument. I realized that I couldn't read the Bible in front of her. I had to do it in private.

The next day, after Donna left for work, I noticed some radical changes. The words I read in the Bible were filled with life. It seemed as if God Himself was talking directly to me through those printed words on the pages. I opened the Bible to the Gospel of John, chapter 3, verses 1 through 7:

> There was a man of the Pharisees, named Nicodemus, a ruler of the Jews:
>
> The same came to Jesus by night, and said unto him, Rabbi, we know that thou art a teacher come from God: for no man can do these miracles that thou doest, except God be with him.
>
> Jesus answered and said unto him, Verily, verily, I say unto thee, Except a man be born again, he cannot see the kingdom of God.
>
> Nicodemus saith unto him, How can a man be born when he is old? can he enter the second time into his mother's womb, and be born?

Jesus answered, Verily, verily, I say unto thee, Except a man be born of water and of the Spirit, he cannot enter into the kingdom of God.

That which is born of the flesh is flesh; and that which is born of the Spirit is spirit.

Marvel not that I said unto thee, Ye must be born again.

I now understood what Jesus was saying. All of us are first born of the flesh. This describes the physical birth from our mother's fleshly womb, and "the water" describes the embryonic sack bursting forth its water. However, Jesus was telling Nicodemus that man must have a second birth, without which he cannot even understand the Kingdom of God. This second birth is a birth in the Spirit, and Jesus gives the only way one can obtain this second birth, further down in the same chapter, verses 16 through 18.

For God so loved the world, that he gave his only begotten Son, that whosoever believeth in him should not perish, but have everlasting life.

For God sent not his Son into the world to condemn the world; but that the world through him might be saved.

He that believeth on him is not condemned: but he that believeth not is condemned already, because he hath not believed in the name of the only begotten Son of God.

God was confirming in his Word the steps of faith I had already taken. Yet, the greatest witness that God's *Ruach Hakodesh* (Holy Spirit) was truly within me came as I set out on the routine course of daily living. It was then that the miracle of deliverance was made manifest in my life.

I went upstairs to work on a new script I was writing. I opened my desk drawer and saw a bag of Mexican Gold marijuana. Previously, I would have immediately started rolling a joint. No one had preached to me that it is ungodly to use drugs. Nor had I read anything about it. I just realized that I didn't need drugs anymore. Even the *idea* of drug use seemed detestable. I took the bag into the bathroom and flushed it down the toilet. I went back into my room and gathered together all the drug paraphernalia, cigarette papers and pipes, and threw them in the garbage. I never would have done this on my own, without the *Ruach Hakodesh* giving me the power to overcome my addiction.

I thought to myself, *What else is in my life that I need to get rid of?*

I went downstairs and flipped through my rock music record collection. All of them brought back things of the past that I no longer wanted to associate with. So much of the music I had listened to was drug-related, or stressed illicit sex, liberal philosophies, and eastern mystical thoughts inconsistent with biblical teaching. I started throwing out all my albums. Yeshua gave me a clean slate, and I wanted to get rid of anything that would hold me back from living a holy life.

I went through the refrigerator and the closets and pulled out every bottle of liquor and wine, dumping the contents into the sink. I threw the empty bottles into the garbage.

I thought about the other area in my life that needed deliverance. I remembered the pornographic books, magazines, and films in my upstairs office. I went upstairs and threw them all away.

Next, the books in my library needed cleansing. I had collected various titles on radical thought. I threw away my leftist political books, including a copy of *The Communist Manifesto*. Then I gathered all the false religious titles, including *I Ching* and other books on the occult and eastern philosophies. I had filled dozens of paper bags with the vestiges of what once composed my thought life. I was so involved with the task at hand that I didn't hear Donna return from her day at work. She stood at the door of my office, staring at me.

"What are you doing?" she asked.

"I'm getting rid of some things that are displeasing to the Lord," I told her.

Donna had a puzzled look on her face as she reached into one of the bags and pulled out the hardcover edition of the authorized autobiography of the Beatles. She knew how much I loved this group. I had collected all their records.

"You're throwing away this book? You better not throw away anything of mine," she warned, as she turned and walked downstairs.

I followed her down as she walked into the kitchen, inspecting some of the other garbage bags. She couldn't believe that I had thrown out all the booze.

"Why did you throw all this away?" Donna confronted me.

"Donna, I want to honor God in all the things I do. We don't need all this garbage in the house. I got rid of all my porno books and my drugs. I even cleared off my record shelves. Don't you realize who Jesus is? He is the Messiah, God's only begotten Son. He died on the cross for you and me! Donna, you went to the Catholic church, and you don't know who He is? What did they teach you there?" I challenged her.

I now know I was being unfair to sincere Catholics, yet I was angry that she didn't seem to understand her own religion. It seemed that all my Christian friends from the neighborhood had negative appraisals of their religious upbringing.

"I can't take this. You've really flipped out. I mean, you've gone nuts!" Donna said in disgust.

"I've never been more sane in my life. Donna, you don't know what type of person I really was—deep inside. If it wasn't for the Messiah, I probably would have wound up dead with a drug overdose. Donna, please try and understand. Jesus wants you to believe in Him, too," I tried to convince her.

"I believe in God, but in my own way. I don't need to hear you preach to me," she said as she made her way to the door.

"Where are you going?" I asked her.

"To my parents' house. I've got to get out of here," she said as she slammed the door. I prayed hard, asking God to help me deal with Donna in the same way that He gave me power to overcome the bad habits in my life. Yet, I realized that the things I had thrown away were subject to *my* desires and mine alone. I couldn't make Donna believe in the Messiah. She was an individual, and no matter how much I hurt for her, she had to make that choice on her own. I remembered the Scripture I had read in the Gospel of John, chapter 6, verse 44, "No man can come to me, except the Father which hath sent me draw him. . . ."

I knew at that moment I needed to beseech the Lord to draw Donna to Himself by His Spirit.

• TWENTY-THREE •

CHARIOTS OF FIRE

I began attending Evangel Church on a weekly basis, including Sunday school at 9:30 A.M., the morning worship service at 10:45, and the evening service at 6:30. Donna didn't like me going so much, but after several months she accepted it as part of my life. She remained true to her promise of not setting foot in the place.

Evangel was a body of believers composed of a healthy mix of rich and poor, black, white, and Hispanic. Pastor Tate was a dedicated man of God who loved people and demonstrated it by hugging everyone walking out the door after the morning worship service. In the evening service he would open the altars for a time of prayer.

He would tell the congregation, "The service is dismissed. Those who wish to fellowship, please leave silently and go to the fellowship room for some coffee and cookies, but this sanctuary is now a place of prayer."

I found myself kneeling at the altar, along with at least a third of the congregation. I spent time on my knees, beseeching God to save my wife and all my loved ones and friends. It was a time of tears and deeper commitment in my life. Sometimes, Pastor Tate and other members of the church would walk behind me and lay their hands gently on my back, encouraging me with prayers of their own. I quickly realized that Evangel Church was full of electricity. It was alive with the reality of God. I felt as if I were back in the early church during the days of the Bible, as I witnessed dozens accepting Yeshua as their Messiah at the altars week after week. People from all walks of life were becoming believers. I was amazed to see not only businessmen, laborers, and hippies giving their lives to God, but prostitutes, alcoholics, and drug addicts as well. They were all set free from their former lifestyles and becoming vibrant followers of the Lord God of Israel. I had never seen such a dramatic demonstration of God's power while growing up in the synagogue or in any church. This was something new and exciting as I looked forward to every service, wondering what miracles God would perform next.

Pastor Tate had his own miraculous testimony. He had been reared by parents who were loyal to the Lord and brought him to church while he was still in the cradle. In October of 1935, at the age of four, he had contracted infantile paralysis, better known as polio. It damaged the muscles in a leg and an arm, making it difficult for the young boy to walk without dragging his left foot. The illness was confirmed by a local health officer and later by a district health officer of the state of New Jersey, and as a result the Tate residence was quarantined. Pastor Tate showed me old newspaper articles that told the story of the controversy that ensued between his parents and the New Jersey Board of Health when the Tates refused to call a physician, believing that God Himself would heal their child. A newspaper article reported that just before the state could take any actions against the Tates, a miracle occurred. Within a week after a minister prayed with little James Tate he began to walk, and was seen riding his scooter outside his home. The newspapers reported the miracle in a series of articles, and God was given all the glory. To see Pastor Tate today, you would never know he had had such a dreadful disease. He walks without a limp and has full mobility of his arm.

The pastor referred to his miracle from time to time. "You know, to this day, I have hardly any muscle joining my left arm to my shoulder. Almost all of it was completely destroyed by the polio. Just the other day, my doctor saw an X-ray of my arm and said, 'I don't understand how you could move your arm without any muscle.' I just answered him by saying, 'I just move it, like this, and God does the rest!' as I rotated and waved my arm in the air."

The congregation would break out in applause, praising God for the miracle the Lord had performed with our pastor.

As I look back, there were many reasons God was alive in Evangel Church. First of all, Pastor Tate would conduct a period of worship, praise, and prayer, creating an atmosphere helping free the congregation to receive fully that which the Holy Spirit would impart. The second reason was Pastor Tate's commitment to teaching the inerrant Word of God.

When I was a child at the synagogue, the Torah would be carried through the congregation, and we would kiss the end of our prayer shawls and touch the Torah in respect. However, when it was read in Hebrew, we had no idea what the words meant. Pastor Tate taught me a new way to reverence the Word of God, by reading and studying it everyday.

Pastor Tate often reinforced the importance of God's Word in our lives by quoting from Second Timothy, chapter 3, verses 16 through 17:

All scripture is given by inspiration of God, and is profitable for doctrine, for reproof, for correction, for instruction in righteousness:
That the man of God may be perfect (mature), thoroughly furnished unto all good works.

He would not usually preach topical sermons, with cute titles and themes. Rather, he would teach us directly from the Bible in an expository manner.

He announced from the pulpit, "For the next six months I will be preaching on the book of Romans."

Every Sunday morning he'd dissect the book, word by word and chapter by chapter. We would be taught the historical background of each book as well as the impact it had on the early church. Then, he helped us apply it to our daily lives. When Pastor Tate taught, the congregation hung on his every word. People came from miles away to hear his anointed teaching.

"The Bible is not some ancient book written for times past," he said. "It has relevance for us today. God can speak to us through His Word, and our lives can be dramatically changed." He instilled in us the basic doctrines of the Bible. One of the most important biblical doctrines he taught us was sanctification:

Daily, we must read the Bible and ask God in prayer to illuminate His Word and show us areas in our lives that need correction. The Bible declares that every one of us has been born with a sinful *old nature* which we inherited from the fall of Adam and Eve. Once we are born again, God's Holy Spirit takes up residence in us and guides us into all truth. The Holy Spirit helps us comprehend the Word of God, and He convicts us (causes us to be sorrowful) for those areas of our lives in which we have fallen short. The next step is to confess these shortcomings and ask God to empower us by His Holy Spirit to overcome these sins. By practicing this everyday, we are doing what the Bible commands in the book of Ephesians, chapter 4, verses 22 through 24: shedding off the old man (the old sinful nature) and putting on the new man (the character of Jesus). Our main goal is to day by day become more like Jesus Himself and truly become a new creature in Messiah, "created in righteousness and true holiness."

He would often cite the words in the book of James: "But be ye doers of the word, and not hearers only, deceiving your own selves" (James 1:22).

Another important lesson he taught us was that the measure of the fullness of the Spirit in a believer was not in how many gifts he has, but in how much fruit. He would point to the Gospel of Matthew, chapter 7, verse 20: "by their fruits Ye shall know them." Pastor Tate explained the difference between the fruits of the Spirit and the flesh (the works of the old sinful nature), referring to the book of Galatians, chapter 5, verses 19 through 24:

Now the works of the flesh are manifest, which are these; Adultery, fornication, uncleanness, lasciviousness,

Idolatry, witchcraft, hatred, variance, emulations, wrath, strife, sedition, heresies,

Envying, murders, drunkenness, revellings, and such like: of the which I tell you before, as I have also told you in time past, that they which do such things shall not inherit the kingdom of God.

But the fruit of the Spirit is love, joy, peace, longsuffering, gentleness, goodness, faith,

Meekness, temperance: against such there is no law.

And they that are Christ's have crucified the flesh with the affections and lusts.

"Each one of us must make choices between the Spirit and the flesh every day, moment by moment," he would often admonish us. "It's as if we have two bears within us, one is the Spirit Bear and the other is the Flesh Bear. Each is kept in its own cage, until temptation comes. Then the cages are opened so the bears can fight. Whichever bear we have fed the most will be the one who wins."

He would bolster this illustration with the Scripture found in Galatians, chapter 5, verses 17 through 18:

> For the flesh lusteth against the Spirit, and the Spirit against the flesh: and these are so contrary the one to the other: so that ye cannot do the things that ye would.
> But if ye be led of the Spirit, ye are not under the law.

He told us *how* to feed the Spirit Bear: "His food is prayer, and study in the Word of God. The degree to which we feed the Spirit determines how successful we are in overcoming the temptations we face everyday."

Though he was one of the most godly men I have ever known, he would *never* talk down to his congregation. Whenever he came to a difficult area of exhortation or rebuke as revealed in the holy Scriptures, he included himself as needing to hear what the Spirit of God was saying: "Here's an area in which God has been dealing with me." Often he would say, "I really need to repent of this one!"

He continually emphasized that we should never elevate any man to take the place of God. "People will almost always disappoint you," he warned us, "but Jesus will never fail you. He is the only one who is perfect. We are all on the way toward becoming perfect, but we will never reach perfection until we see Him face to face. If tomorrow you were to hear that I did some horrible thing, don't you dare let it shake your faith in Jesus. I might fail you, but He never will."

Little did I realize how many times these words would help me during my years in the ministry.

Pastor Tate taught us that Jesus in the Great Commission gave charge to all believers in the church to "preach the gospel to every creature" (Mark 16:15). It was not the job of the clergy only, but the duty of every person in the body to reach out to the unsaved. He would also cite First Peter, chapter 2, verse 9:

> But ye are a chosen generation, a royal priesthood, an holy nation, a peculiar people; that should show forth the praises of him who hath called you out of darkness into his marvelous light.

He strongly urged new believers to get involved in ministry immediately. I was shocked when he asked me if I would publicly give my testimony in church after I had attended the services for only several weeks. My immediate reaction was to hedge.

Seeing my hesitation, Pastor Tate told me, "Just pray about it. I know that many people would be reached, hearing your testimony."

After that I went home and began agonizing over whether I was even capable of speaking publicly. The phone rang, and Pastor Tate was on the line encouraging me to step out in faith.

I was not the only one whom he called on to do these things. He would persuade everyone in the assembly to do his or her part. Yet, his warm, compassionate spirit helped instill faith in every individual to perform far and above what was humanly possible. Some of the old-timers in the church didn't like the pastor's approach in allowing new believers to be used in ministry so quickly.

"That fellow's only been saved a few weeks. How does Pastor Tate know he won't backslide tomorrow?" I heard one ask. "I just don't feel people should be even singing in the choir until they have proven that they are truly saved!"

Pastor Tate knew of their apprehension and would address it from the pulpit.

Some of you are concerned that I allow a new believer to get involved immediately in the life of this assembly. I tell you that the rewards far outweigh the risks. I have tried it both ways, and I have found that the bad apples show themselves much quicker. But even greater than that, the majority of these "babes in Messiah" become vibrant soul winners and dedicated followers of the Messiah. Besides, these new believers are so fired up for the Lord, maybe some of us old-timers will catch their spirit and get off the pews and do something wonderful for the Lord.

Not only did Pastor Tate ask me to give a brief testimony before the congregation, but as he got to know me better, he allowed me to preach the entire service. I was humbled by the fact that he would consider me for such a mission. I would take hours and hours studying the Bible and praying before preparing notes for my sermon. From the first time I stepped in the pulpit, I felt as if I belonged. It was in the pulpit that I experienced the greatest sense of fulfillment, even greater than producing religious feature films. I could actually sense the anointing of God, His *Ruach Hakodesh*, in a powerful way inside me and all around me as I preached God's Word.

It was so strong the first time I preached that I was shaking by the end of the message, unable to effectively give an altar call. After preaching, I began to wonder if God was calling me to become a full-time minister.

What if the desire He placed in my heart to produce religious motion pictures was only His way of leading me to this point in my life? I rationalized. *How can any motion picture I would produce ever compare with the power contained in the greatest script of all time, the Holy Bible?*

I was ready to give up my entire film career to become a pastor. I was convinced that God wanted me in the pulpit. I had a meeting with Pastor Tate about this idea.

"I believe that God has a special calling for your life. I am amazed at how young a believer you are, yet you have an amazing grasp of the Scriptures," he told me.

"Pastor, I believe that the highest calling anyone can have is to be a pastor. I realize that there is a high price and responsibility, but that doesn't frighten me! There is only one problem," I began explaining to him.

"What is that, Warren?" he asked.

"It's my wife, Donna. She isn't even a believer. I'm sure she would be against it," I answered.

He opened his Bible to First Timothy, chapter 3, verses 2 through 7.

"Let me read you the qualifications needed for any man seeking a full-time office in the ministry," he said, then read the Scripture:

> A bishop (or pastor) then must be blameless, the husband of one wife, vigilant, sober, of good behavior, given to hospitality, apt to teach;
>
> Not given to wine, no striker, not greedy of filthy lucre; but patient, not a brawler, not covetous;
>
> One that ruleth well his own house, having his children in subjection with all gravity;
>
> (For if a man know not how to rule his own house, how shall he take care of the church of God?) Not a novice, lest being lifted up with pride he fall into condemnation of the devil.
>
> Moreover he must have a good report of them which are without; lest he fall into reproach and the snare of the devil.

"Warren, as you can see, the scriptural criteria for a full time minister are quite formidable. In the book of James, the Bible admonishes, 'My brethren, be not many masters (teachers), knowing that we shall receive the greater condemnation' (James 3:1). This alludes to how serious a calling the pastorate is, because of the effect our lives have on so many people."

Then Pastor Tate encouraged me by pointing out that with God all things are possible. However, God would have to do a work in Donna's heart before I could ever become a pastor.

After my meeting with Pastor Tate, I went home to talk with Donna. At what I felt was the appropriate time, I told her my deepest desire.

"Donna, I feel God is leading me to change my career."

"Yeah? Change it to what?" she asked suspiciously.

"I believe that God would have me become a pastor," I said, looking her squarely in the eyes.

"Fine! You could do that!" she said smiling.

"You mean you'll let me?" I jumped up in excitement.

"You can do whatever you like, but I won't be around when you do it!" she said in anger.

"But, Donna, I can't proceed without you. I can only be a pastor if you are with me," I pleaded.

"We'll get a divorce, so I won't be in your way," she responded.

"Donna, a divorced man cannot be a pastor!"

"Well, then, I guess you've got a problem, haven't you? Because I didn't marry you to become a pastor's wife," she announced as she walked upstairs to go to sleep.

I was devastated as I weighed her words.

How could God be calling me if He has not put that same desire in Donna's heart?

I came to the conclusion that either God was not calling me into full-time ministry, or Satan was using Donna to stand in the way.

During the next few weeks, my faith was put to the ultimate test. Donna would turn the heat of her displeasure up to an unbearable temperature. I began to feel that there were truly evil spirits provoking her to try my faith.

Donna became extremely angry when I told her I was taking baptism classes at the church and asked her if she would at least come to my baptism.

"There's no way that I'm setting a foot in that church. So, you're getting baptized? Don't you think it's about time you told your parents?" she challenged me.

"I will tell them after I am baptized," I promised her.

Donna was true to her promise. Though I coaxed her right up to the very evening of my baptism, she did not come to the church.

Initially, I had immense problems with the idea of baptism. As a Jewish believer, this concept seemed foreign to me. As a Messianic Jew I had not "converted" to a new religion called Christianity. The name Christianity simply means "followers of Christ (or Messiah)." The church is composed of Jews and Gentiles who believe that there is only one god, the Lord God of Israel. Yeshua (Jesus) and His early followers never renounced their heritage. As a matter of fact, the early church was composed of Jewish believers who still attended the synagogue on Saturdays and fellowshiped with one another on Sundays. These followers of Messiah still celebrated all the Jewish holidays and observances, including circumcision. The main difference between a Jew who believes in Messiah and one who does not is that we who are Messianic Jews know that the observance of Jewish festivals and rituals does not bring about salvation. The only way for any person to be saved is through belief in Yeshua. In light of this, Gentile believers do not need to follow the Jewish customs, but there is nothing more beautiful than observing the same Jewish customs that Jesus and the early church observed, but with New Covenant understanding.

Finally I asked a fellow Messianic Jew about this practice of baptism.

"I guess you weren't raised as an Orthodox Jew?" he smiled. "We still practice ritual bathing for purification. It's called a *mikveh*. This bath is also required when a Gentile decides to convert to Judaism."

Having been reared in the conservative branch of Judaism, I had never heard about the mikveh. I purchased a book from a Jewish religious bookstore and studied all about the mikveh ritual and discovered that it was a Jewish practice that went back before the time of Jesus and John the Baptist. Suddenly, I understood that the nice Jewish boy, John the Baptist, was not doing something strange in the sight of the Jewish people of his times, but rather, mikvehs were quite common.

The early church baptized, using full immersion, since it was composed of Jewish Messianic believers who understood this to be a New Covenant mikveh. At Evangel Church they also baptized by full immersion. The candidates would first give brief testimonies in front of the congregation and then make their way down into the tank. Pastor Tate would be inside waiting.

Once the candidate was in the tank, Pastor Tate would say, "Based on your confession that Jesus Christ is truly your Lord and Savior, I now baptize you in the name of the Father, the Son, and the Holy Spirit." He would then immerse the person fully under the water. When the believer came out, the band would play the candidate's favorite spiritual song, and the congregation joined in and sang.

The night of my baptism I was dressed in a black gown, which symbolized the color of death. I stepped up to the microphone. "God had been trying to reach me ever since I was a little boy," I said. "He used a childhood dream, religious movies, and another Jewish boy in my bar mitzvah class. I got involved with the drug scene and radical political ideology, but God sent His witnesses on the street and in the Port Authority Bus Terminal to confront me with the Gospel. I want to thank two people who are sitting here tonight for being obedient in bringing me to Evangel Church—

Gary and Debbie King. Let me close by saying that I thank God for Pastor Tate for the way he shares his faith in the Word and in his deeds. I am so happy that he is my pastor."

As I made my way to the baptismal tank, I realized that this was only the outward sign of what had already taken place inwardly. Through my belief in Messiah, my old sinful nature was already crucified with Him, and I had now become a new creation. As I was immersed in the waters of baptism, I realized that it represented my death and burial with the Messiah. As I rose out of the water, it symbolized my being raised with Messiah in newness of life. The Bible calls baptism the circumcision of the heart. The congregation sang my favorite song, "I Have Decided to Follow Jesus."

When I returned home, Donna was quite cold to me. She was watching a television show that I didn't find particularly edifying, so I went upstairs to my office to spend time reading my Bible. I no longer read the Bible in front of Donna because it upset her.

As my hand touched the Bible, I heard Donna yell from downstairs, "What are you going to do, read the Bible?" A chill ran down my spine. I felt as if Satan himself was using Donna to challenge me.

How did Donna know that I was reaching for the Bible? I wondered.

I immediately ran downstairs to confront her.

"Yes, I was going to read my Bible. Is that such a sin? What's wrong with reading my Bible? Tell me."

"You're away at church all day and you have no time for me anymore!" Donna exclaimed.

"Donna, you know I hate television. Whenever you watch it, I've always done something else. In the past, I'd put on earphones and listen to my music. I'd roll up a joint and smoke it. You didn't seem to mind when I did that. But here I am, reading the Bible, the Word of God, and you're putting this trip on me," I reasoned with her.

She began to shout, releasing her pent-up emotions, her frustrations. I realized that Satan was provoking her because the Bible says that Satan is the author of confusion.

I pointed her toward the mirror.

"Look in that mirror at you and me. Donna, see my face? There is perfect peace written all over it. Now, look at you. Look at how flustered your face is. You don't realize this, but Satan has been using you. . . ."

Donna flipped into a rage.

"So you think I'm possessed! That's it, Warren, I've had it! I can't take any more!" Nothing I could say would calm her. While she screamed at me, I began to pray silently.

"Satan, I come against you in the name of *Yeshua HaMashiach* (Jesus the Messiah)," I prayed. "Satan, get out of my house and out of my marriage. You have no place here. This is God's home, and it is sanctified. Now, Lord God, put a hedge of protection around Donna and me that Satan will never penetrate again. I pray this in Yeshua's name."

The moment I finished praying, Donna stopped yelling. Tears began to stream down her face. I got up slowly and put my arms around her to comfort her.

"Donna, I love you. You don't understand what I was saying. You aren't possessed. I was merely pointing out how Satan was influencing you to be upset with me."

"There you go again," she said, pulling away from me.

"No, Donna, please don't pull away. I really love you. It's all over. Please believe me. This will never happen again," I said to her, once again putting my arms around her. The Lord seemed to answer my prayer. Things became much calmer in the weeks ahead. Daily, I would bind Satan in the name of Yeshua and ask the God of Israel to protect my marriage.

Twenty-Four

Tender Mercies

Donna invited her parents over to our apartment for dinner. It was an informal meal. I always got along well with Donna's folks and had decided that they would be the first to know of my new faith in Messiah. Donna already knew what I was going to share, and she was nervous about how her parents would accept it, since they were Catholics. Donna began prodding me to tell them.

"Warren, you have something you wanted to share with my parents, didn't you?"

"You're pregnant?" Donna's mother guessed wrongly.

"No way!" said Donna laughing.

"No, it's just that you might have been wondering where I've been every Sunday the last several months," I explained nervously.

"Yes, Warren. I meant to ask you, where have you been on Sundays?" my father-in-law, Joe, said in a joking manner.

"I've been going to church," I stated.

There was complete silence in the room.

"What do you mean, you've been going to church?" Joe asked me.

"I have become a believer in Jesus the Messiah," I clarified.

Instead of getting upset, as Donna and I thought, both of her parents had tears in their eyes. They were touched by what God had done.

Donna, seeing their tears, said jokingly, "You're both crying? You're happy he became a believer? I don't believe it. My own parents are going against me!"

Her parents scolded her for not seeing the wonderful miracle that had taken place in my life. They knew that only God Himself could have reached me.

Telling my parents wouldn't be as easy. I agonized over how to break it to them. I decided to confide in my mother first, since she was always the easiest to talk to. After spending many hours of prayer on my knees, I believed it was the right time. I rehearsed the words I would say to her over and over again in my mind as Donna and I drove up to my parents' home.

Once inside, I told my mother to sit down at the kitchen table because I had something very important to tell her. Donna sat down opposite my mother.

"You're having a baby?" she said, causing Donna and me to burst out in laughter.

"Why is it that you and my parents all think alike?" Donna remarked.

After the laughter subsided, I began.

"Mom, I need to tell you about some of the things I did in my life when I was living at home before I was married. Your son was not the little angel you always thought him to be. I used just about every drug in the book."

Concerned, my mom asked, "You used drugs? What kind of drugs?"

"Marijuana, LSD, speed, and probably many you've never heard of. While Dad was up here drinking with the police chief, I was downstairs smoking grass," I revealed.

"That plant you had growing downstairs, was that LSD?" she asked in all seriousness.

Donna started laughing. "LSD doesn't grow on trees!"

"No, Mom. That was a marijuana plant that I was growing in the downstairs bathroom," I chuckled.

"Oy vey! The chief of police used that bathroom. He didn't even know what that plant was," she laughed too.

I disclosed more.

"Mom, there are so many things that I never told you. Deep inside, I was always unhappy. I felt there had to be more of a purpose for life than waking up, going to work, and going back to sleep. I was searching for real peace. I looked into radical politics, and it wasn't there. Then I tried drugs, but that didn't help."

"I can't believe you used drugs!"

My voice shook as I divulged the truth.

"Mom, I finally found something that changed my life forever.

It gave me real peace. I'll never be the same again. I asked *Yeshua Ha Mashiach* (Jesus Christ) into my heart. I've been born again."

"You mean you became a Catholic?" she shouted.

"No, Mom. I was born a Jew and I'll die a Jew. I've become a Messianic believer. Jesus is the promised Jewish Messiah whom the rabbis rejected. They can't change the fact that He is our Messiah. It's time we Jews take Him back! The Gentiles have had Him for almost 2,000 years. It's our turn!" I declared, pounding my fist on the table.

All my mother could say was, "But I can't believe you used drugs."

I had expected my mother to disown me, or at least to call me a traitor to the faith. Yet, all she was concerned about was that I had used drugs.

I later shared with my father the same story. He reacted in a similar manner. However, God did a marvelous thing with my dad and me. No longer did I find myself arguing with him on political issues. I felt a tremendous love and burden for him. Every time I visited, I would put my arms around him, kiss him on his cheek, and tell him how much I loved and appreciated him. I had consistently done this with my mother, but there had always been a distance between my dad and me. Yeshua had forgiven me for my wrongdoing and showed compassion, and now it was my turn to demonstrate the character of Messiah to my dad and mom.

I began to tell everyone—my brother and sister, my aunts, uncles, and cousins. Most looked at me like I was crazy, but they treated me respectfully. Several called my mom and asked what is going on with Warren.

She would tell them, "Look, I don't care what Warren believes in. All I know is that he is a good kid. His belief in Jesus has made him a completely different person. He doesn't drink, smoke, gamble. I don't have to worry about him cheating on his wife and getting a divorce. The bottom line is Warren is a great son. You know what? Maybe some of the family should try believing in what he does. Maybe they'd be as happy as him."

Even my film company, Sunrise Productions, was prospering. At every shoot, I would share my testimony with the freelance crew I had hired.

At Evangel Church, Pastor Tate asked me to go into training to be a future elder of the church. I began attending meetings at his church office and looked forward to a time of special teaching and prayer.

At the same time, I studied Messianic Jewish thinking on my own. I read everything I could get my hands on and I began appreciating my heritage. Finally, I understood why God instituted the Jewish festivals. Everything in the Jewish Scriptures spoke either directly or in types about the coming of Messiah. I never realized how Jewish Jesus was. Judaism came alive for me as I celebrated the Passover seder, but for the first time as a believer in Messiah.

My burden was that all my family, friends, and even strangers that I met would get saved. I began to desire a chance to minister more using *all* my talents. If I couldn't become a pastor, then perhaps God would allow me to use my filmmaking talents to advance His kingdom. My seventh-grade prayer was reactivated on a daily basis.

"Oh, Lord God of Israel. I come to You in the name of my Messiah, *Yeshua Ha Mashiach*. You've given me the techniques and creative abilities to produce, write, direct, photograph, and edit films. Nothing would please me more than to be able to use my talents to reach millions with the Gospel through creative films and even religious commercials. Please God, provide a way in which I can be used by You in a mighty way. Amen."

At the same time, I was burdened with Donna's animosity toward my religious beliefs and finally asked Pastor Tate for a special meeting.

"I just don't know what to do," I poured out my heart to him. "Donna is so hostile toward the Gospel."

"Your marriage should be improving, not getting worse, with Jesus in your life. Does she pray with you?" he asked with deep concern.

"She definitely wouldn't pray with me. Pastor, I can't even talk about God in front of her. I have to read my Bible in secret. She treats me as if I were cheating on her with some woman instead of understanding that I am spending time with the King of kings," I complained.

"Warren, Donna surely knows that you are a true believer by now. You don't need to flaunt your faith in her face everyday. All you need to do is love her to the Messiah. Ask God to show you how you can express your love to her in new and different ways. She needs you to pay attention to her. Buy her some flowers! Is there anything that she always wanted but thinks she could never get?"

I couldn't think of anything in particular. As usual, Pastor Tate ended our session with a time of prayer. As we finished praying, I received a revelation.

"I believe that God has revealed to me the answer," I blurted out. "Donna always wanted to be a beautician, but never had the opportunity to go to beauty school."

"If you could afford to send her, this might be the very thing that will turn her around. Just tell her that the Lord has shown you that you should send her," he said encouraging me to proceed.

As soon as I came home, I confronted Donna with the good news.

"Honey, if you could have anything you wanted, what would it be?"

Donna looked at me strangely and answered sarcastically, "One million dollars and a trip far away from you."

I smiled, not taking her remark seriously.

"I was in prayer today, and I asked the Lord how I can be a blessing to you and show you that I love you very much."

"Oh, no! Here it comes," she said, rolling her eyes.

I put my arms around her.

"Donna, I want you to quit your job, because I want to send you to beauty school!"

I could see in her eyes that I had struck the right chord. At first she argued that we couldn't afford her going to school. I encouraged her, saying that if God was truly in this, then He would supply the finances needed. Little did I realize how my desire to show Donna love would end up leading her to make a decision to receive Jesus as her Savior.

God provided the necessary finances for Donna to begin attending school, and He showed me other ways to begin building back the love and respect that Donna once held for me. I would surprise her with flowers, cards, and with hand-written notes of love.

Then one day while in prayer, I remembered the words, ". . . What therefore God hath joined together, let not man put asunder" (Matt. 19:6). I thought about these words from Scripture and looked them up in the Gospel of Matthew. I wondered why these words popped into my head during prayer. Then I remembered my promise to Donna's parents that we would get married in the church. I knew that this was the Lord telling me that not only will this be a blessing to Donna's parents but it would also bind Donna and me together in a closer union under God.

When Donna came home I told her what I had received from the Lord.

"Donna, I really feel that God showed me that we are to get married a second time in the church. After all, we *did* promise your parents."

"That's a great idea, but, they're gonna want the wedding to take place in the Catholic church," she insisted.

I hesitated, then responded.

"I will do it, as long as they don't make me sign a paper saying that I must bring my children up Catholic."

Donna made the appointment with the priest. On the way over to the church, she broke the news to me. We were going to see Father Eilit, the priest we had seen prior to our first marriage. He was the one who had insisted on our signing papers to bring our children up in the Catholic church. I began to doubt that God was really in this as we made our way into the rectory.

When we entered his office, I noticed that his hair had turned gray since we had last seen him, just six years earlier. When he saw us he jumped up from his chair and immediately moved toward us and gave us each a hug. There was a glow on his face that I didn't remember seeing the last time.

"Didn't we meet once before?" he asked as he looked right at me.

"Yes, we were here several years ago to see if we could get married in the church, but there were problems then," Donna answered.

"What problems are you talking about?" he asked with concern.

"You told us that Warren would have to sign papers that he would allow the children to be raised Catholic. Warren is Jewish," she said calmly.

"Oh, that's all changed. You don't have to sign any papers. Not any more. Not since the Vatican II reforms," he assured us.

"Since last time we met, there have been some changes in my life," I interjected. "I became a Messianic believer. I received Jesus as my Messiah and Lord!"

A huge smile came over the priest's face as he got up and again hugged me. "That's wonderful, brother! Praise the Lord!" he exclaimed.

I was puzzled at the change in his attitude. This was not the same priest. Besides, I had never heard a priest call a lay person brother.

"There's been some changes in my life too, Warren," he said as he sat down. "Several years ago, I had a heart attack and almost died. While in the hospital, I recommitted my life to God. I was born again. My life will never be the same. Before this, I would never pray to God. I figured that when I prepared the Eucharist that this was as good as prayer. Boy was I wrong! Were you baptized, Warren?"

"Oh, yes. I had my *mikveh* at Evangel Church," I answered.

"You go to Evangel Church? Pastor Tate? He is such a wonderful man of God! I love him very much. So you were fully immersed? Just like the early church," he continued.

We must have conversed for an hour before Donna and I committed to getting married in the Catholic church. As we left the parsonage, Donna confessed that she was amazed that Father Eilit had become born again. She admitted being stunned when she heard he knew Pastor Tate.

Only a handful of people attended the wedding. However, God used this to bind Donna and me together spiritually. It was the beginning of a new, revitalized marriage. To this day, Donna and I wear a second wedding band, celebrating our second marriage to one another, this time in the church. Yet, the greatest miracle was yet to happen.

Returning late one night from a film shoot, I saw Donna and several young women sitting around the kitchen table. I had hardly laid my camera equipment down before I heard my name being called from the kitchen.

"Warren, come in here!" Donna yelled. I entered the kitchen. The women looked like they had seen a ghost.

Donna introduced me to her friends.

"Warren will know what to do. Pat, tell him what is happening."

Donna's friend Pat was shaking as she talked.

"There are some students at school who claim they are witches. They told me that they're going to put a curse on me."

I realized how upset these girls were. I began to ask them some questions.

"Are all of you here Christians?"

They told me they were Catholic.

"Do each of you believe in Jesus," I continued, "that he is your Lord and Savior?"

Each indicated that she believed in Jesus, except for Donna, whom I did not embarrass with the question.

I continued to minister.

"If you truly believe in Jesus as your Lord and Savior, then you have nothing to fear. The Bible declares, '. . . greater is he (the Holy Spirit) that is in you, than he (Satan) that is in the world' (1 John 4:4). Each one of you needs to confess your sins and commit your life to Jesus, if you haven't already. I promise you, if you do this, God will protect you."

We ended in prayer. The women left, thanking me for the prayer and counsel. I began to put away my camera gear as I felt Donna tapping me on the shoulder. I turned toward her.

"Warren, I don't want you to go crazy when I ask you this. Do you promise not to go crazy?" Donna asked.

"Of course. What is it?" I asked.

She continued, "Will you please pray with me to accept the Lord?" she continued. "I want Jesus in my heart as Lord and Savior."

My eyes immediately welled up with tears as I embraced Donna, asking her to repeat the sinner's prayer after me. God had answered my prayers, and Donna became a born-again believer that night. If it wasn't for Pastor Tate's wise advice about loving Donna to Jesus, I would have never sent Donna to beauty school, and who knows when she would have come to accept the Messiah?

• TWENTY-FIVE •

UNCERTAIN GLORY

Two months after Donna became a believer, she was attending the morning services with me at Evangel Church. It was a miracle that I never would have believed could happen. For three years, I had faithfully attended Evangel Church and had been taught the essentials of the faith.

I was still petitioning the Lord daily, asking Him to open a door of full-time ministry that would utilize my talents as a filmmaker. Though Donna had become a believer, she still opposed my becoming a pastor. However, she said she wouldn't object if I could get a job in my field with a ministry.

Everyday at twelve noon, I watched a Christian TV show called "The 700 Club" on WPIX, one of New York City's independent television stations. I felt encouraged watching the host, Pat Robertson, as he interviewed people who had made a profession of faith in the Messiah. I also enjoyed his analysis of world events from the Christian perspective. One day there was a TV spot asking for believers with experience in television production to send in their resumes to the Christian Broadcasting Network (CBN) in Virginia Beach, Virginia.

I immediately sent a letter and resume to CBN. Weeks later, I received a form letter saying that my resume would be kept on file. It stated that at this present time there was no need for a person with my abilities. To say I was disappointed would be an understatement.

I continued developing my Madison Avenue company, Sunrise Productions, making five-minute films for Platinum, Kodak, and the Apple Growers of America for a new division of J. Walter Thompson Advertising, though my heart wasn't in it.

I was tired of producing commercials for products I didn't necessarily believe in. The truth was that I'd rather tell people about the Messiah than deodorant, cereal, or how to have cleaner underwear!

In the midst of shooting a major infomercial for J. Walter Thompson, I received a call from Tom Dennis at CBN. He said he was very interested in seeing some samples of my work. I shipped my sample reel to CBN and received a call back later that week. Tom said he wanted me to fly down to Virginia for an interview.

He met me at the airport and brought me to CBN's executive offices in Virginia Beach. The job he was considering me for was with CBN's in-house agency, Victor King Advertising. This group had the task of producing all the TV commercials that went into "The 700 Club" TV show. At that time, the spots were rather archaic and simple. They wanted more of a "Madison Avenue look." However, Tom told me that the studios were overbooked, and they needed someone who could overcome the obstacles. He took me on a tour of CBN's TV studios, then in Portsmouth, Virginia. They consisted of two studios, one housing "The 700 Club" set and the other open for various production. Tom introduced me to an executive of network operations. As I shook his hand, I asked, "Do you have any film equipment here?"

He stared at me.

"Film equipment? We don't use film here! This is a video house! Film is a thing of the past," he exclaimed.

"Well, Tom wants a Madison Avenue look. And every national advertising agency in the country still uses film because it has a better quality look," I responded.

His face became red:

"Well, I'll fight you on this one! There will be no film used at CBN!"

As we drove away from the studios, Tom asked me, "What do you think we need to do to get the job done?"

"The first thing you should do is get rid of your colleague. If that's the way he carries on I wonder if he is even a Christian," I said in disgust.

Tom Dennis laughed at my observation and continued, "I believe that you'll fit in just fine here."

I flew home with the job offered to me. I told Tom that I would pray about it, after talking it over with Donna. They told me that they could pay me $15,000 a year plus benefits. This was far less than what I was earning at the time. Furthermore, I would move from being the president of my own production company on Madison Avenue to a company that didn't even have the film equipment necessary for me to use my skills competently. I was disappointed, but for some reason beyond my rational mind, I felt I should move to Virginia Beach and take the job.

As far as I was concerned, the real test was what Donna would think. To my surprise she agreed that I should take the job. She wanted me to go there for six months without her, to see if I really liked it. I agreed. Donna had a great job as a beautician in a posh beauty parlor. Furthermore, both our parents lived in Linden, and Virginia Beach was 400 miles away. For her to consent to a possible move was a miracle in itself, especially in light of the low salary.

Early the next day, Donna had left for work. I was alone in the apartment asking God for an answer. Pastor Tate had agreed that this could be of the Lord. Yet, I realized that I would miss Evangel Church and Pastor Tate. Deep inside, I felt that CBN was the answer to my daily prayers to have my filmmaking talent used by God. Yet, I wondered what would happen to my family and friends who still had not accepted Jesus as their Messiah. Who would be around to tell them the truth concerning Messiah?

I cried out to God in prayer, asking Him to clearly let me know His perfect will for my life. As I prayed, a Scripture number and verse came to mind. It was from the book of Jeremiah, chapter 6, verse 10. I immediately opened my Bible and read:

> To whom shall I speak, and give warning, that they may hear? behold, their ear is uncircumcised, and they cannot hearken: behold, the word of the Lord is unto them a reproach; they have no delight in it.

As I read the Scripture and the verses that directly followed it, I realized that the God of Israel was talking about the nation of Israel. These were the circumcised, yet God was saying that it was possible for His people to have uncircumcised ears, unable to hear the Word of God. I began to pace the apartment and cry out to God for the salvation of my family and friends.

I said to myself, *How could I leave them? They need to hear the truth. There are no other believers in the family. Surely, I can't leave.*

I glanced out the window. There was a morning fog that misted the street. I noticed a silhouetted figure in what appeared to be a robe coming down the street.

I asked myself, "Is this real or is it a vision?"

I watched as the figure got closer. It was a man dressed in a dark monk's robe. A giant cross dangled from his rope-like belt and moved with his every step. I had to find out if this was some kind of apparition.

The man was passing my apartment, and I couldn't find my shoes. I grabbed my keys from the kitchen counter to open the dead-bolt lock on the front door and ran outside looking for the man. He was walking quickly across the street, half a block away. I ran after him in my bare feet.

As I ran, I yelled, "Hey you, please stop!"

The man didn't seem to hear what I was saying. Finally, as I approached, several yards away, he stopped walking and turned toward me.

I was out of breath from the pursuit, but managed to speak, "You must tell me, what are you doing here, walking on this street? Please tell me why you are here!"

The man shrugged his shoulders as if he didn't understand what I was saying.

"Do you speak English?" I asked him.

In broken English, he responded, "No English. No English."

I motioned for him not to leave as I tried to communicate, "Are you a Christian?"

He smiled slightly, "Si, Christian, Christian!"

I smiled back and continued, "Are you Catholic?"

"Si, Catholic," he motioned with his hands as he talked.

I only knew of one Catholic order and that was the Franciscans. This I knew from the movie, *Brother Sun, Sister Moon*. I asked him, "Are you a Franciscan?"

He smiled broadly, "Si, Franciscan!"

I smiled back and proclaimed, as I pointed to myself, "I'm a Christian, too!"

He nodded as if he understood, then went on his way. As I walked into my apartment, I wondered what this was all about. It was strange that someone dressed like him should walk in front of my apartment just when I was seeking the Lord about whether or not I should go into full-time ministry.

I thought to myself, *Is this some coincidence that doesn't mean anything, or did God cause this to happen for a reason?*

I reread the Scripture that I had been given in prayer.

> To whom shall I speak, and give warning, that they may hear? behold, their ear is uncircumcised, and they cannot hearken: behold, the word of the Lord is unto them a reproach; they have no delight in it.

I analyzed the situation. This Franciscan monk was walking down the street. He was called of God and obviously knew where he was going. I saw him walking and immediately recognized that he was a man of God. He didn't have to say anything. When I tried to address him, I found out he spoke another language.

I began to ask God if there was some lesson in this and if there was, that He would reveal it to me. Then, it came to me. God was indeed calling me into full-time ministry. I was to be that man. I was to have a purpose and continue in my Messianic walk. If I did, my family and friends would be attracted to me and seek to know what I was doing, just as I sought out the monk. Right now, they couldn't understand what I was saying. My family and friends' ears were unable to hear, their ears were uncircumcised. When I talked to them, they couldn't understand the language of Zion I was speaking. God's promise to me was that if I obeyed Him and followed Him, my family would see my Christian walk and turn to God.

I felt a special peace. God had truly imparted a significant truth to me. I decided that I must take the job at CBN. I closed down Sunrise Productions and drove to Virginia Beach.

TWENTY-SIX

FANTASTIC VOYAGE

During my eight-hour drive to Virginia Beach, I spent time singing spiritual songs to the Lord and prayed for God to guide me through every step I'd take in my new job at CBN. On arrival, I ran upstairs to the corporate office, where CBN'S advertising division, Victor King, was located. I was excited. I wanted to tell my new boss, Tom Dennis, that I had arrived and would start work the next day. However, the minute I showed my face at his door, I was ushered into a production meeting with Tom, another television producer, Alan Winters, and the agency writer, John Jenney.

Tom introduced me to the others, then explained, "We are going to shoot a CBN University recruitment commercial in about an hour. It's great that you're here, Warren. You can help."

"Where is the school?" I asked in shock.

"Right over there!" Tom answered, pointing to an empty Victor King boardroom. He laughed out loud at my puzzled look. "The school begins its first semester in the fall. They have not yet completed the facilities."

After videotaping the mock classroom scenes with the new dean of the School of Communications, Dr. David Clark, and Professor David Gyertson, Alan Winters and I drove over to the CBN studios in Portsmouth for more shooting. We used my Bolex 16mm film camera which I had bought with the money given to me at my bar mitzvah. We filmed behind-the-scenes shots of "The 700 Club" cameramen and other personnel in the TV studio control room. The film was developed at a local TV station. This was the first spot I ever filmed for CBN. When it appeared on "The 700 Club," the response was tremendous. The video portions with Dr. David

Clark and Dr. David Gyertson appeared in sharp contrast to the dramatic behind-the-scenes footage shot on film. Everyone including Pat Robertson was excited by this new TV commercial. That fall the School of Communications began its first year with more students than anyone thought it would have.

After my first tumultuous day, I should have known what was in store for me at CBN. Everything at Victor King was a crisis. As I sat in my first agency production meeting, the head of the agency, Stan Ditchfield, went through a long list of TV commercials that needed to be produced. As I took notes, I realized that there were over twenty-five commercials, all with production deadlines which were past due.

"How can we ever get ahead with this many productions and only two producers?" I raised my hand and asked.

"Brother, with Jesus, all things are possible," Stan responded in dead seriousness.

For Alan and me, producing commercials for "The 700 Club" was frustrating. We spent late nights and many hours without getting the quality production the agency desired. We were several weeks behind the deadlines on most spots, and we were getting orders for new TV spots on top of the ones we could not complete. Tom Dennis, because of my Madison Avenue experience, made me the head of the spot production department. Several months after I arrived, Stan Ditchfield became quite upset that we were not able to obtain more editing and production time at CBN's studios, so he called for a production meeting with Network Operations. One executive brought in a number of his staff. On the table in front of him, I noticed a thick black notebook.

He was quite upset with me, since I used film on CBN University's first TV spot. The first words from his mouth were, "Victor King shouldn't be wasting CBN's money using a costly media like film."

"On Madison Avenue, all the major television network commercials are produced on motion picture film as opposed to videotape," I responded.

"We can give you a film look on video by just throwing our lenses out of focus!" he fired back. His staff broke out in laughter.

Ignoring his comment, Stan Ditchfield laid out his feelings of frustration.

"Brother, Victor King is not getting enough studio and editing time. We are behind on our deadlines, and Pat is on my back every day wanting to know the problem."

The notebook-toting executive rose up in his chair in anger. "We've given you more time than even "The 700 Club"! The problem is that the time is often wasted by Alan Winters and Warren Marcus who never come prepared to a session."

"What do you mean we don't come prepared?" I asked. "On the contrary, many times we have problems with machines breaking down and videotapes missing."

The executive opened the black notebook and began reading notes that were taken by the various directors and editors.

"Warren, you were in a session on December 4th at 6 P.M. You came without one of the source tapes you needed. It took my staff two hours to find the exact tape. This should have been researched prior with the necessary takes transferred in an off-line session, and you should not have taken valuable CMX time to look for that tape."

I was flustered by his attitude and what I considered Gestapo tactics. How can this be? This is surely not the way that Christians should treat one another, I thought to myself.

"I had ordered the tape in advance, but for some reason, it was not in the editing suite," I explained.

The executive defended his staff:

"There is no way that you ordered it in advance! If you had, it would have been there!"

He went on to cite ten other instances in which we were supposedly unprepared. However, what really upset me was when he accused me of saying negative things about Stan Ditchfield, the head of Victor King:

"Warren, I have reported here that you said some derogatory remarks about Stan Ditchfield. You said on December 19 at 6:15 P.M. that you wished that Stan Ditchfield would stop throwing so many projects at you."

By this time, I could no longer speak. I could feel the corners of my mouth quivering. In the world, I would have stood up and angrily shouted at this man. I would have possibly thrown a punch or two, but here I was a Messianic Jewish believer who never expected to have a confrontation of this nature with another believer. After the meeting, I apologized to Stan Ditchfield for the remarks I was accused of making, but I told him that they were taken out of context. He was a gentleman and a good Christian man.

"Don't worry about it. I've had my own problems with the man. Just do the best you can," he told me.

If Pastor Tate hadn't taught me not to put my trust in any man, but only in the Messiah, I would have been devastated by this incident, I thought.

After the meeting, I called Alan Winters into my office. Alan was not only a TV producer but a pastor of a local church. He told me to read Pat Robertson's book, *Shout It From the House Top*.

"Warren, things have always been hectic around here," Alan explained. "CBN is going into foreign countries with the Gospel, and whenever we do, Satan gets angry. He is the author of confusion, and he wants to divide us and weaken us."

We prayed over the situation. As we prayed, a Scripture from the book of Ephesians, chapter 4, verse 15, came to mind: ". . . Speaking the truth in love. . . ." As I meditated on this Scripture, I recognized that we needed to be able to tell our side of the story, but as the Scripture says, in the spirit of love, not confrontation.

"From now on," I told Alan, "we're going to keep our own records of every session and every conversation we have on the phone with network operations. Everything that happens in production and in editing shall be recorded on a piece of paper."

Over the next few months, we compiled our notebook, which documented our side of production foul-ups. It honestly reported where others were at fault and when we were in error. At the next production meeting, I went with my notebook in hand. My old adversary had his notebook sitting right in front of him on the boardroom table. We remained silent as the meeting progressed. I didn't bring up anything negative.

Then the executive began to lay into Alan Winters.

"Alan, on June 6, in the production studio, you took twelve hours instead of eight hours to complete the shooting of your spot. My director reports that you were unprepared. You ad-libbed many of the shots instead of preparing a script in advance."

While he was speaking, I turned to Alan's report on that same day. When he was finished, I politely spoke up.

"I think you have that wrong. My notes show that on June 6, the reason the session took twelve hours instead of eight was that your videotape room did not have the source tapes that were ordered one week prior. Also, there were major technical difficulties with two of the videotape machines. Therefore, Alan had to change his entire script to compensate for these problems. Between the down time of searching for alternate takes and the equipment dilemma, this resulted in his having to shoot overtime."

I looked at the executive. He was in shock. He had no idea that I could play the same "blame game" he was playing. However, I was not stacking the deck with half-truths and innuendos. I had the facts, and I was also quick to note when *we* were at fault. After two more attempts to discredit us, he became angry and frustrated that I had explanations, memos, and paperwork to deal with every area of contention.

He slammed his book on the table.

"I refuse to sit in this meeting any longer! This is certainly not pleasing to our Lord. My people are the best in the business, and I refuse to have Warren Marcus and Alan Winters sit there running my department down."

With that he left the room. Several of the others who worked for him remained, gathering up their papers. By this time, I had developed a rapport with most of the people. Two of the other department heads came over and shook my hand, congratulating me for the way I handled myself.

"I just wanted to set the record straight. I pray that he is not too angry," I told them.

The next day I went to visit him in his office. He asked me to sit down. I shared with him from my heart.

"There is no way that I want to hurt you or your department. I'm here to do the best job possible to tell the story of the wonderful things God is doing through this ministry. I want you to know that I am sorry if in any way I hurt you by the things I said yesterday in the meeting. Please, if there are things I'm doing that bug you, just come directly to me and tell me."

He shook my hand, and we prayed together. He never gave me

any problems from that day forth. A number of years later, he came over to me as we passed in the hallway.

"Warren, I need to talk to you, brother. I want to tell you that I am so sorry for the way I have treated you in the past. You are a talented and creative producer. Now that I am a producer, I can see how bureaucratic my operation really is. I had no idea of the problems you and other producers were going through. I created a monster, didn't I?"

I was touched by his apology, and a new respect welled up inside me. I realized that we could all make mistakes, but any man who admits his faults is a man to be admired.

My first six months at CBN were without my wife Donna. She continued to work for the posh beauty parlor in New Jersey until I was sure I liked the job. With the problems of my first months at CBN now solved, I called her and said that I felt as if I belonged in this ministry. She promised to come to Virginia Beach in three short weeks. In light of my crazy production schedule, I didn't have time to put our apartment in order. Most of the furniture was still in the same place the movers had left it.

It was my first Friday night with no production. I was too exhausted to begin unpacking so I went to a Christian Night Club called The Fire Escape out at the beach that faces the Atlantic Ocean. This ministry was run by a group of CBN employees who had a Christian rock group called Isaac.

The best part of all was that The Fire Escape was located on the main strip of Virginia Beach, right in the middle of all the bars and secular night clubs. The doors of The Fire Escape were left open, blaring out music so that the steady stream of tourists and Navy personnel could hear it as they passed by. The sign outside read: "The Fire Escape——No I.D. or age requirements." Many individuals would wander into the doors and climb the stairs to the second floor, attracted by the music. Once inside, I would observe them wander over to the bar and ask for a drink. It was fun to watch their countenances change to surprise as they were told that no wine, beer, or liquor was served. Too embarrassed to leave, they would inevitably sit down and hear a refreshing presentation of the Gospel. Many would give their hearts to the Lord.

"Charles" was a young Navy man who sat down at my table.

He was one of the many who walked into the club without knowing that God was about to touch his heart. As the leader of the band, Stan Majkut, ministered the Gospel, I could see how the Holy Spirit was convicting Charles. Several times he would drop his head in sorrow, and when it came time to pray the sinner's prayer, he raised his hand, recognizing the need of God in his life.

After he prayed, I began to talk with him about the decision he had made. I told him how all his sins were forgiven. He began to weep openly. I put my arm around him to comfort him and began to pray for God to touch him in a special way.

He stayed until after midnight when the club closed. He needed a ride back to the base. I figured it was the least I could do.

As I drove, I noticed that Charles sat silent, even though I tried to make conversation. I popped an audio cassette of a new Phil Keaggy album into the car stereo.

As the music played, I suddenly felt Charles' hand touch my knee. He left it sitting there for some time. I couldn't figure out why he was doing this. It seemed odd, but I didn't want to embarrass him. I ignored it and tried to move my leg, but his hand remained on my knee. Slowly, he began to move his hand up my leg. I realized that he was making a sexual advance. I couldn't believe this was happening to me. I grabbed his hand and pulled it away from my leg. He tried to pull my hand toward himself, but I strongly held his hand in mine and kept it raised in the air.

"You don't want to do this!" I said.

"Oh, yes I do," he replied.

"No, you don't! This is *not* of God! A moment ago you asked Jesus into your heart. If you really meant that, you've been forgiven for all your sins. The past has been erased. Now, if I would let you continue with what you were going to do, you could be sure I didn't care about you. I love you with the love of the Messiah. His love is greater than any sexual attraction."

Charles lowered his head and began to weep as he said, "Nobody ever told me that before. Nobody ever rejected me!"

I spoke up boldly: "I'm not rejecting you. On the contrary, I love you more than any man who has had sex with you. This is not of God, and you know it. Do you only have sex with men, or do you also like women?"

Charles bared his soul to me.

"There's this sailor who is married, but he won't leave me alone. He got me into this stuff. He told me that I was born a homosexual, and I will always be one."

"Can't you see that he doesn't care about you? He only wants to use you as a sex object. You were not born a homosexual. That's a lie from Satan! Your choice to have sex with someone is up to you. God can give you His Holy Spirit to enable you to overcome this habit," I told him.

"What do I do?" he said.

"First, I will lead you in a prayer and ask you to confess that homosexuality is a sin and that you realize that God hates the practice of any sex outside of marriage. Then, we will ask God to give you His Holy Spirit to overcome your sexual urge and to protect you from any temptation you are unable to bear. But you must promise me, after we pray, that you will find a Bible-believing fellowship with people who know that homosexuality is sin. I also want you to commit to going there regularly. You must give up all your relationships with homosexuals and tell them you have now committed your life to God."

Then Charles prayed with me, and I realized that the first time he had prayed at The Fire Escape, he did not fully understand the invitation. After that night, I saw him from time to time at The Fire Escape with a girl whom he introduced as his fiance. God had miraculously delivered him from homosexuality.

The experience with Charles was another illustration of God's power to deliver and cleanse us from sins. Belief in the Messiah allows one to truly become a new creature, free from the sins of the past. God had taken the bad experiences of my youth and used them to help me minister to Charles. How wonderful are His ways!

God gave Donna the ability to adjust, even though we were over 400 miles from northern New Jersey where our parents lived. We found a body of believers in which we were comfortable. On January 15, 1979, God blessed us with the birth of a beautiful baby girl, Tara Lynn. God continued to make our marriage fulfilling and stronger.

The Lord protected me from going astray with false doctrines and erroneous biblical teachings during my time at CBN. As good as CBN was in screening personnel, some employees would slip in who were not believers. Others were unstable in their understanding of the faith. And still others were experts in their profession but spiritually immature.

At CBN, I would get into lengthy discussions with many individuals from various denominations. The contradictions would seem bewildering. I thank God that Pastor Tate had given me a solid foundation in the Bible. He taught me to think for myself, testing all doctrine against that which is in God's Holy Scriptures. The Lord kept me from falling into the various religious trends that would sweep through some of the staff at CBN. Most of these fads were an over-emphasis of a specific area of scriptural truth. I witnessed as the prosperity doctrine, the "name it and claim it" philosophy, became the fashionable dogma of the moment. In the Bible, God *did* promise prosperity to his children. Yet, there were also instances of chastisement and adversity experienced by the saints of God, even when they were walking in righteousness.

Another short-lived movement that overtook some at CBN in 1981 was the "doctrine of deliverance." The principle wrongly taught that *every* problem or bad habit one cannot overcome is attributable to some demon who needs to be cast out of the believer. My Bible told me that once we invited Messiah into our hearts, we have become new creatures and that old things have passed away. Though the enemy of our soul may tempt us, we have the enabling power of the Holy Spirit to help us overcome. We read in the book of First John, chapter 4, verse 4:

Ye are of God, little children, and have overcome them: because greater is he that is in you, than he that is in the world.

Pat Robertson, to his credit, held a staff meeting in which he shared a balanced view on the subject of deliverance. He stated that it is possible for "principalities and powers of the air" to *oppress* us, but it is impossible for demons to *possess* a believer.

"Know ye not that your body is the temple of the Holy Ghost which is in you? Wherever there is light, darkness cannot dwell," Pat reminded us.

To this day, I thank God for putting me in a balanced fellowship with Pastor Tate who taught me the pure Bible and not strange doctrines that were based on some Scripture taken out of context.

My work at CBN continued to be difficult in meeting the unrealistic deadlines for completion of TV commercials for "The 700 Club."

One day, Tom Dennis called me into his office and asked what could be done to increase productivity.

My answer was instant. I told him that the agency needed to purchase some film equipment—a sound camera, a Nagra tape recorder, and portable lighting so we could have a self-contained film unit. This would help us produce quality commercials in a timely fashion without any interference with CBN operations.

The best Tom could do was allow me to find used film equipment on a rental basis with an option to buy. I had thirty days to prove the merit of commercial production using motion-picture film versus using videotape.

The first two film productions I produced with the used equipment were extremely low budget. They were testimonies based on letters from viewers of "The 700 Club." One dealt with a prostitute who prayed with Pat Robertson while watching "The 700 Club" and became a born-again believer. She was now married and was leading a dynamic life as a Christian. The second TV spot was the story of an eighty-five-year-old woman who was extremely lonely and depressed. Every night she would look forward to watching "The 700 Club," until she finally prayed with Pat Robertson to receive Jesus as her Lord and Savior. Now she had many friends in the church she was attending.

I shot both of these spots on 16mm motion-picture film and transferred the dailies onto videotape. I edited the spots in the CMX editing suite and used voice-overs of the actors instead of on-location sync-sound. I cast a professional actress to play the part of the prostitute and another to play the old woman. The rest of the cast were Victor King employees and friends.

While I was working on mixing the sound at the CBN Portsmouth studios, John Cardoza, the executive producer of "The 700 Club," popped his head into the audio room and started watching the unfinished spots. He became highly excited at the quality, power, and impact of these TV commercials. He watched them several times.

"These need to get on 'The 700 Club' immediately," he finally said. "Let's put them on the show tomorrow!"

I was glad about the positive reaction. However, I also knew this might cause a problem at Victor King, which operated procedurally like a secular advertising agency. Normally, a producer did not show the client, namely "The 700 Club," a new TV commercial. Rather, this was done by an account executive.

I hesitantly brought up this act.

"John, I've got to show this first to the people at the agency. They have procedures."

He cut me off. "Oh, hogwash! These things are great, and we need them on TV right away!"

He poked his head out of the room and saw Pat Robertson. He called out to him.

"Pat, Brother Pat, come here! I've gotta show you something!"

"Who is John talking to?" I asked Bob Wiley, the sound man.

"Pat Robertson, of course." he answered, laughing.

I was nervous, because I had never met Pat, and I knew that my boss at Victor King would be upset if he saw the commercial without the account executive present. Pat came into the room. He was much taller than I thought he was. I sensed an incredible anointing on Pat Robertson, one that humbled and silenced me.

"Pat, take a look at these spots that Warren Marcus produced," John Cardoza told him.

Pat smiled as the spots ran.

"This is great, brother. Glory to God!" he kept saying.

After he saw both spots, he turned to John and said, "Get these on tomorrow's show!"

John saluted in a joking gesture, "Yes, sir!"

Then Pat looked me in the eyes and said, "Brother, keep up the good work! These are exactly the type of spots we need. Great to have you here!" He turned and walked out.

When I got home, I found John Jenny, the agency writer and his wife, Julie, sitting at the dining room table. Donna reminded me that she had invited them over for dinner. I shared my concern with John, and he told me to call Tom Dennis and share the problem with him.

"Tom is a great guy. He'll tell you not to worry," John assured me.

I followed John's advice and called Tom, explaining what had happened. He was a little concerned about the possible reaction of his direct superiors, yet God worked things out. As a result of those two commercials, Pat Robertson approved the purchase of new film equipment, and the CBN Film Department was born!

Twenty-Seven

The Miracle Worker

In October of 1983, I was made the Director of Special Projects. I had over fifteen people working for me, plus another twelve in Network Operations who were designated to help the film department. We produced all the TV commercials for CBN's various outreaches including "The 700 Club," telethons, CBN University (now called Regent University), Operation Blessing, and the Freedom Council. I was also in charge of prime-time specials and CBN motion picture development.

There was a vast difference between our film crews and those I had worked with on Madison Avenue. On location, we would always begin with prayer. The crew would gather in a circle, and I would pray through a megaphone. I was always conscious of the curious bystanders watching as we prayed.

I would pray, "Oh God of Israel, we come before You in the name of *Yeshua HaMashiach*. Please bless this shoot. You know the many people who will see this production, and we pray that You will save many of them. We pray for protection over the actors and for Your anointing on the crew and equipment. Lord, please touch the hearts of those who are bystanders here tonight. Help them to know that Jesus will change their lives forever if they will only let Him. In Yeshua's name, we pray. Amen!"

Many bystanders were saved on the sidelines. Some of the actors we used did not know God. By the time we finished production, many would pray the sinner's prayer. The reputation went out that the Special Projects Division really cared about the people who worked with them. Our film unit tried to exhibit the fruits of the Spirit in everything we did.

On assignment in Puerto Rico, we were producing a testimony of a Puerto Rican man who had become an alcoholic but was saved through a "700 Club" partner. Some of the hired crew were not Christians, and I found out that several embraced socialism. One man in particular criticized the church for ignoring the plight of the homeless. As we shot the scene with an actor named Carlos Cestero portraying the alcoholic, a *real* homeless person began to watch. He interrupted the shoot a number of times, causing us to stop production. When he approached a crew member who was an avowed Socialist, he pushed the man away from him in disgust. Carlos and I went over to the homeless man as the Socialist and the other crew members looked on. They didn't want to go near this dirty man.

"What is your name?" Carlos asked him.

"Unghill," the man responded.

Carlos told me that in English his name meant *Angel*.

God gave me a real burden to minister to Angel. Carlos interpreted my words into Spanish.

"I was just like you—a person wandering, with nowhere to go. I was lost. All of my dreams were shattered. I wasn't an alcoholic, but I was addicted to drugs. Yet, Jesus changed my life. You may be dirty on the *outside*, but I was dirty on the *inside*, full of sin and rebellion against God. No matter what your dreams and hopes once were, Jesus can restore them if you make Him your Messiah and Lord."

The homeless man told us that he wanted to receive Jesus into his heart. Carlos and I laid hands on him, and Carlos led him in the sinner's prayer. Tears were flowing from his eyes.

After praying, Carlos didn't want him to return to the streets. Carlos decided to bring him to his home and clean him up. This was a sacrifice far above the call of duty. It was a witness to us all.

A week later, we were filming a different testimony with the same crew. Carlos came by with a strange, well-dressed man. No one recognized him as being the homeless alcoholic. When Carlos told me that this man was Angel, I was shocked. He was now going to church and working in a new job. I praised the Lord and wept.

I yelled to the rest of the crew, "Look, everybody, this is Angel!"

The Socialist on the crew, upon hearing Angel's testimony, was so touched he said, "I must ask your apology for criticizing the church. I told you that it was filled with hypocrites. It is I that am the hypocrite. I didn't even want to touch Angel, he was so dirty. Yet, here I was talking about the attributes of Socialism over Christianity. You two really care about people. If Jesus can help Angel, I know he can help me too!"

Carlos and I prayed with the Socialist to receive Jesus as Lord and Savior.

While shooting another spot in Puerto Rico, God provided one of the greatest miracles I have ever witnessed. We were shooting a scene at the historic fort, El Moro. It was the only day we could shoot this complicated scene with period costumes and fifty extras playing Spanish and British soldiers. Just as we finished setting up the film equipment and assembled the cast for the first shot, wind from a hurricane began blowing. The rain poured down forcing everyone, cast and crew, into a tunnel for cover. One of the unbelievers on the crew came over to me.

"Warren," he said, "there is no way we can shoot this today. It is a hurricane, and it will be raining all day, and tomorrow, too."

I looked outside the tunnel and watched as the wind whipped the rain into the ancient stone walls of El Moro.

"If we don't shoot this commercial today, then we can't shoot it at all," I lamented. "Our budget is limited!"

As I spoke, I felt the urge to pray. I told the crew that we were going to ask God to stop the storm. If He did, we would shoot the spot. If the storm continued, then perhaps God didn't want it to be produced.

The crew looked at me as if I were crazy. Only one other member of the group, Craig Cummings, my associate producer, was a Christian from CBN. I instructed them to make a circle and hold hands.

I began to pray, "Father God of Israel, I come to You in the name of *Yeshua HaMashiach*. If You want us to shoot this today, then please stop the rain. Stop it long enough for us to get the production done. You know the reason why we are shooting this. It is to bring the Gospel to millions. We leave it in Your hands. In Yeshua's name I pray. Amen."

I opened my eyes, only to see a number of the crew laughing at what they considered foolishness. However, five minutes later the rain stopped. Not only were we able to shoot the entire sequence for nine hours, but we also had God's wind from the hurricane, blowing the capes of the soldiers. The hurricane wind was far better than the wind a Hollywood wind machine could have generated. In addition, the earlier rain brought out interesting patterns on the stone walls of El Moro, causing the site to appear to be a painting on the canvas of film. We finished the *entire* shoot without any rain. As we put the last piece of equipment in the car, it began to pour. For the rest of our time in Puerto Rico, the Spanish crew members would come to me and Craig, asking us to pray for them and their loved ones. God continually performed miracles during our productions, to the point where it became commonplace.

In my first four years at CBN, God had the Film Department produce award-winning public service announcements that can be seen to this day on Christian TV stations across America. One of the most effective ones was "Tell Them." This TV spot was a montage, set to Andrae Crouch's classic song "Tell Them." I had loved that song from the first day I heard it on a Christian radio station. Over and over again, I would listen to the words. One day, images came to me as I listened to the words. In my mind, I saw a prostitute, a woman with a child, a man in a bar, and a homeless person standing in the rain with hundreds of other lonely, isolated city dwellers. The commercial looked as if we shot it documentary style, capturing real scenes on the city streets. Yet, every shot was dramatized and planned to fit the words and music of the song. The only dialogue added was an announcer saying, "Jesus loves you. He gave His life, so you can count on it!" The spot was given by CBN to any TV station that would air it. The results were amazing. An unsaved TV station manager told us that when he viewed it, all he could do was weep. Nobody had ever told him that God loved him.

Andrae Crouch was a guest on "The 700 Club" and had seen the commercial. He asked the guest coordinator if he could meet the person who produced the TV spot.

When I was brought into the green room, the place where "The 700 Club" guests waited before and during the show, Andrae asked me where I got the idea for the spot.

"I just listened to the song, and I believe the Lord gave me those images," I answered. "Why do you ask?"

"The prostitute, the man in the bar, those images in that spot were *exactly* the ones God gave *me* when I wrote the song," Andrae said.

"No wonder God used that sixty-second commercial to reach so many people! The Spirit of God had given us the *same* vision, even though we live miles apart! God used us both to communicate the message He wanted us to deliver," I said excitedly.

Another TV commercial we produced which has been seen around the world is called "Everything But." It is about a young man driving a red Morgan sports car. He has everything—a car, a house, girlfriends, and a great job. As his car pulls out and then comes to a stop, we see a tear fall from his eye, and the announcer says, "You've got everything, but you're not happy. Read the Bible and find out what true happiness is all about."

A new producer in CBN International, Robert Moses, once told me how the "Everything But" spot changed his life.

"Warren, I was just like that young man in the sports car. I had everything, a great job, girls, but I was not happy. Then, in a hotel room, I turned on "The 700 Club" and saw your TV spot. It touched me so much that I fell on my knees and gave my heart to Jesus."

Robert Moses was just one of many who were changed forever from watching one of these TV spots. I considered it the greatest compliment when my peers would stop me in the halls of CBN and communicate with me how these TV spots influenced them.

Jay Lindsey, an advertising executive from J. Walter Thompson in Detroit came to work for CBN.

"I saw your TV spots on 'The 700 Club.' I told my wife that if they can produce TV spots as good as these, then someone there is on the ball. I came to CBN because of your productions," he explained.

These were just a few of the many testimonies I heard about the TV spots. During my nine and one half years at CBN, I personally directed and photographed over 200 film commercials and developed 500 more TV and radio spots.

During the all-staff CBN prayer meetings, Pat Robertson began lauding my work. I was humbled by the praises he would utter.

"I challenge all of you at CBN to use the same innovation, creativity, and integrity in your areas of expertise that Warren

Marcus does when he produces those marvelous spots," he said.

To this day, I give the glory to the Lord and all the creative people God brought to CBN to work with me on these productions. My closest associates were John Faulk, my main writer; Craig Cummings, an on-line producer; Alan Winters, a producer; Barbara Simpson, our casting and pre-production planner; Laura Eastman, a producer; and John Hanke, a close friend and prayer partner.

I found Pat Robertson to be a man of God with great integrity in all he did. Pat had a burden to see the country of Japan reached with the Gospel. It was a country with less than five percent of the population claiming to be Christians. Pat had the CBN marketing team working with a Japanese advertising agency in designing a contemporary Bible cover. The CBN marketing director, Dick Thomas, worked with the Japanese agency to produce a TV commercial advertising the Bible. As a result, the Bible became an overnight best-selling book in all the Japanese markets in which the commercial was aired.

In further discussions with the Japanese advertising agency, CBN was told that the Japanese television networks would be willing to air animated Bible stories if we would have the series produced in Japan. Dick Thomas asked me to go to Japan to oversee the production of "SuperBook" and "Flying House." On my twelve-hour flight to Japan, I read the English translation of the contracts between CBN and the Japanese animation company. I discovered that CBN was funding the *entire* production. It would not, however, own the series. I couldn't believe that we had not secured the international rights.

Once I reached my hotel in Tokyo, I called Dick Thomas and told him that this animation could be translated into other languages and distributed world-wide after we covered the Japanese nation. Dick told me that as soon as I returned to the United States I should work with the CBN attorneys to renegotiate the contract, procuring all the rights to the series.

On my second trip to Japan, I had the privilege of watching the first episode of "SuperBook," the story of Adam and Eve. The TV and advertising agency executives were gathered in the screening room. Although the program was in Japanese, I could understand clearly what I was watching. I began to weep as it really hit me that this would be airing all over Japan, and that many children and their parents would be hearing the Bible story of creation for the first time in their lives. I didn't want anyone to see my tears so I kept wiping them with my shirtsleeves.

Later that day, as I knelt in my room in prayer, I could see a vision of millions in America watching this same episode in English. As I continued praying, I saw a mental picture of Arabs and Israelis watching "SuperBook." Little did I realize how real my vision would become. After airing in Japan, "SuperBook" and "Flying House" were translated into English and broadcast in America on CBN Cable for many years. After I left CBN in 1986, the international market began to open. In 1991 and 1992, "SuperBook" aired in Russia. Millions of Russian adults and children have responded to these animated Bible stories, hearing the Gospel on Russian television and in some of the schools.

Yet, I was most ecstatic when I heard that CBN was airing the series on MidEast Television. Arab and Jewish children now had the opportunity to see these animated Bible stories and learn about the same Messiah whom I had come to love.

After the success of the Japan Bible Blitz, Pat had the vision to reach America with a contemporary version of the Bible. He instructed CBN Marketing to do research on American Bible reading habits. The research uncovered the fact that while many Americans have Bibles at home, most don't read the book because it is too hard to understand. Millions thought that the Bible was a book without significance for today.

Pat instructed the CBN Marketing people to test various translations of the Bible to find out which was easiest to read. The Living Bible, though a paraphrase, won hands down. He then had them test various names and cover designs. The name that tested best was simply: *The Book*, which was the English translation of the Greek word *biblios*, more accurately translated *books*.

CBN Marketing worked with a Madison Avenue advertising agency to develop an ad campaign for prime-time television. CBN spent over $400,000 to produce these commercials. But when Pat Robertson saw them, he was disappointed. I happened to walk down to "The 700 Club" set in Studio Seven to see Pat's reaction to a new commercial our department had produced. He spotted me, and I sensed that he was anxious to talk with me.

During the commercial break, he confronted me.

"Brother, those spots for *The Book* are terrible! Did you produce those things?"

"Pat, I had nothing to do with them," I told him. "Marketing produced them. Though I had suggested a different approach, they chose to hire a Madison Avenue agency!"

Pat then turned to me.

"I want you to produce some new spots. Use your creativity. Do something great, brother! I want to see celebrities!" he said excitedly.

"That's exactly the concept I had, to use known celebrities who will endorse *The Book*," I responded. "But Pat, I can't just start producing something without being asked. This is a Marketing project."

"Don't worry. I'll take care of it," Pat promised.

The next thing I knew, I was called into David Clark's office. He was now the head of CBN Marketing.

"Warren, we are going to give you a chance to show off your creative talents. We need you to produce a new series of spots for *The Book*," he said to me.

He did not mention Pat's dislike for the Madison Avenue commercials. We developed a campaign called "Discover The Book," using fifteen Hollywood celebrities, such as Ben Vereen from "Roots," Michael Gross from a sitcom called "Family Ties," Susan Howard from the TV show "Dallas," and the rock singer Donna Summer. The first series of spots were celebrity endorsements set to a new jingle composed by writer John Faulk and a CBN sound man, Steve Peppos. The lyrics, "Come on America, Discover The Book," were sung by Glen Campbell.

The second commercial was a montage of everyday people from all across America holding up *The Book*. A businessman reads *The Book* at the breakfast table; a messenger holds up a copy of *The Book* while on roller skates; a cowboy on a bucking horse holds up *The Book* for all to see. This second commercial also included a modern dance troupe on a city street with acrobats and children representing all of America as they celebrated the greatest book of all time.

The Madison Avenue people were upset by the fact that Pat did not like their commercials. They decided to test my spots against theirs.

The account representative from their agency contended that the problem with our new commercials was that they didn't clearly state that *The Book* was the Bible. The commercials, he said, should have words in the jingle, or provide an announcer, saying that *The Book* is easy to read and that it is a modern translation.

My contention was that our commercials would visually communicate these concepts. I felt that the main goal of the spots was to provoke the viewer to purchase a copy and read it him- or herself. The New York agency set up focus groups to test their spots against ours. The focus groups came away with negative reactions to the ones that the agency had produced. One of their spots, which I personally liked, showed an English king reading the King James Version of the Bible out loud. He complained that he didn't understand what he was reading. Then a pageboy gives him a copy of *The Book* after which the king says, "Now this is a good translation."

However, many of the people in the focus groups did not like this spot because it put down the King James Version. When it came to the commercials which I had produced, ninety-five percent of the people rated them very highly.

To the amazement of the New York agency, the people, when asked what the product was, answered, "It's the Bible!"

The group was then asked how they knew *The Book* was the Bible and virtually everyone responded in the same way:

"What other book would celebrities carry all over the place with them if it wasn't as important as the Bible?"

As a result of these focus groups, CBN Marketing ran *The Book* spots that I had produced on prime-time television. In just three months over one million books were sold. It was a record for Tyndale Publishing and was something never before accomplished with *any* version of the Bible.

The most exciting project I was asked to work on while at CBN was the prime-time religious special, "Don't Ask Me, Ask God!" Pat Robertson commissioned a Gallup Poll which asked Americans, "If you could ask God any one thing, what would it be?"

The poll gathered the ten most-asked questions America would like to ask God, and from this, Pat Robertson wanted a prime-time special developed. Initially, some work had been done on this TV special, but I was called into a meeting with Michael Little, then head of Ministry Programming.

He told me that Pat did not like the direction the special was headed and asked if I could head up the production. When Michael told me the concept, my initial reaction was that it was a *machugana* (crazy) idea. However, as I drove home and prayed, God began to impart to me that I should get involved. It was already decided that the questions should be presented by celebrities. I came up with the further idea that not only should each question be presented by celebrities, but that an entertaining dramatic vignette would explore some facet of each question. I added man-on-the-street interviews, and experts such as Alvin Toffler commenting on the future and Mother Teresa speaking on the subject of suffering.

We attracted stars such as Tony Danza, Michael J. Fox, Dean Jones, Steve Allen, Jayne Meadows, and Vincent Price. I functioned as the executive producer, director, and director of photography. I also wrote some of the scripts. God supplied an outstanding producer in Jeffrey Wyant and associate producer in T.N. Mohan, who did a great job overseeing the editing. And, if it hadn't been for Michael Little placing his complete trust in us, we could have never completed the project.

Once we consummated the first cut we showed it to Pat Robertson and he appeared to like it. Yet, there were several CBN vice presidents who didn't. Some said it was not religious enough while others said it was too religious.

We aired this first cut in a nationwide video conference. In it Pat showed supporters the entire special and shared how he was going to syndicate it on prime-time television. After this screening, I went on a two-week vacation. By the time I returned, there was talk of dumping the special and never letting it be seen on network television. I couldn't figure out why this had happened. I believed that we had an award-winning program that would be heralded as one of the greatest religious television specials ever produced. I also knew the prayer and the work that had gone into producing this quality production. I became convinced that Satan was trying to keep it from being seen. Even Pat, who initially liked the production, was now acquiescing to the naysayers and was willing to shelve the project.

I went to David Clark and asked him to have it tested by a focus group composed of the intended audience.

"Please, David," I begged him, "let's see if there are problems with the special. If there are, I know we could correct them."

David set up the focus groups. I attended every one of the meetings. Over 95 percent of the people said that the production was good to excellent. They also said they would watch the production if it was aired on television. They had various comments on how some of the drama segments could be improved. But there was little negative criticism from these focus-group sessions. After listening closely to their comments, I listed ways that the show could be improved in the editing room. David Clark caught the vision and wrote a memo to Pat Robertson.

In it he told Pat that if the recommended changes were made, he knew "Don't Ask Me, Ask God!" would be successful.

However, what really turned David around was the answer to the question, "Did any of you pray with Pat to receive Jesus as Lord and Savior?" In front of the other participants over half of each focus group admitted that they had prayed the sinner's prayer at the program's conclusion.

The special aired in January of 1984, and the results were staggering. In a number of markets, we beat out network shows like "M*A*S*H," movies, and sporting events. In other markets, we were tied for first or second place. The Nielsen rating for the show was the highest that any religious special had ever received, a 10.5 average. Fifteen million people watched this prime-time special on syndicated stations all across America, with an additional one million watching it on CBN Cable.

This was the high point of my production days at CBN. I personally read over 114,000 letters that were written to the ministry from people who had been touched by this special. Entire families had come to the Lord. Others who had never seen "The 700 Club" were commending CBN for producing the program. Less than a month after airing "Don't Ask Me, Ask God!," CBN received a 30 percent increase in support during its January telethon, "Battle for the Family." Many of the vice presidents directly attributed the success of this telethon to the prime time airing of "Don't Ask Me, Ask God!"

• TWENTY-EIGHT •

WITNESS

During my time at CBN, God began to fulfill His promise to me as revealed in the vision of that Catholic monk who passed in front of my apartment in New Jersey in 1978.

It was my belief that God would win my family and friends to Himself if I went into the ministry at CBN and continued to be true to the faith. Just as I had been attracted to that monk and his purpose and direction, so, too, God caused many of my friends and family to observe my purpose and direction.

I had tried to share my faith with my sister, Fran, when I was in New Jersey. However, nothing I said seemed to get through. Her husband was an atheist, and Fran, though she was the one who first told me about God during that thunderstorm, now claimed to be an agnostic. The two of them had reared my niece, Janice, and my nephew, Richard, without any knowledge of God.

Fran began to watch "The 700 Club" to see my TV commercials. As she watched, she began to wonder if what I had told her was, in fact, true.

She said an innocent prayer, "If Jesus is real, then please give me a sign."

A month later, God provided the sign that convinced her of the reality of the Messiah. She found out that her husband, a physician, was being sued by a patient. They had just dropped their malpractice insurance because of the high cost. Fran knew that the review board usually sided against the doctor in favor of the patient. She was afraid that they would lose their home and everything they owned if the plaintiff was awarded a settlement. My brother-in-law was quite upset with the matter because he knew he was innocent. My sister also believed he was innocent because she had been the assisting nurse at the time of the incident.

Fran dropped to her knees to pray.

"If You have mercy on Jean-Claude and me, and You do not allow the patient to win, then I will turn my life completely over to You."

Miraculously, the patient could not defend herself. Her tongue seemed tied, and she appeared to be quite nervous. My sister told me that the woman's body was shaking. Fran watched in amazement as the patient seemed to be silenced by God Himself. When the board cleared her husband of any wrongdoing, Fran knew that God had answered the prayer and she accepted Yeshua. Several months later, her two children also became believers.

God moved on Donna's mother and father as they watched "Don't Ask Me, Ask God!" The two of them told me that they prayed with Pat Robertson to receive Jesus as their Lord and Savior, which renewed them in their Catholic faith.

I had the privilege to minister the Gospel to my cousin Floyd. I shared my testimony with him and he prayed the sinner's prayer with me.

I prayed with Floyd's dad, my Uncle Ben, when he was on his deathbed, to receive his Messiah.

In 1974, I shared my belief in Yeshua with my cousin Sam Pomper when I first became a believer. Sam was in my daily prayers as I sent him two rather lengthy letters explaining why I believed that Jesus was the promised Jewish Messiah. On several occasions, I played contemporary Christian music for him and he was quite impressed with several of the groups. Yet, none of this seemed to penetrate Sam's heart. In 1981, while producing the "SuperBook" animated television series, my travels took me through the city of Chicago on my way to Japan. At this time, God was moving sovereignly upon Sam's heart in his Chicago apartment. The day I stopped by to see him, I was amazed to hear him tell me that he had already become a Messianic Jewish believer. I immediately discerned God's hand in the matter as we joined together in a time of prayer and praise unto the God of Israel. Today, Sam is still serving God faithfully.

Since that time, several other cousins have become believers in the Messiah.

My own mother prayed with Pat Robertson while watching "Don't Ask Me, Ask God!" She heard me give my testimony at my sister's church and committed her life to God. By the time I left CBN, I became deeply burdened with my dad's spiritual condition. My sister and I tried to share the Messiah with him, but he continued to be resistant to our outreach. During this time, Mom confessed to me that she saw little chance that Dad would ever believe in God.

"Your father is just too far gone. The god of booze has got a solid grip on him," Mom lamented.

"With God all things are possible," I told her, however bad things looked. "We just need to keep him bathed in prayer!"

During my CBN years, I witnessed to many individuals who came across my path. In my travels to other cities across America and as I traveled to other countries, I shared my testimony with others.

While in New York City, Craig Cummings and I were working on a TV spot for "The 700 Club." We went to eat at a Chinese restaurant around the corner from the editing facility which we had rented. As we ate, we were having an in-depth discussion concerning the things of the Lord.

As we talked, I realized there was a woman at the next table listening intently to our conversation.

Finally, she could remain silent no longer.

"Excuse me, but I've been listening to your conversation and I find it very fascinating. Are you ministers or something?"

Craig and I laughed, and we told her we were just lay people who loved the Messiah. We both shared with her how she could get to know Jesus in a personal way, but she was resistant.

"You know, life is so short," I told her. "We never know if this could be our last day on earth. You can be sure you are going to heaven just by saying a prayer similar to this . . ." I went on to pray the sinner's prayer.

As she listened, I noticed her eyes close and her head start to nod. Suddenly, her head dropped right into her plate of Chinese food.

Craig and I looked at one another in shock. Realizing something serious had happened to her, we called the waiter and told him that he should call an ambulance. Then she regained consciousness and insisted that she was all right.

She looked at her watch and said, "I must get back to work. I'll be late."

We were so concerned about her that we walked with her to the building where she worked. She thanked us for our kindness. Just as she got into the lobby, she collapsed. It was the end of lunch hour, and a crowd of people were returning from lunch. They crowded around us and stared.

"Don't just stand there, somebody get an ambulance!" I yelled at them as I knelt beside her.

Then I asked Craig to join me in a prayer. We knelt by her and prayed until the ambulance came.

Several people from her office came over to us as the ambulance workers attended to her, still lying on the floor.

"Do you know her?" one of her co-workers asked me.

"No, we just met in a restaurant and she fainted there," I answered. "So we walked her back to her office, in case she had any problems."

The woman became conscious again, and the ambulance attendant asked her if she remembered where she was.

"I'm in my office building!" She tried to focus her eyes.

"Do you recognize those two young men over there?" asked another worker, pointing to us.

She craned her head to look at us.

"Yes. Those were the two nice young men who walked me back from the restaurant."

As she was put into the ambulance, several of her co-workers asked me for my business card. I gave them one and asked that they contact us about their friend.

"We will be praying for her," I added.

A number of weeks later, I received a letter. It read:

Dear Mr. Marcus,

I just wanted you to know that Mrs. O'Connor, to whom you were so very kind when you were in New York, died two days later from a massive stroke.

It was a great shock to all of us, but we want you to know how very grateful we were to you for being so kind and thoughtful. None of us will soon forget it.

I called the office number on the stationery the letter was written upon. I learned that Mrs. O'Connor had asked for a Bible while in the hospital. She talked about Jesus to her friends and family before dying. I was encouraged by the mercy of God in her life. It taught me an important lesson; we can truly be an instrument of God on this earth if we do as the Bible commands us to do in Second Timothy 4:2:

Preach the word; be instant in season, out of season; reprove, rebuke, exhort with all longsuffering and doctrine.

On another occasion, I was on my way back to Virginia Beach from a film-to-tape transfer in New York City. As I stood in line at the airport waiting my turn to walk through the metal detectors, I saw a rabbi open his briefcase for inspection. Inside, I could see religious articles from Israel.

In my heart, I had this feeling that God wanted me to talk to the rabbi. I was extremely tired and wanted to sleep on the ride home.

Please. If there is any chance, have him sit somewhere else, just this one time, I begged God.

As I walked aboard, I noticed that he was sitting in the back of the jet. I was happy as I sat down in my seat by the window. I had just begun to doze off when I felt a hand on my shoulder. It was the rabbi.

"Excuse me. You mind if I sit here? I hate cigarette smoke. They gave me a seat in the smoking area," he spoke in a broken accent.

I told him I didn't mind his sitting next to me.

As the plane taxied for take off, I lowered my head and prayed silently as I always do for a safe journey.

After I finished my prayer, the rabbi asked me, "Were you praying?"

"Yes. How did you know?" I answered.

"I'm a rabbi. It's my business to know when someone's praying," he said smiling. He continued, "What religion are you?"

Not wanting to get into controversy, I answered, "I'm Jewish."

The rabbi got excited.

"A Jew who prays? But you have no yarmulke on your head. You must be Reformed?"

As the trip went on, I asked him questions about the Torah. He was stunned at my grasp of the Torah and the Prophets.

After some conversation I asked him two questions:

"Why is it that so much of the Torah centers on sacrifices and priests? What does that have to do with us today?"

The rabbi pondered my words. "Well, that's where we get our kosher laws from," he finally said.

"Yes, but what about all the rest of it? And what about Leviticus 17:11 where it reads, 'For the life of the flesh is in the blood: and I have given it to you upon the altar to make an atonement for your souls: for it is the blood that maketh an atonement for the soul.' Is this just talking about kosher laws, or is it pointing to the significance of sacrifice?" I countered.

The rabbi's eyebrows were raised.

"I have never thought about such a thing before. You never went to yeshiva?"

I laughed and told him, "No, I just went to Hebrew school, but my knowledge of the Torah comes from self-study."

"Where do you work?" he asked.

The airplane was landing as I replied:

"I know you are going to find this controversial, rabbi, but I work for the Christian Broadcasting Network, CBN. I am a Messianic Jew. I love the God of Israel and I love you, rabbi."

He was so shocked that his mouth flew wide open. I gave him my card and told him that I would love to have us stay in contact. He told me that he would keep in touch.

A few days later, I received a call. It was another rabbi who said he was a friend of the one I met on the airplane.

"The rabbi said he liked you very much, but was concerned about you spiritually," he told me. "He wanted me to ask you some questions to think about. Now, you must promise that you won't ask Pat Robertson the answer to these questions, but you will seek the answers for yourself."

"I promise you," I answered him, "I won't ask Pat Robertson the answer to any of these questions!"

He began by trying to undermine the credibility of the B'rit Hadashah (New Covenant). He read me a Scripture in the New Covenant and told me it was misquoted from the Tanakh (Jewish Scriptures). I opened my Thompson Chain Reference King James

Version of the Bible and looked for the Scripture he was referring to. I found that the footnotes gave another Old Testament reference as the actual verse being quoted.

I interrupted the rabbi.

"I beg to differ with you, but the New Covenant writer was quoting a different verse of Scripture with a similar meaning. Here it is." I read it to him.

He became extremely angry because I was able to answer his every objection. During the whole conversation, I was extremely respectful and meek as I answered his charges.

Finally in great anger he said, "Look, as a Jew, if you believe in Jesus as the Messiah, I fear that you will not go to heaven!"

I spoke up with confidence, "What God is it to whom the Christian Gentiles pray, when they pray, 'Father who art in heaven?' Is it not the God of Israel?"

The rabbi answered, "Of course it is! But what does that have to do with you?"

I further asked, "Are only Jews going to heaven, or can these Gentiles go to heaven, too?"

"Of course they can go to heaven!" the rabbi answered.

"Then, if I am praying to God the Father, too, are you telling me that I will not go to heaven?" I reasoned.

"Absolutely not! For you, it is different. You should know better, being a Jew," he argued.

"Rabbi, what if I am right and you are wrong? What if Jesus *was* our Messiah? If I am right, then you, by your own assertion, are saying that you would be the one to be kept out of heaven!"

The rabbi got so angry he hung up on me. I got on my knees and prayed for his salvation. Unfortunately, I never heard from him again, but I felt sure that my being able to answer his questions caused him to ponder the words I spoke. After all, I protested just as loudly with Richard Gallagher without ever giving him the satisfaction of knowing that his answers were getting through. Perhaps, some other believer would in the future reap the harvest of the seeds I planted in that rabbi's heart.

I am grateful to God that Pat Robertson had respect for me and opened many opportunities for me to serve God at CBN. To this day, I think very highly of Pat Robertson and love him as a brother in the Lord. God has done marvelous works through CBN and through his obedient servant, Pat Robertson. When I first came to CBN, the staff had only a tiny production facility in Portsmouth, Virginia. They were just beginning to build the complex in Virginia Beach. During the nine and one half years that I was there, I saw CBN and its cable network grow in an enormous way. This gave me the courage to believe that God could fulfill *all* of my visions and dreams concerning the use of motion pictures and television to reach millions with the reality of Messiah.

In December of 1985, after seeking God in prayer and with the counsel of others, I decided to leave CBN to raise the money necessary to produce Christian feature films.

TWENTY-NINE

THE KING AND I

Immediately after leaving CBN, I began writing several feature films scripts that were deep in my heart. At the same time, I embarked on a joint venture with a former CBN vice president, John Gilman, in Virginia Beach. He was the founder of a ministry called DaySpring Productions International. He had a vision to produce the life of Jesus with actors from India, Africa, China, and other nations for the purpose of evangelization. He had already found a film on the life of Jesus produced in India, and he was financing film teams to show the movie in village after village. The movie would be projected on a blanket spread between two trees, using a portable 16mm projector and generator. Thousands were receiving Jesus as a result of viewing the movie all over India.

For the most part, our vision was similar. However, John was committed to producing only the life of Jesus. He believed that the film should be produced with actors from the particular country in which the feature film would be used. However, I wanted to produce various Christian films that could be shown in America as well as distributed world-wide. I was feeling uncomfortable each day we worked together, though I loved and respected the vision God gave him.

An old friend, Alex Von Saher, called me. Alex used to work with me at CBN as a lighting director on many of my TV spots and on "Don't Ask Me, Ask God!" He had left CBN in 1984 and briefly worked at another TV ministry, Jim Bakker's PTL in North Carolina.

Alex brought me up to date.

"I'm no longer with PTL. I've been working in Lynchburg for the Liberty Broadcasting Network (LBN)," he explained

"What is the Liberty Broadcasting Network? Is it Christian?" I asked.

"Yes, of course it's Christian. I'm working with Dr. Jerry Falwell," Alex responded.

"Jerry Falwell? What are you doing there?" I inquired.

Alex was such a phenomenal creative lighting director that I couldn't envision him working for Jerry Falwell on a weekly church service.

"Warren, you need to come to Lynchburg to witness what is happening. Jerry Falwell has brought in Dr. Jerry Nims as CEO. He has a vision to produce original programming for Christians," Alex said.

He informed me of the 24-hour-a-day Christian cable network that Falwell was launching. Already gathered in Lynchburg was a production team of some of Christian television's heavy-hitters from diverse ministries including CBN and PTL, plus a former employee of Ted Turner's CNN. I was reluctant to visit Alex for fear of getting side-tracked from my own vision to see Christian movies on the screens of America and the world. Alex called me several more times, each time with more enthusiasm. He talked about exciting programs being developed to reach teenagers and senior citizens. I could no longer resist.

How could it hurt to just look? I reasoned.

I expected everyone to have fundamentalist haircuts and suits as I drove up to the Old Time Gospel Hour headquarters in Lynchburg, Virginia. As I parked, I spotted Alex walking into a building. He hurried over to my car, accompanied by several of his co-workers.

"Warren," he said, "this is Chuck Elder, formerly of PTL. And this is Lee Cantelon, another friend from PTL."

As I shook their hands, I couldn't believe that these individuals, with long hair and dressed casually in jeans could be working for Jerry Falwell. Alex signed me in as a guest and walked me over to Dr. Jerry Nims's office. He opened the door, revealing Dr. Nims sitting back in his chair with his feet up on the desk as he talked on the phone. He put the phone down and welcomed us into his office.

"Alex! Come in! So, is this Warren Marcus? I've heard great

things about you from Alex. Is he your agent?" Dr. Nims asked laughing as he warmly greeted me.

Dr. Nims filled me in on Jerry Falwell's vision for Liberty Broadcasting Network. It was to be a 24-hour Christian cable network that produced the finest in original Christian programming.

"Jerry is willing to bring in the right individuals to accomplish this dream," he told me.

"I can't believe that there are people like Alex and Chuck Elder here," I exclaimed. "I mean, they don't exactly fit the fundamentalist image."

Dr. Nims laughed and said, "I'm sure I've ruffled the feathers of some of the old-timers, but Jerry Falwell and I want the best born-again believers in Christian television. There's a revolution happening here."

I gave him a copy of my latest resume. Dr. Nims seemed impressed.

"Would you consider coming to work for LBN as the president and chief operating officer?" Dr. Nims asked.

"I am honored that you would even consider me in that capacity, but my vision is to develop and produce Christian feature films," I said.

"That's great! There's room here for that, too," Jerry Nims told me.

He invited me over to his home in Lynchburg to meet his family. His wife prepared a wonderful southern dinner. I felt at home with Dr. Nims and his family.

I promised him that I would pray over his offer, but I couldn't understand how Dr. Falwell would allow me to pursue my vision of producing Christian motion pictures, as he didn't allow his Liberty University students to attend movies.

I returned to Virginia Beach. The plans were moving forward on my joint venture with John Gilman of DaySpring Productions. He had begun building new quarters, which included a large executive office for me. As I stood in the middle of that empty office, I felt an incredible sickness deep inside me. I had never experienced this before in my Christian walk. I was looking through a catalog of office furniture and had to stop because the feeling was so intense. I initially thought it was Satan trying to keep me from pursuing this venture with John Gilman.

After all, I thought to myself, John's vision is so close to mine. Why wouldn't God want me to stay here instead of going to Lynchburg?

Yet, the more I considered moving forward with John, the more intensely sick I felt inside. I prayed to God to help me understand what He wanted me to do.

That week, I received another call from Dr. Nims. He asked if I had had any revelations from God.

"I showed your resume to Dr. Falwell, and he was very impressed. He would like you to come to Lynchburg to meet him," Dr. Nims revealed.

I decided to go meet Dr. Falwell. If nothing else, I might obtain a better understanding of God's will for my life.

I was nervous on my first meeting with Jerry Falwell. He was sitting in the Old Time Gospel Hour boardroom at the head of an enormous table. He was surrounded by key staff members when Dr. Nims ushered me into the room and introduced me.

Jerry Falwell made me feel at ease.

"Warren, we're in the middle of a marketing meeting. Sit down right next to me, and after we are done, I want to take you on a tour of our ministry."

I felt an immediate part of Falwell's ministry as I listened and even participated in the meeting. After the meeting was over, Jerry Falwell took me and Dr. Nims in his truck on a tour of Liberty University, the LBN TV Studios, the Liberty GodParent Home, and the Thomas Road Baptist Church. I was impressed with Dr. Falwell. I found him to be completely different from his TV image in the Moral Majority days. On television, he appeared to be dogmatic and almost overbearing as he debated the liberal opposition. In person, I found him to be full of warmth, and a compassionate individual with a pastor's heart.

As we talked during our tour, I realized that he had a terrific sense of humor. He would sneak up behind an employee and begin tickling him. I watched as he grabbed one of his star college football players from behind in a bear hug. The young man laughed at Jerry's antics. It appeared to me that Jerry had great rapport with the students at Liberty and his employees. He would wave at everyone, and they reciprocated with a warm greeting or a kind word.

As he drove his truck, I sat in the front seat next to him. Dr. Nims was seated in the back. Without warning, Falwell suddenly yelled and shot his arm out toward me, causing me to jump half-way out of my seat.

Laughing, he said, "Just checking to see if you're still awake." I felt good being around Jerry. He made me feel comfortable, as if I had known him for years. He was the direct opposite from Pat Robertson—Pat was more aloof and harder to approach, but Jerry was extroverted and extremely friendly.

As we sat in a restaurant for lunch, Jerry stopped in the middle of our conversation to chat with an elderly waitress who thanked him for helping her through the trial of her father's death. Then he turned to me:

"Warren, you are the perfect one to head LBN. You have a great track record. You love the Lord, and as long as you're not a thief or a liar, we can have a lot of fun doing some great television."

I told him about my hesitation: "Jerry, I really think what you are doing is great. I had no idea so much is going on here in this ministry. The university is impressive; so is the church. The Christian programming LBN will produce is so needed, but I have a vision of producing Christian motion pictures, and I feel I need to pursue that dream."

"What kind of films do you want to produce?" Jerry asked.

"Films like *Chariots of Fire* and Billy Graham's *The Hiding Place*. I want to use movies to win souls to Christ," I explained.

Jerry nodded his head in agreement, saying, "I think that's great! Why can't you come here and head up our television ministry and pursue your dreams at the same time? There's no conflict in that."

I promised Jerry that I would pray about his proposal.

Back in Virginia Beach, I was feeling pressure to make a decision one way or the other. I felt extreme peace every time I thought about Lynchburg, but enormous turmoil when I considered a future in Virginia Beach with John. My wife also had enormous reservations about my going forward with John. She liked him, but something deep inside her was confirming that this was not the direction we should take.

Then, it dawned on me. Donna loved living in Virginia Beach and had told me a number of times that she would never move. I decided to take her to Lynchburg to see the area for herself and meet Jerry Nims. I felt that God could speak through Donna. If she was against the move, I'd have to assume that God was not in it.

To my amazement, Donna seemed to love Lynchburg even better than the Beach.

"You wouldn't want to move here, would you?" I asked her.

Donna turned to me and said, "If you took the job at LBN, I'd definitely move. I love it here!"

I called Jerry Nims and told him that I wanted the job, but I had to talk with John Gilman first and discuss my decision. I wrote a lengthy letter to John, explaining how Donna and I felt the Lord was leading us. I was concerned that John might misunderstand our decision.

I loved John and his ministry, but by that time I knew without a doubt that God wanted me at Liberty Broadcasting Network. John Gilman was understandably upset. He had his heart set on our working together. However, after a lengthy meeting at a restaurant, he and his business partner said they understood. To this day, I support John Gilman and DaySpring Productions and the great vision God has given him to reach the world through using full-length motion pictures about the life of Jesus Christ.

In February of 1986, I joined the Falwell ministry. My duties were carefully laid out by Dr. Falwell and Dr. Nims. I was to be the executive producer of the "Old Time Gospel Hour," the ministry's weekly church service, which also promoted Liberty University, the GodParent Home for unwed mothers, Elim Home for alcoholics and drug addicts, and related ministries. My other area of responsibility was as president and chief operating officer of the Liberty Broadcasting Network. In this capacity, I reported to Dr. Nims and oversaw the entire cable network, including network operations, programming, and production.

As President of LBN, I was the executive producer of eight different television programs on an extremely low budget. There was "Act It Out," which was an outreach to teenagers. It had an African-American host named Alfonzo Wesson, and a live TV audience of Liberty University students. "Act It Out" used creative dramatic vignettes to provoke discussion. It quickly became our most successful original program.

"Over the Hill Gang" with host Doug Oldham was geared to

reach the older crowd. It included Doug Oldham riding a Harley motorcycle in a fast-paced magazine format. The program featured senior citizens and the important message that life is not over, but just begins at the age of 60.

Another program we produced was "Back Stage with Gary McSpadden," in which Gary would interview various Christian musicians and songwriters. The program featured videos and live performances by the artists.

LBN also produced college-level football and basketball telecasts, including Liberty University's own sporting events.

I helped develop and produce a five-day-a-week live Christian talk show called "The Pastor's Study with Dr. Jerry Falwell." The program shared the great things God was doing through Falwell's ministry. Many of these television shows are still airing today on Christian television stations.

The first week I started with the ministry, Jerry had received word from several ministers that there was a scandal brewing at the PTL ministry which, if true, could cause irreparable harm to all TV ministries. I was part of an initial fact-finding team including Dr. Nims and Jerry Falwell's spokesperson, Mark DeMoss. We met with PTL's Richard Dortch to find out the truth about vicious rumors concerning Jim Bakker and Jessica Hahn. The *Charlotte Observer* was about to break the story. Here I was a Messianic Jew put right in the middle of one of the most publicized defaults of the modern-day church. Soon, Jim Bakker handed PTL over to Dr. Falwell. I was asked by Jerry Falwell to head up the PTL television division and oversee the programming of the Inspirational Network, as well as serve as the executive producer of "The PTL Show." I spent six months five days a week at PTL and never received any salary for this work. I continued as president of Jerry's television network in Lynchburg and did receive a salary from LBN. I had to wear two hats, keeping oversight of the Falwell ministry back in Lynchburg, as well as keeping the peace at PTL. I would travel back and forth between PTL in Charlotte, North Carolina, and Lynchburg, and on the weekends to Virginia Beach where Donna and my daughter were still living. The hardest part of the time at PTL was being away from my beloved wife and daughter.

Much of my time at PTL was spent ministering to the employees in my department who were hurt over the Bakker default and the malevolent publicity that continued to make major headlines in the newspapers and on the network news. I would wind up praying with many of these people, who communicated horror stories of the way they had been treated.

Many in the ministry and in the church seemed to be blown away by what was happening. However, I had a totally different perspective. First of all, I was already prepared to handle the scandal, having learned so much from Pastor Tate's biblical teaching at Evangel Church. My nine and one half years at CBN helped me recognize that Satan himself had been trying to destroy Christian broadcasting since its inception, because it had been so effective in reaching millions with the life-changing message of Yeshua the Messiah. Secondly, being a Messianic Jew, I was removed enough to perceive that God was not just singling out PTL for chastisement, but rather this was a warning to all ministries and the entire church. God was calling us to repentance and to turn back to our first love, *Yeshua Ha Mashiach*.

At my first meeting with the more than 150 employees of the PTL television ministry, I shared from my heart what I believed:

"Only if we love one another, and treat each other with the love of Messiah, will God bless our work here. It's easy to look at the great things being accomplished by any ministry and think that God will overlook unrepentant sin. Looking externally at the PTL Ministry and the wonderful buildings of this complex, most Christians passing through would say, 'How can the rumors be true? Look at the wonderful things God has accomplished here.' Yet, you and I know that every ungodly thing that the press is reporting is true. It really *did* happen! In God's mercy He allowed more than seven years from the Jessica Hahn episode for Jim Bakker to repent. Instead, he and others continued in sin. But God is holy and when repentance did not come, he allowed the sin to be uncovered. Just as He chastised the children of Israel who were the children of promise, so, too He will chastise sin in the church. God cares more about who we are and how we treat one another than He does about the lofty goals of this ministry. If we can truly be like the Messiah in the way we treat one another, God will allow us to reach the world with the Gospel. If we fail to reach out in love to one another, this ministry is doomed to failure."

Many of the employees that day made a renewed commitment to try to work together in love. Yet, the tension between pro-Bakker partners, Falwell loyalists, and some employees who had plans to take over the ministry themselves made every day at PTL a challenge. Crew members were fighting with one another. Some charismatic people loyal to Jim and Tammy Bakker were fighting with the other PTL partners who just wanted to see PTL continue as a ministry. The press was having a field day, putting a microscope on the sensational scene. My main concern was for my dad. I figured that all the bad publicity would reinforce his disbelieving mind. I truly began to believe that perhaps there was no hope for him, as my mother had stated.

As I walked through the hallways of PTL, I saw Christians divided against Christians. I would take the time to try and reason with all sides in the conflict.

I would tell them, "The eyes of the world are on the church. What is happening here is turning millions off from the saving knowledge of the Messiah of Israel."

I preached in the Grand Hotel of PTL, and in the shopping area called Main Street, in front of the shops and restaurants.

I remember one day in particular. I saw a group of Christians holding up signs that read, "Jerry Falwell, go to hell." I watched as the secular TV cameras recorded the disharmony.

I went over to the protesters and confronted them.

"How can you hold up signs like those and call yourselves Christians?"

"We're upset with Dr. Jerry Falwell," they told me. "We want him to get out of here and give the ministry back to Jim Bakker." Rather than defend Jerry Falwell, I avoided that issue altogether.

"When I was a little boy and walked the streets of New York holding my mother's hand," I told them, "I saw Christians who were holding up signs. But they didn't have the words that you have on them. They had the words, 'Repent and be saved.' I was provoked enough to ask my mother, 'What does that mean, Mom?' Even she had to examine her beliefs, because these street witnesses were confronting us with the Gospel. Yet, you are standing here with words of hate written on your signs toward another Christian brother."

They continued to defend their actions.

"We believe Jim Bakker's story that Dr. Falwell orchestrated the takeover of PTL. He's a liar and a thief!"

I inquired, "If you were to go home to be with the Lord this night, which sign would you rather be holding in your hand for the Lord to see. Would you rather have 'Jerry Falwell, go to hell,' or would you rather be holding a sign that reads 'Repent and be saved?'"

As I continued talking, the Holy Spirit convicted hearts. The protesters put down their signs and expressed sorrow for what they had done. I told them that they were forgiven. We all agreed that this tragedy had hurt the church. I told them that they could help make a difference because Jesus said, "Ye shall know them by their fruits. . . ." (Matt. 7:16). We ended in prayer together, right in the middle of the Heritage Grand Hotel.

Little did I realize that Jerry's son, Jonathan Falwell, was standing in the large crowd that had gathered, listening as I ministered to the protesters. I found out later that Jonathan told his dad about this incident because he was deeply touched at the way I had allowed God to use me. This resulted in Jerry Falwell having a deeper trust in me.

THIRTY

AGAINST ALL ODDS

Jerry Falwell had no intention, from the very day he set foot on the grounds of PTL, of remaining there. Once the scandal broke, he tried to assemble a team of interdenominational experts to rescue the ailing ministry. I left PTL the same day Jerry and the entire board resigned. I went back to Lynchburg to my job as president of the Liberty Broadcasting Network.

The key lesson I learned at PTL was that our daily witness truly affects the lives of those around us. Nothing etched this truth into my soul better than a TV newscast I saw in my hotel room while still working at PTL. In the midst of the negative news reports about religious broadcasting, I eagerly watched an investigative report on Mother Teresa of Calcutta. The news reporter spent weeks with her, observing her every move.

At one point, she held up a newborn baby and showed her to the camera, saying, "This is what America is afraid of, a little baby. So you would rather murder it with abortion. Look at what you are so afraid of. She is just a beautiful little baby!"

The liberal news reporter surely didn't share Mother Teresa's anti-abortion stance. Neither did he share her enthusiasm for God. Yet, he chose to show her talking openly about her belief in Jesus. Even with her broken English accent, she spoke as eloquently as any born-again preacher I had ever heard, including Billy Graham. Her pulpit was the poverty-stricken streets of India. Her sermon was not only in her words but in her deeds as I watched her care for the needs of the poorest of poor. After the news clip was completed, the anchorwoman turned to the news reporter, who now sat in the studio with her.

"You spent weeks following Mother Teresa every day," she said. "I'm curious, was she real?"

The newscaster thought about the question for a moment, then said, "Yes, she was real! She was definitely real."

With all the bad publicity concerning Christianity as a result of the PTL scandal, here was one woman who transcended the skepticism of the liberal press. They could not find fault in her testimony, because she exhibited the reality of Jesus in her talk and her walk. I thought to myself, *This Catholic woman has found the key to true faith in the Messiah. It doesn't matter whether we are Catholics, Protestants, or Messianic Jews. She owned no property and hadn't acquired any wealth. Yet, she was far richer than Donald Trump.* It was then that God reemphasized the key spiritual truth that Pastor Tate had taught me at Evangel Church: as individuals, we can truly help change the world around us, not by power or earthly might, but by how much fruit of the spirit we exhibit.

Many believers were overcome by the tragedy of PTL, and later, by the revelations concerning another TV evangelist, Jimmy Swaggart. The faith of multitudes was shaken by these abominable events. Some tried to excuse the sins of these defaulting Christian leaders by comparing their sins with those of David in the Jewish Scriptures.

"Warren," they would tell me, "look at King David. He was an adulterer and had the husband of Bathsheba murdered. Yet, God called him a man after His own heart. Therefore, shouldn't we just forgive Bakker and Swaggart and leave them alone?"

I responded, "Yes, we should forgive these men as God forgives them. Yet, according to the Bible, they have lost their effectiveness to minister. They have hurt the cause of Messiah. King David was forgiven by God after he repented, but he wasn't restored to the same place he had before his trespass. He suffered many tragedies. God loved David in the end because, though he sinned, his heart became humbled and repentant before almighty God. God is a merciful and forgiving God, yet the damage and hurt we inflict upon others and the reputation of God's kingdom tragically remains tarnished in the eyes of those around us."

The hardest part for me after the PTL scandal was that many of my Jewish aunts, uncles, and cousins didn't make any distinctions between practicing Christians and the several backslidden TV evangelists. Tragically, many of my unbelieving friends pointed to Jim Bakker and Jimmy Swaggart with ridicule.

"What hypocrites!" they'd tell me. "All of these born-again Christians are a bunch of hypocrites. Those televangelists are a bunch of thieves!"

What made matters worse was that I worked in Christian television and all my relatives knew it. In their minds, Christian television was just a big business ripping off little old ladies' Social Security checks. To them it was all one big scam! Rather than try to defend Jim Bakker or Jimmy Swaggart, I had recognized that my job was to repair the damage done against the name of my Messiah. I believe God gave me the right words to say:

"Look, the Torah and the Prophets declare that every one of us is capable of sinning. In the Psalms we read that the Lord looked down from heaven upon mankind and said: 'They are all gone aside, they are all together become filthy: there is none that doeth good, no, not one' (Ps. 14:3). God tells us in the Torah that He hates sin. We can look at the sins of others and point our fingers. Yet, one day every one of us will stand before God, and He will judge us for the choices we have made. We can't point to Jimmy Swaggart and Jim Bakker as our excuse for not choosing to follow God's commandments. He will say to you in that day, 'I'm going to deal with *them* when *they* stand before Me. I'm talking to *you*.' All the excuses we have will be inadequate. You might say, 'Well, I've done some things wrong in my life, but I've also done some good.' God tells us in the book of Isaiah that 'All we like sheep have gone astray; we have turned every one to his own way; and the Lord hath laid on him (the Messiah) the iniquity (the sin) of us all' (Isa. 53:6). I know what I will do when I stand before the God of Israel. I will fall down on my face before Him and tell God that I am a sinner. Anything I have done good is as filthy rags in His sight. I would ask for His mercy, not because of anything good I accomplished, but because the Messiah, His only begotten Son, paid the price as my sacrifice."

After leaving PTL, I noticed that the negative newspaper headlines and network newscasts seemed to have taken their toll on my dad. He seemed harder to reach than ever, and alcoholism definitely had a stranglehold on him, clouding his receptivity. My mini-sermons seemed to be falling on deaf ears. However, I was able to convince Dad that not all believers were like Bakker and

Swaggart. I pointed to my sister's life and my own as examples of the reality of God in true believers.

"I know that you and your sister are real. I can see the difference religion has made in your lives. I'm glad for you. But I'm too old to change," Dad said to me during one of his sober moments.

Both Mom and Dad had watched the "PTL Club" every day during the six months that I produced the program for Jerry Falwell. During this time, my dad developed a great respect for Jerry. After the production of the show, I would often telephone my parents from the Heritage Grand Hotel, and they would tell me how much they enjoyed the singing of Doug Oldham, Ron Aldridge, and Gary McSpadden. How wonderful are the ways of God. He took the tragedy of PTL and turned it into a blessing in disguise in my parents' lives. Even though they were tuning in just to watch the program their little boy produced, they were hearing every day about the life-changing message of the Messiah. Yet, as great a miracle as this was, my father still was resistant to having any serious discussions with my sister and me concerning the truths contained in the holy Scriptures. It seemed as if there was nothing Fran or I could do but hold Dad up in prayer.

I began to pray unceasingly for my dad in the following manner: "Oh God of Israel. Please don't let my father perish from this earth without becoming a Messianic believer. Somehow, someway, please bring him to Yourself. In Yeshua's name I pray. Amen."

I didn't see any immediate results from my prayer. As a matter of fact, things got worse. Dad was always afraid of doctors. If he could avoid them, he would—like the plague! He was not feeling good. He was weak and tired, but he did not want to get a medical examination. My sister Fran asked her husband, Jean-Claude the doctor, to give my dad a blood test at home to check him out. Jean-Claude found that my father was losing blood. He insisted that Dad should be admitted into a hospital.

At the hospital, they found that his heart had been taxed because of the loss of blood. He needed a blood transfusion, but he was frightened of receiving blood from the hospital because of the recent publicity of the AIDS epidemic. Fran told her pastor about my dad's need for blood and the members of his congregation gladly volunteered to help. My father was deeply moved. He felt better knowing that the blood came from Bible-believing Christians since he knew that the Bible taught against homosexuality and illicit sex. My father understood that the odds of getting infected blood from born-again Christians was far less than receiving blood from other sources. He was deeply touched, but it still wasn't enough to make a believer out of him.

X-rays showed that there were growths in his intestines. My reaction was to prepare myself for the worst. I began to pray to God for Him to spare my dad's life. I knew he was not ready to accept Yeshua as his Messiah.

When they operated, they had to remove a significant amount of the intestine. But even worse news came when they told us that the growths were cancerous, and that they had to leave a spot of cancer on his liver. It had spread from the intestines as a result of my father's neglect in seeking prompt medical assistance. It could not be removed.

Separately, Fran and I prayed that God might heal my dad so he could get out of the hospital and come home. Dad was like a baby in that hospital. He felt as if he would never get out—as if he were going to die right there. All he wanted to do was to go home to his accustomed surroundings, his favorite chair, and all his friends who would constantly stop over to have a few drinks with him. But he had lost so much weight, he had come close to death's door.

Throughout the ordeal I went to the hospital, visited with him, and prayed for him. He didn't want to hear anything about God, and he even resisted my praying for him. When my sister visited him she tried praying for him, too. We hoped for the best—that the cancer would just go away.

Finally, he was released from the hospital and went home. He was grateful. He stopped the heavy drinking that he had done all his life. It wasn't that he *wanted* to stop, but alcohol bothered what little stomach he had left. There was one thing he didn't know. The family had made the decision not to tell him that there was a spot of cancer remaining on his liver. We felt it would really dishearten him and make things worse.

In one year, the cancer had spread. By October of 1988, my dad didn't know exactly what was wrong, but the cancer was taking a toll on him. His legs were blowing up like balloons filled with water. He couldn't figure it out. Jean-Claude increased his visits to the house, trying to talk dad into returning to the hospital.

"Even if I was dying I would not go back to the hospital!" my father would say with all the strength he could muster.

Whenever I could, I'd visit. I would sit in the living room and talk to him, trying to discuss the things of the Lord. However, he would make jokes or change the subject. It was so frustrating, knowing that he was dying and not being able to get through to him on spiritual matters. I was so afraid that he would die without ever knowing the Messiah. Sometimes he would seem to be listening, but more often than not he would cut me short with his usual excuse.

"That's fine that you believe in God, but it's not for me."

I became quite frustrated and depressed on my nine-hour drives back to Lynchburg. To me, it seemed that no one had more chances to hear about the Messiah than Dad. He had seen the television productions I produced for "The 700 Club" and the CBN prime-time special, "Don't Ask Me, Ask God!" My mother reminded me that he even shed a tear as Pat Robertson led the nation in a prayer for salvation at the end of the show.

Not only did Dad hear the Gospel when he saw my TV productions, he heard me attempt to explain my beliefs time and time again. My sister and her two children continually tried to witness to him without apparent success. It was hard for me to leave this in God's hands. I kept telling myself that there had to be something I could do. The only comfort I seemed to have was in remembering that God could still do a miracle. God had used me to pray with my Uncle Ben even as he lay on his deathbed. If God could change the heart of an atheist, why couldn't he do the same for my agnostic father? The question was, could lightning strike twice in the same way?

"This would have to be some miracle," I said to myself as I pulled into the driveway of my Lynchburg home.

THIRTY-ONE

IT'S A WONDERFUL LIFE

The next day, I went to work, but my heart was not in it. Just before Jerry Falwell's daily talk show, I walked into his dressing room. In spite of his own heavy schedule, Jerry noticed that I was downcast. He asked if anything was wrong, and I told him about my dad. I disclosed to Jerry that my father knew he was sick, but he didn't know that he was dying of cancer.

Jerry asked me if my father knew the Messiah, and I told him the sad truth, that Dad had once prayed but there was no evidence or confession of the faith in his life. I could have never anticipated what happened next.

"Would it help if I called him?" Jerry asked.

I thought that if Jerry called, it might be the very thing needed to get through to Dad. For one thing, I knew my father would be thrilled to hear from Jerry. After all, my dad was a man who all his life wanted to be known by others—to rub shoulders with the powerful and famous of the world—even if they were just the local mayor, the police chief, or some political cronies. He'd often brag about once knowing many of the old-time boxers, actors, and entertainers. For some reason knowing influential people made Dad feel important.

I thought to myself, *There couldn't be a more perfect person to call my dad.* I told Jerry, "Yes, I think it definitely would help!"

To my surprise, Jerry Falwell immediately lifted the receiver of his dressing room phone and asked me for Dad's number. It was less than half an hour before the live broadcast of his TV show, and there were so many things to do to get ready. Yet, Jerry had a true pastor's heart and ministry always came first! He asked me my parents' full names as he dialed the number.

Mom answered the phone, "Pearl Marcus?" Jerry asked. "This

is Jerry Falwell in Lynchburg, Virginia. I'm with your son, Warren. He told me your husband is not well. I would love to talk with him."

My mother's first thought was that this was a practical joke by my elder brother, Stan. He was famous for such pranks. However, when she realized it really was Jerry Falwell, she quickly got my father to the phone. Jerry began with light conversation, making a friend of my dad first.

"Charles, Warren told me you're not feeling well," Jerry began.

Dad and Jerry talked for at least fifteen minutes. Most of the conversation centered on Jerry asking questions, trying to get to know my dad on a more intimate basis. He asked Dad about his past work as a tool-and-die maker, how long he was married, and the ages of his other two children. I kept looking at my watch, nervous that Jerry wouldn't get to talk about anything spiritual, in light of the fact that he would be needed on the set in less than five minutes. Looking at his own wristwatch, I heard Jerry say, "Charles, Warren and I will be going into the TV studio in just a moment to do a program. I would like to take the time to pray for you. Would that be okay with you?"

Tears came to my eyes as I heard Jerry begin to pray with my dad. I had never heard my dad pray. Ever since I had become a Messianic believer, I tried to share about the Lord with him, yet he was not open. I never thought I would see the day that he would pray with anybody. I bowed my head in agreement with Jerry's every word.

Jerry concluded his prayer, "Father, we come before You and ask that You minister to Charles Marcus. We ask, if it be Your will, that You heal him of his infirmities. Comfort him and his wife, Pearl. We ask that You do this in the name of the Messiah of Israel, Jesus Christ. Amen."

Later, I found out from my mom that dad had actually closed his eyes during that prayer and was very touched by it. Jerry then asked my father if he could call back in a few days. Dad told him he certainly could. What else could he say to such a well-known figure as Jerry Falwell? The tears continued to fill my eyes as I witnessed God in his own wonderful way attempting to reach my father when I had thought there was no hope. My mom told me that it lifted my father's spirit just to talk to Jerry. He was very moved that someone so important would even take the time to call him. Little did my dad know right then what would happen later!

My parents were greatly surprised that Jerry would take the time from his overwhelming schedule to call a second time. This time I was not with Jerry. However, there was an additional "audience" at the Marcus house. The next-door neighbors were visiting as were several of my mother's cousins. It was an entire household of my Jewish relatives and neighbors. My mother had to quiet them down several times so my father could hear. When she told them it was a long-distance call from Jerry Falwell they were impressed.

Jerry talked to my father for a considerable time, asking him more questions about the Marcus family. Jerry showed that he cared by taking the time to get to really know my dad in an intimate way. He didn't just rush in insensitively about spiritual matters.

Then Jerry Falwell asked my father an unbelievable question. "Would you mind if Warren and I flew to Linden so I can meet with you personally and talk to you about the Messiah of Israel, Jesus Christ?" My father agreed—but added that Jerry shouldn't take time out of his busy schedule just to see him.

"I *want* to do that, Mr. Marcus," Jerry said firmly. It was settled! Jerry then prayed again with my father.

When my dad got off the phone with tear-filled eyes, he told everyone that Jerry Falwell was coming to visit him in person! No one could believe that Jerry Falwell would actually do this. One of the neighbors was so excited that he suggested that they call all the local media to cover the event. My father withstood this tempting idea and firmly said, "No! He's coming to see *me!*"

Seven days later, Jerry and I got on a private jet and flew to Linden. My mother met us there and drove us to my boyhood home. She told us that my father's health had gotten so bad that he could hardly walk because of the pain in his legs.

Once inside the house, Dad appeared at the top of the stairs, where he stopped and just stared in amazement as he looked Jerry over once, twice, and a third time. It was as if he could hardly believe his own eyes. Standing there in his home, in his own familiar living room was Jerry Falwell—the man he had seen on TV. There were tears in his eyes as he stood still at the top of those stairs.

He just said in humbleness, "I cannot believe that you would do this for me. For *me!* That you would drop your busy schedule to see *me*. Who am I that you would come to see me?"

The stairs still separated us, and I had to say a number of times, "Dad, c'mon down. C'mon down, Dad!"

Stunned, my father walked slowly down the stairs to meet Dr. Falwell. I formally introduced them and they shook hands. Dad made his way over to his favorite living room chair—he could not stand up for long without great pain and he looked worse than I could have imagined. His muscle tone was gone. His once chubby face was sunken and drawn. Mom and I walked down to the lower-level recreation room, leaving Jerry and my father alone to talk.

And talk they did! Like my dad, Jerry has a very full, booming, powerful voice. Downstairs Mom and I could hear every word. For nearly an hour Dad and Jerry talked, Dad covering many of the trivial subjects he had loved to chat about with visitors over the years. He went through the "laundry list" of things he was proud of. He talked about his brother, Uncle Sol, who wrote many famous songs performed by Nina Simone, Elvis Presley, The Animals, and others. He shared the usual anecdotal stories about the actor, Edward G. Robinson—especially noting that he was his cousin. He went on about the famous and not-so-famous people he had met in his lifetime. My father told him about the plaque he received from the mayor of Linden, and other prized possessions.

Every time someone would visit, my dad would repeat all the same stories again and again. My mom and I began to laugh because whether the visitor was a neighbor or a national leader, as far as my dad was concerned, everyone was equal in one respect: they all had to hear the same routine of outrageous stories, corny jokes, and anecdotes.

Then, Mom and I heard Dad make an unprecedented proclamation, "But Jerry, of all the people I have ever met, you are the most important. You are the greatest!"

Things seemed to get quieter as Jerry chatted a little longer with Dad. We tried our best to listen in on their conversation.

Then, all of a sudden, Dad started yelling, "Pearl! Pearl!"

We ran up the stairs, worried, not knowing what to expect.

"Jerry is going to pray for me now—and I want you to be here with me," my father informed Mom as we entered the room.

I went into the adjoining kitchen, leaving the three of them together. Sitting in silence, I realized that Dad's eternal life was at stake. I knew that this was the moment of great reckoning in my father's life, but I could not help doubt even a great preacher like Jerry Falwell's ability to make my dad understand. In my flesh, I had forgotten that faith is a gift of God and does not come to any man through intellectual understanding alone.

I listened intently as Jerry took my father through the Jewish Scriptures. He explained the true meaning of Isaiah, chapter 53, one of the most amazing Messianic passages in all of Scripture. These were the very same Scriptures that had convinced me that Yeshua was indeed my Mashiach (Messiah). My dad listened carefully. Then, Jerry turned to the New Covenant and showed Dad where it was recorded by witnesses of that time that Yeshua fulfilled all the many prophetic passages about the coming of the Messiah. My father said very little, while I sat in the kitchen wishing I could peek into the room to see his visage. I was afraid of distracting them, however, and that was the last thing on earth I wanted to do. My heart pounded as I discerned the great stakes involved.

Jerry talked about his own life, telling Dad how he came to the Lord on January 20, 1952! My father spoke up in amazement.

"January 20 is my birthday! I was born on January 20!"

A chill ran down my spine as I perceived this to be no coincidence. I was now convinced that God had this whole thing planned, even down to this very detail! I began to pray that my father would respond.

Jerry talked about his own father's deathbed conversion. I couldn't believe how it paralleled my dad's situation. Jerry told how his father was an alcoholic and was dying of cirrhosis of the liver. This had to have a powerful impact on Dad because he himself was an alcoholic.

Then Jerry explained how his father had received Jesus as his Messiah on his deathbed and is now alive in heaven. I could feel the tension in the air. Jerry was about to pop "the big one." Dad would either accept Jesus and receive eternal life or be lost forever. I bowed my head and prayed more intensely. Jerry was clear and authoritative as he talked:

"Charles, I would like to pray for you because God *can* heal you. However, if He should choose not to heal you at this time, if He should choose to take you home, you can be assured of heaven just as my *own* father was after *he* received Jesus into his heart. You could take the same step that your son, Warren, took—that my dad took on his deathbed—the same step that your daughter, Fran, took. You can be born again! You can be a completed Jew just by praying a simple prayer. Do you want to pray with me to receive Jesus into your heart?"

"Yes! Yes, I do!" said my father unequivocally.

As I heard my father's response, my heart began pounding so hard that I was sure they could hear it in the other room. Still, I had my doubts. Maybe he was just saying it to be nice to Jerry Falwell, this important man, who had come a long way to visit him. I prayed fervently, "Oh God, let it be true! Open his heart that he might receive!"

Tears began streaming down my face as Jerry prayed a simple prayer with my father. It was the same type of prayer I had prayed to receive the Messiah of Israel into my heart.

The prayer ended and I walked back into the living room and embraced my dad. Tears were streaming down his face.

Jerry talked a little while longer with all of us, and we finally stepped outside to leave. I still had questions running through my mind as I prayed, *Did he really receive Jesus into his heart? God, please let me know. I just have to know if he really believes! Please let me know the truth concerning my father.* As I entered my mother's car, I realized that I had forgotten my briefcase. I ran back into the house and opened the door. Dad was still sitting in his favorite chair. He looked up at me, and a big smile came over his face. I was amazed as I saw that the sick, pale, yellow look that he had before was gone! In its place was a healthy glow—as if he had never been sick. That wonderful smile remained on his face. I will never forget the miraculous transformation that I saw occur in the space of just a few minutes. If that were all that happened, I would have left convinced he had become a believer.

Dad then said, "Well, I prayed that prayer. You know, I was never a religious man. I never was really much of a Jew. I was never bar mitzvahed."

"Dad, you are more of a Jew right now than you have ever been! Because now you know the Messiah of Israel!" I exclaimed.

"But you know," he continued, "I feel great! If I die, I'm ready now. And if the family wants to have a rabbi to bury me, that's fine. I could always have the other guy, too," he said, pointing out the window in Jerry's direction.

Now I *knew* it was true. My dad had become a believer. Though I realized he was in fact now prepared for the first time in his life for death, I was still grieved to hear him talk about it.

"Dad," I said, "first of all, you don't even need to talk that way, because you don't know what God's going to do. You never know. God might even heal you."

However, my father knew something more than I did at that moment and spoke with a new-found courage:

"No. No, Warren. I know what's happening. But now, I'm not afraid to die."

I hugged him once more and promised, "I'll be praying for you, Dad."

I told both my mother and Jerry what my dad had said as Mom drove us back to the airport. Jerry listened intently and made an interesting observation:

"Warren, your dad's heart had been prepared to receive. You and your sister's faithful prayers and your fruitful lives as witnesses finally took root."

The following day, after Jerry had prayed with him, Dad was so incapacitated that he could no longer even get out of bed to walk down the stairs. He stayed in bed, getting weaker and weaker over the next few days. Thank God, my sister, Fran, was a nurse and could help my mother care for him.

He declared to her and my mom, "I am born again."

Fran's daughter, Janice, also a believer, read to him from the holy Scriptures about heaven. This greatly comforted him. And true to his word, he was not afraid to die any more. His only prayer during the closing days of his life was, "God, I'm a born-again believer. Take me. Take me. Don't let me suffer. Just take me home!"

Five days after Jerry's visit, he was gone from this earth, but alive forever in heaven. The Scripture promises: ". . . to be absent from the body (death), and to be present (alive) with the Lord!" (2 Cor. 5:8).

To demonstrate just how wondrous God's works really are, my father, a man from a little town in central New Jersey who desperately wanted to be known by others, to make his mark on the world, and who always enjoyed meeting famous people, became known by countless people all across the nation. For Jerry Falwell told the story of Charles Marcus to millions of people through "The Old Time Gospel Hour" television program. Millions heard how an agnostic Jewish man on his deathbed found the true Messiah and inherited eternal life with God. Only God could pull off something like that! My father's earthly dreams were fulfilled in his death. And Dad himself was totally fulfilled as he began spending eternity with God.

Dad's funeral was a large one. Our family itself was very large. Then there were the many, many friends, politicians, mayors, police chiefs, and police officers—many were drinking buddies of my father. They were all there to pay their respects. The man who did not want to be forgotten was truly remembered!

At that funeral, my sister Fran, her daughter, and I spoke about my father in front of all who were gathered. Many knew that we were Messianic believers. I told about Jerry Falwell's visit, and how my dad turned to God in those final days of his life. My sister told about the new home where my dad was now abiding—heaven!

She quoted the Scriptures, "And God shall wipe away all tears from their eyes; and there shall be no more death, neither sorrow, nor crying, neither shall there be any more pain: for the former things are passed away" (Rev. 21:4).

We found out later that many hearts were touched. The rabbi who performed the funeral services told my sister that he was deeply affected and fascinated by the concept of heaven she talked about.

THIRTY-TWO

THE GREATEST SHOW ON EARTH

Both my Uncle Ben and my father received their Jewish Messiah in the final, fleeting moments of their lives. My dad did many things in his life which he was ashamed of. I'm sure that was the case with Uncle Ben, too, because that's the case with every human being on earth. We have all done things against the holy character of God. Thanks to God's amazing grace, all our sins can be forgiven through a simple prayer, in just a moment, when there is true repentance, a sincere turning away from sin and desire to walk in a new direction. God's promise to us is that He will put our sin as far as the east is from the west. God promises in the Scriptures that He will remember our sins no more. We don't have to wonder whether or not we are going to heaven. We can know for sure! All can be forgiven. In a single moment. With a single prayer!

My fellow believer, the only person worth defending is the Messiah and His name. We will only be effective in our witnessing to others to the degree that we are allowing the fruits of the spirit to be evident in our lives. I truly believe that we are living in the end times. So many believers missed the real lesson God was trying to teach us concerning the Jim Bakker and Jimmy Swaggart scandals. God was clearly saying to the church, "I will judge sin!" Yeshua (Jesus) will return, but He will come to receive a bride (the church) who is spotless and blameless, adorned in white.

Whether we believe in a pre-, mid-, or post-tribulation rapture, most of us in the church today, whether we are Catholics, Protestants, or Messianic Jews, feel that the Messiah's return is eminent. Even Orthodox Jews, though they don't realize that Jesus is their Messiah, are for the first time taking full-page ads out in the Israeli newspaper, *The Jerusalem Post*, proclaiming, "Repent and study the Torah. Do good works of charity. The Messiah is coming soon!"

When Orthodox Jews begin to proclaim that Messiah is coming soon, the world had better stand up and listen. Time is short. Paul spoke to the Gentile church concerning the future which will soon come to pass. His words are recorded in Romans, chapter 11, verses 25 through 27:

> For I would not, brethren, that ye should be ignorant of this mystery, lest ye should be wise in your conceits; that blindness in part is happened to Israel, until the fulness of the Gentiles become in.
>
> And so all Israel shall be saved: as it is written, There shall come out of Zion the Deliverer, and shall turn away ungodliness from Jacob:
>
> For this is my covenant unto them, when I shall take away their sins.

While the church continues to lose political clout in America and the world, the worldwide mission fields are more fertile than they have ever been in the history of the church. Nations such as Russia, once closed to the Gospel, are now open for a short period before Yeshua returns. The times of the Gentiles will soon be coming to an end. Then as Paul promises, the eyes of the Jewish people will be opened so they can see. Jewish people in record numbers are already returning to Israel from Russia. More importantly, record numbers of Jews are becoming Messianic believers. Messianic fellowships are being established around the world, even in the nation of Israel itself. Time is short. We must be ready and working in the fields of harvest when Messiah returns.

Since 1974, I have known Yeshua as my Messiah and my Lord. I have not regretted one day and have found that the closer I walk with Him the more He comes through for me. He has helped me face the most difficult trials of my life. I would surely have fallen into deep sin had it not been for the reality of Messiah in my life. I don't have any doubt that I would have been divorced and possibly dead from a drug overdose had Yeshua not come into my life. Yeshua has given me by His Spirit the enabling power to overcome the lusts of the flesh that every human is subject to. Only through belief in Messiah have I been able to walk in the way of righteousness. Ever since I became a Messianic believer, I have been able to say before man and God that I have never violated my marriage in any way. I have been a loving father to two wonderful children, Tara Lynn and Joseph Charles. I believe now that God is going to use me in ways I never before believed or dreamed possible. He has cleared the way for me to speak in churches and give my testimony that others might know that God is reaching out to them.

No matter how circumstances may look in your life, no matter how bad you think things are, God is always there reaching out to you. He loves you and He has a plan for your life. He is giving everyone the same opportunity to come. There will be no excuse. My story is about a God who is sovereign. He revealed Himself to me in a dream as a five-year-old. He heard my prayers while I was yet a sinner. In spite of my sinful and rebellious ways, God used difficult circumstances and all types of people to point me toward the Messiah. He used Catholics, Protestants, and even non-believing Jews to bring about His plan for my life.

Whether or not God supplies the finances needed for me to produce another Christian program or motion picture, I have learned that, more important than accomplishing some lofty vision in His name, God wants me to use my talents to reach out to the lost souls around me. God has given each one of us many abilities. God has given the talents of writing, acting, singing, music, oratory, and a variety of other gifts to be used to declare His glory. Yet, Satan constantly tries to overcome us with our past by reminding us of how wretched we really are apart from God. Or, he entangles us with the preoccupation of looking so far into the future that we get frustrated in chasing our elusive dreams. God would have us learn to concentrate on the here and now, living each moment of our lives, conscious of the *Ruach HaKodesh* (Holy Spirit) who dwells within us. We are not alone. God is with us every moment of the day. Yet, often we act as if He doesn't exist at all. We no longer have the past; it is gone. The future is not ours either, for who knows whether this is our last day on the earth? We only have this very moment, right now, in which to make some real choices that can count for all eternity. We need to allow God to mold us and shape us into the new creatures He has designed us to be.

Let us not be discouraged in doing good unto others. Let no trial, or circumstance rob of us of the joy of Messiah reigning in our hearts. May the words of Paul in Second Corinthians, chapter 4, verses 17 and 18, encourage us:

For our light affliction, which is but for a moment, worketh for us a far more exceeding and eternal weight of glory;

While we look not at the things which are seen, but at the things which are not seen: for the things which are seen are temporal; but the things which are not seen are eternal.

APPENDIX A

Here are a number of Scriptures that teach sexual purity.

None of you shall approach to any that is near of kin to him, to uncover their nakedness: I am the LORD.

The nakedness of thy father, or the nakedness of thy mother, shalt thou not uncover: she is thy mother; thou shalt not uncover her nakedness.

Thy nakedness of thy father's wife shalt thou not uncover: it is thy father's nakedness.

The nakedness of thy sister, the daughter of thy father, or daughter of thy mother, whether she be born at home, or born abroad, even their nakedness thou shalt not uncover.

The nakedness of thy son's daughter, or of thy daughter's daughter, even their nakedness thou shalt not uncover: for theirs is thine own nakedness.

The nakedness of thy father's wife's daughter, begotten of thy father, she is thy sister, thou shalt not uncover her nakedness.

Thou shalt not uncover the nakedness of thy father's sister: she is thy father's near kinswoman.

Thou shalt not uncover the nakedness of thy mother's sister: for she is thy mother's near kinswoman.

Thou shalt not uncover the nakedness of thy father's brother, thou shalt not approach to his wife: she is thine aunt.

Thou shalt not uncover the nakedness of thy daughter in law: she is thy son's wife; thou shalt not uncover her nakedness.

Thou shalt not uncover the nakedness of thy brother's wife: it is thy brother's nakedness.

Thou shalt not uncover the nakedness of a woman and her daughter, neither shalt thou take her son's daughter, or her daughter's daughter, to uncover her nakedness; for they are her near kinswomen: it is wickedness.

Neither shalt thou take a wife to her sister, to vex her, to uncover her nakedness, beside the other in her life time.

Also thou shalt not approach unto a woman to uncover her nakedness, as long as she is put apart for her uncleanness.

Moreover thou shalt not lie carnally with thy neighbour's wife, to defile thyself with her (Lev. 18:6–20).

Woe unto him that giveth his neighbour drink, that puttest thy bottle to him, and makest him drunken also, that thou mayest look on their nakedness (Hab. 2:15).

Thou shalt not lie with mankind, as with womankind: it is abomination (Lev. 18:22).

Wherefore God also gave them up to uncleanness through the lusts of their own hearts, to dishonour their own bodies between themselves:

Who changed the truth of God into a lie, and worshiped and served the creature more than the Creator, who is blessed for ever, Amen.

For this cause God gave them up unto vile affections: for even their women did change the natural use into that which is against nature:

And likewise also the men, leaving the natural use of the woman, burned in their lust one toward another; men with men working that which is unseemly, and receiving in themselves that recompence of their error which was meet (Rom. 1:24–27).

There shall be no whore of the daughters of Israel, nor a sodomite of the sons of Israel.

Thou shalt not bring the hire of a whore, or the price of a dog (a sodomite, male cult prostitute), into the house of the LORD thy God for any vow: for even both these are abomination unto the LORD thy God (Deut. 23:17–18).

And even as they did not like to retain God in their knowledge, God gave them over to a reprobate mind, to do those things which are not convenient;

Being filled with all unrighteousness, *fornication*, wickedness, covetousness, maliciousness; full of envy, murder, debate, deceit, malignity; whisperers,

Backbiters, haters of God, despiteful, proud, boasters, inventors of evil things, disobedient to parents,

Without understanding, covenantbreakers, without natural affection, implacable, unmerciful:

Who knowing the judgment of God, that they which commit such things are worthy of death, not only do the same, but have pleasure in them that do them (Rom. 1:28–32).

Now the works of the flesh are manifest, which are these; Adultery, fornication, uncleanness, lasciviousness,

Idolatry, witchcraft, hatred, variance, emulations, wrath, strife, seditions, heresies,

Envyings, murders, drunkenness, revellings, and such like: of the which I tell you before, as I have also told you in time past, that they which do such things shall not inherit the kingdom of God (Gal. 5:19–21).

But *fornication, and all uncleanness*, or covetousness, let it not be once named among you, as becometh saints;

Neither filthiness, nor foolish talking, nor jesting, which are not convenient: but rather giving of thanks.

For this ye know, that no *whoremonger, nor unclean person*, nor covetous man, who is an idolater, hath any inheritance in the kingdom of Christ and of God (Eph. 5:3–5).

But the fearful, and unbelieving, and the abominable, and murders, and *whoremongers*, and sorcerers, and idolaters, and all liars, shall have their part in the lake which burneth with fire and brimstone: which is the second death (Rev. 21:8).

ABOUT THE AUTHOR

Warren Marcus, a Messianic Jewish believer since 1974, is known as one of the creative forces behind Christian television. His award winning work including, but not limited to, "Superbook," "The Flying Horse" and "Don't Ask Me, Ask God!" has been seen on the daily syndicated television program, "The 700 Club."

Today, Warren Marcus is founder and president of New Day Pictures International, a ministry whose sole purpose is to produce uncompromising Christian motion pictures for world-wide distribution.